WRITING AND POWER

WRITING AND POWER

A Critical Introduction to Composition Studies

Candace Mitchell

Paradigm Publishers
Boulder • London

Published in the United States by Paradigm Publishers, 3124 Noble Court, Boulder, Colorado 80301 USA.

Paradigm Publishers is the trade name of Birkenkamp & Company, LLC, Dean Birkenkamp, President and Publisher.

Library of Congress Cataloging-in-Publication Data

Mitchell, Candace.
Writing and power : a critical introduction to composition studies /
Candace Mitchell.
p. cm.
Includes bibliographical references and index.
ISBN 1-59451-020-2 (hardcover : alk. paper) — ISBN 1-59451-021-0
(pbk. : alk. paper)
1. English language—Rhetoric—Study and teaching—Social aspects.   2.
English language—Composition and exercises—Study and teaching—Social
aspects.   3. Report writing—Study and teaching—Social aspects.   4.
Power (Social sciences)   I. Title.   II. Series.
PE1404 .M58 2003
808'.042'071—dc22
2003018110

Printed and bound in the United States of America on acid-free paper that meets the standards of the American National Standard for Permanence of Paper for Printed Library Materials.

Designed and Typeset by Straight Creek Bookmakers.

09 08 07 06 05 04 03
5 4 3 2 1

For Darien,
my wise and wonderful son,
who may someday write a book of his own.

CONTENTS

ACKNOWLEDGMENTS

Throughout this book I argue that writing is a social activity linked in its many guises to cultural, ideological, and historical circumstances that shape and re-shape its discursive form and intent. The reality of what I argue takes on a powerful and personal significance as I write these acknowledgments, allowing me to recognize that *Writing and Power,* though authored by me, is truly a socially constructed text. This book would not have come to fruition without the many lectures, discussions, and critical and supportive feedback from colleagues and friends that helped shape it, as well as the availability of the published work of so many others and the help of the committed employees of Paradigm Publishers.

I thank first James Paul Gee—my dissertation advisor, mentor, and true friend—whose linguistic arguments and brilliant text analyses led me from a constrained view of language dominated by syntax and pragmatics to a whole new world of radical, social literacies that links language and culture in a manner that would forever change my view of the world. James Gee also led me through the primary research component contained in *Writing and Power* and relentlessly prodded me into completing my dissertation; he was determined not to give up on me. Thank you, Jim.

I thank Henry Giroux—my comrade, my brother, my friend—for teaching me so much during the years we worked so closely together to bring radical, cutting-edge work in the sociology of education and critical pedagogy to publication in the *Journal of Education* while it was situated within the conservative confines of John Silber's Boston University. It was a decade's ride well worth taking. I have learned, and continue to learn, so much from you. Thank you, Henry.

I thank Donaldo Macedo—my mentor, my colleague, my friend—for his intellectual integrity and his continuous support, encouragement, and critical reading of this book in manuscript form. When even I doubted I would ever complete this work, Donaldo assured me that I would and, moreover, that I must. He gave me books and articles to read, suggested revisions, and questioned me *very often* about my progress. I had no choice: finish the book or listen to Donaldo's questions forever. We have worked together for more years than I care to mention, and through them all I have remained energized intellectually in good part due to the enormous critical intellectual power and stature Donaldo brings to every project and enterprise he undertakes. Thank you, Donaldo.

I thank Ellen Rintell, who was the teaching assistant in the first course I ever took at the graduate level. I wanted to learn what Ellen knew and was thus inspired to continue on for a master's and then a Ph.D. We have been the best of friends for years, supporting one another through the raising of children and the maneuvering of the hurdles academia places in one's path. Her support and encouragement throughout these years have meant a great deal to me. Thank you, Ellen.

I thank my colleagues in the Applied Linguistics Program at the University of Massachusetts Boston (UMB)—Chuck Meyer, Pepi Leistyna, Corinne Etienne, Maureen Hawkins, and Lilia Bartolome—for their support and for taking up the slack. And to Lauren Mayhew at the Center for World Languages and Cultures: I thank you too. Without the help of my colleagues this book would not exist. I also thank Nancy Smith-Hefner, my former colleague, for her guidance, wisdom, and devoted friendship during the years we worked together at UMB. I miss you, Nancy, and thank you for all that you have done for me.

I thank Charles Tontar for handling all things technical, for I do not have a clue. Without your help I might have deleted my entire manuscript and had to begin anew.

Thanks also to Wendy Tsapatsaris, Nick Tsapatsaris, Sheryl Norris, Norma Audy, Chris Tunstall, and all my comrades on Jefferson Street and thereabouts—Cary, Rob, Kay Kay, Kay, Gary, Evelyn, Maria, Mindy, Ron, Sharon, Steve, Robin, Carole, Doug, Douglas Ford, and my *whole* family—especially Jenni, who transcribed all taped dialogues, classes, and meetings! Thank you to Laurie Fraser for helping put my body back in working order, Dr. Daniel B. Carr for continuing to fight the physical pain, and to my lawyer, Amy Carlin, for winning my case. Without your help this book would not have been written.

I thank Dean Birkenkamp, president of Paradigm Publishers, for having the faith and courage to support *Writing and Power,* Julie Kirsch for her prompt and careful copyediting, and Michael Peirce for his contribution to the process of pulling the book together. It was a pleasure to work with all at the press.

I thank the extraordinarily helpful employees of WGBH public television in Boston, who led me to their affiliate in Pittsburgh, WQED. Linda Anderson and Quilan Murphy kindly directed me to Steve Friedman, copyright expert and computer whiz extraordinaire. After many, many more calls I learned that the fabulous *American Roots Music* series was produced by Ginger Group Productions in New York City. The kind people at Ginger Group led me to Carla and Sue, and to the opportunity to cite a compelling stanza from Floyd Red Crow Westerman's song "Wounded Knee." I thank you all, and apologize for not asking everyone with whom I spoke for their name.

Finally, I thank Sarah, Alan, Zola, Tan, and Araya, who so generously and willingly gave of their time.

INTRODUCTION

> Critical educators need to challenge those educational discourses that view schooling as a decontextualized site free from social, political, and racial tensions. What has to be stressed . . . is the primacy of the political and the contextual in analyzing issues of culture, language, and voice. —Henry Giroux, *Teachers as Intellectuals: Toward a Critical Pedagogy of Learning*

In early June 2003 I met with my son's high school Honors English II teacher to discuss a writing assignment just returned to him. I sought a conference with Darien's teacher because Darien was dismayed by the fact that he had received a B on the paper—he had worked very hard on it and was proud of the outcome. On the rubric handed back with the graded paper the teacher had noted that the paper needed more details to enhance its believability and that there were more than two errors in grammar. I had no intention of asking, or arguing, for a higher grade for my son. I just wanted to know what "more details" meant and why minor typos counted as grammar errors, when Darien had appropriately used two colons and two semicolons in the paper—the points of grammar/punctuation the class had just finished addressing. We never got to the grammar issue, just to the details one, after initial pleasantries. The teacher is truly committed, energetic, and determined to teach her students to read and write in ways that will serve them well as they move through school, so the initial discussion was far more than mere formality: I like and respect her. I also understand that she is dealing with far too many students in each class—in her two honors classes alone she has twenty-six and twenty-seven students.

1

The assignment—extraordinarily creative in conception—required students to write "page 214 of their autobiography." Think what this entails: the student must first hurl himself into an imagined future and then reflect back on a life he has not yet experienced. Details must accentuate the fact that this one page contains a portion of an event or circumstance that clearly situates it in the future—my son chose to include travel to other planets to indicate this. Further, he fictionalized his future self as one who copiloted spacecraft that made taken-for-granted excursions to faraway worlds. On page 214 the reader learns—or perhaps is reminded—that he is married and the father of two young sons, and that he would surely be missed if he were not able to get himself out of the fix he was in as a result of a crash landing. I thought the paper was well written and believable in a fictionalized space and displayed a controlled emotional tension fitting of one—Darien—who was responsible for the safety of others, while at the same time worried about his own potential personal losses.

The single restriction the teacher had placed on the assignment was that it could not be about one's wedding day, since the year before each girl in class had chosen this as her topic. The teacher had emphasized further, as I learned from speaking to her, that the final product itself was to appear as if it had come from a book. My son took this to mean that he should single-space the text, as is done in books, and have the beginning and ending of the page contain fragments of sentences so that at the end of his paper one would need "to turn the page" not only to find out what happened next but also to read the complete sentence. I go on at length about this particular assignment because after having spoken to my son's teacher about her expectations regarding the assignment, I was struck by how closely linked her conception of the task is to a major theme I address in this book. By this I mean that the teacher's expectations had more to do with form than with what was written. I learned this when I asked directly what an A paper consisted of as compared to a paper with a grade of B. The teacher responded with much enthusiasm, exclaiming that the A papers looked as if they had been torn from a "real" book. These papers had "214" typed at the top and next to the page number either the author's name (on the right) or the title (on the left) depending on which side of the page one was to assume had been torn out of the imaginary book. One paper even had the aged look book pages take on over time. I was flabbergasted and asked, "What does that have to do with writing?" I did not get a response, and we both laughed. The conversation turned to her expectations for the final project, since my son had obviously missed the main point of the "page 214" assignment. I hoped to learn firsthand about the final required writing assignment.

Later that day, when I gauged my son to be in a good mood, I asked him about the "page 214" assignment. His response—besides reiterating his disbelief that I would dare speak with his teacher—was that no way was he going to make his paper look as if it were torn from a book or yellowed from time. I asked him why not. His response: "That's a girl thing." End of conversation. I knew it would not, nor could it, go any further because this issue had emerged numerous times throughout his two years in high school. At times, for example, when I had suggested he use a certain color, or multiple colors as backing on a poster project, my son had looked at me as if I were from an alien planet. Certain colors were verboten—lavender and pink, in particular—for boys, as was glitter or any other detailed artistic attachment, which I knew would enhance a female teacher's perception of the project. How did I know? Well, obviously I was once a girl and completed a lot of projects in high school. I know what counts in high school project discourse. So too does my son, yet he risks too much—loss of prestige in his male-dominated, athletically oriented peer group—if he were to fully enter the discourse required and fulfill the teachers' often unarticulated expectations.

The example above draws from a population of privileged, white, "honors" students—a status that provides for them the best teachers the school has to offer, or, unfortunately at times, those with the most political clout. Further, the status provides my son and his classmates with many books that, to my horror, I found out were not available to lower-track students, who enter and leave school without even a backpack, while the "honors" kids are so weighted down I worry about their backs. However, "honors" students, though privileged, still experience within their community multiple discourses and implicit, unstated expectations that create boundaries and barriers within this seemingly singular community. The teacher, too, in this "page 214" instance, seemed totally unaware of how her expectations threatened boys, promising "geekdom" or worse for those males who conformed to, or even fully understood, what she was looking for in an assignment. Therefore this single, seemingly benign and therefore neutral, writing assignment, when examined in context, reveals the complex tensions that emerge in what would appear to be an educational situation free from conflict. Even more striking is the fact that the teacher, though completely well intended, failed to note the tension she creates for her male students through her expectations regarding the superficial form into which the writing of the text is to be situated. The males remain silent regarding their discomfort with the expected trappings; the girls, though forewarned not to enter the gender-specific, girl-culture trap of writing about one's wedding day, are quite willing to package their writing as implicitly expected. Surely this example highlights the need for practitioners and researchers to consider, as I quoted from Giroux at the beginning of this introduction, "the political and the contextual in analyzing issues of culture, language, and voice."

I chose not to debate or even raise the issue Giroux emphasizes with my son's young teacher, two years into her career, for in doing so I would have stepped beyond the boundaries of allowable discourse between parent and teacher. In the high school room in which we met I was denuded of my position of power; I was not an expert or even one who could question or critically reflect on the impact of the assignment, but of necessity needed to play the concerned and grateful parent. I was not in a pedagogically neutral zone, for, I would argue, none exists. And though there has been a proliferation of research advocating a movement beyond a stance of pedagogical neutrality so as to incorporate important factors such as culture, language, and voice, very few practitioners or researchers have fully understood the complex and often contradictory interrelation between language and culture. In other words, educators and researchers alike need to understand, as Donaldo Macedo suggests, that the interrelationship between language and culture is an eminently political phenomenon, and, therefore, it must be analyzed within the context of a theory of power relations and an understanding of social and cultural reproduction. Since language and culture do not exist in neutral relationships, but are almost always structured asymmetrically with respect to power, the teaching of writing to all students, and particularly when taught to students who are members of linguistic minority groups, requires that researchers and educators recognize "the role of language (a factor of culture) as a major force in the construction of human subjectivities . . . and the way language may either confirm or deny the life histories and experiences of the people who use it" (Macedo, 1994, p. 131). Taking the role of language as a factor of culture "in the construction of human subjectivities" points to the impossibility of treating language pedagogy, and in particular the teaching of writing, as a mere neutral transmission of skills from the teacher to the student. Since writing in its multiple guises is part and parcel of cultural and class-based discourses, its acquisition will invariably call for a thorough understanding of the interaction of class across culture and language. To do otherwise is to ignore the essence of how these power asymmetries regulate and shape a priori what we often wrongly come to accept as neutral entities.

In addition to questions of power relations between and across languages and cultures, we need also to understand the extent to which all teaching assumes a goal. Thus no educational endeavor is without direction or, by nature, nondirective. As Paulo Freire so eloquently argues,

> Only those teachers who acquiesce their responsibility as teachers to become mere facilitators perceive education as non-directive: I find this to be a deceitful discourse; that is, a discourse from the perspective of the dominant class. Only in this deceitful discourse can educators talk about a lack of direction in teaching. I do not think that there is real education without direction. To the extent that all educational practice brings with it its own transcendence, it presupposes an objective to be reached. Therefore, practice cannot be nondirective. There is no educational practice that does not point to an objective; this proves that the nature of educational practice has direction. The facilitator who claims that "since I respect students I cannot be directive, and since they are individuals deserving respect, they should determine their own direction," does not deny the directive nature of education that is independent of his own subjectivity. Rather, this facilitator denies himself or herself the pedagogical, political, and epistemological task of assuming the role of a subject of the directive practice. This facilitator refuses to convince his or her learners of what he or she thinks is just. This educator, then, ends up helping the power structure. To avoid reproducing the values of the power structure, the educator must always combat a

laissez-faire pedagogy, no matter how progressive it may appear to be. (Freire & Macedo, 1995, p. 377)

Given the unveiling of the ideological pretense of neutrality, I draw here on recent works in critical pedagogy in an attempt to create the foundation upon which to address the issue of theorizing and teaching writing in the academy. This I do through the process of revisiting the past in order to understand the present so as to create a vision for the future that speaks of the possibility for the emergence of a truly democratic education. Henry Giroux argues above that we need to attend to the important notion of the centrality of the political in relationship to language, culture, and schooling; Donaldo Macedo urges us to consider the power of language in the shaping of human subjectivity; and Paulo Freire raises the fundamental issue of the authority of teachers and the nonneutrality of education. These assertions provide the framework for a reconceptualization of writing theory and practice that embraces a view of education that engages "live human beings in activities of meaning-making, dialogue, and reflective understanding of a variety of texts, including the texts of their social realities" (Greene, 1995, p. 305). To do so I adopt as well a "reconceptionized notion of theory, that does not dictate practice" (Kincheloe & Steinberg, 1995, p. 8), and proceed with a reflective rethinking, albeit retheorizing, of form and process in writing theory. Part of what this endeavor entails is

> an effort to overcome debilitating dualisms because we are talking about the impossibility of separating the teaching of contents from ethical formation. Of separating practice and theory, authority and freedom, ignorance and knowledge, respect for the teacher and respect for the students, and teaching and learning. None of these terms can be mechanically separated one from the other. (Freire, 1998, p. 88)

Rewriting Writing

The revisionism to which I alluded earlier in this chapter is afoot within the world at large and within the academic community as well. The derivational morpheme *re* is active in many disciplines challenging sedimented views, accepted theories, and entrenched methodologies. We are rethinking Marxism, rewriting literacy, and reconceptualizing theory in ways that challenge the status quo and seek to create a new era of hope and possibility in a postmodern world filled with the emergence of the once-silent voices of people of color, women, members of the lower and working classes, and of those so oppressed as to constitute the underclass. I join the radical revisionist movement as I critically review and revise theoretical perspectives toward the teaching of writing in an effort to reconceptualize how writing might to be taught within contexts awash with diversity. The revisionist argument that emerges is offered in the spirit of admiration and respect for progressive writing theorists and practitioners—particularly represented within the process school of writing—who have grappled, for the most part from the late 1960s to the present day, with ways in which opportunities could be provided for students to gain access to academic prose. This struggle for access becomes more and more complex to the degree that we acknowledge that academic writing is class-specific and, as such, working-class and other subordinated students need to not only gain entry into white middle- and upper-class discourses but also master and be fully conversant in a variety of these discourses—both social and discipline-based—as a condition of learning how to write.

However, herein lies a caveat, and it is a big one: the structures of social and academic discourses remain a mystery to the uninitiated and unapprenticed, and, paradoxically, practitioners/theorists are often disinclined to reveal these forms. Some argue that writers will find their way on their own to the forms deemed appropriate to the academy; in stark contrast, some contest the right of the academy to impose its forms on members of discourse communities whose forms vary considerably from those of the academy. Some feminists say let women write as women do; some supporters of nonstandard forms such as Black English Vernacular argue for its place in the academy; and so forth. Yet often these arguments are made in "appropriate" academic form and published in "appropriate" academic journals and texts. Students writing in nonstandard forms might get past and even garner an A from the composition instructor convert to the cause, but they won't get past the upper-level status-quo ideologue who adheres to entrenched traditional forms.

(Passive) Aggressive Progressives

Why is it that so many progressives who argue for allowing the use and acceptance of multiple discourses among students as a means of affirmation and finding voice write in the singular, acceptable discourses of their fields? It reminds me of officers sending enlisted men to the front lines. If a battle is to be fought in the academy, I do not believe that students should be the soldiers on the front lines. A specific example of what I argue here is seen in the common use of journals in composition classrooms. As a genre it is said to be feminist—many women historically have kept journals (of course this was the case for women who had access to literacy, already narrowing the class access to the genre)—and it is therefore argued to be a nonthreatening, non-male-dominated form. Journal writing is a form that allows for a free flow of feelings, thoughts, and impressions without the supposed undue constraints of academic writing. Now all of this may in fact be true, but does that mean that journal writing is an appropriate substitution for the essay or research paper at the college level? Is it oppressive to teach students how to reference work, not to mention how to seek information and to formulate critical questions in so doing—which I believe to be at the very foundation of education—or just to learn something of interest, and to present this information in turn to an audience—to perform, if you will? I do not think so. Yet I have seen classroom writing restricted to journals, even at the graduate level, where personal reflection is elevated above academic referencing and argument. And I remember in particular one student, a senior English major at a highly respected university where I once taught, who had never had to write a paper in which a bibliography and internal references were necessary until I required it of her in my linguistics course. She had been writing journals and essays, no doubt with ease, but had never been asked to learn to write in the form her professors would most generally use. As an English major, I wonder if there is anything wrong with the absence of the reference list. Maybe this student was destined to go on to write a newspaper column, a novel, or a book of poems, and not to an academic audience at all. Who am I to decide where students might want to go, or what they may wish to do after graduation? Yet should lack of access to particular forms of discourse ever be allowed to hamper possibilities for future academic recourse?

In sum, central to process writing theory and practice lies the rejection of authoritarian models of teaching and a move to a model of facilitating students' acquisition of language, both written and oral. While I do not share fully the ideological framework underlying the notion of process writing, it is by no means my intent here to reject outright the work that has emerged from process writing theory and practice but, rather, both to assess and build upon it within a critical framework that recognizes the ideological and political underpinnings of all theories and practices.

Ideology

Here I clarify my use of the term "ideology," because it serves as an important thread linking the various components of this book. Ideological perspectives—how they are historically and socially produced and the status they assume within social contexts—serve to privilege certain groups over others. Ideologies are never neutral. Further, ideologies link historical, cultural, political, and even individual concerns, not in a linear fashion as do the threads of the straight seam but in the complex manner experienced and illuminated in embroidery. If you will, multiple ideologies embroider this book, holding it together in complex ways. As a result I feel it necessary to clarify the manner in which I have used the term "ideology" throughout.

I will take as a starting point the following assertion: with such words as "ideology," "it is pointless to ask what they 'really' mean" (Gee, 1989, p. 34). James Paul Gee asserts further that, in defining words, "what is to the point is to say what you (choose to) take them to mean, after careful, thoughtful, and ethical reflection" (p. 34). Gee has committed himself to, as well as engaged in, this sort of reflection. Thus it is his definition of "ideology" that I choose to incorporate at the outset. What then is ideology? To Gee, ideology is intimately related to the "distribution of 'goods' in society." The "good" to which I refer throughout this book is, of course, academic literacy. In much the same way a capitalist economic system concerns itself with the attainment, acquisition, and distribution of goods to those who, as the myth goes, work the hardest to obtain these goods, so too does the ideology of academic literacy assume that those who work the hardest will obtain their goal: competence in academic literacy, a college degree, a graduate degree, or, in other words, a road through education to a better tomorrow.

How then is ideology linked to the distribution of goods? Ideologies are, maintains Gee, theories that "involve claims about how this 'good' is distributed" (p. 44). It is worth quoting at length Gee's further claims regarding ideology. To Gee,

> Ideologies are important because, since theories ground beliefs, and beliefs lead to actions, and actions create social worlds ("reality"), ideologies simultaneously explain, often exonerate, and always partially create (in interactions with history and the material bases of society) the distribution of "goods." And since everything that makes us human in the honorific sense of the term (the ability to freely think, believe, desire, feel, and create with others in a material world whose resources we share) are "goods" in probably all, but at least some, societies, the ideologies are what construct not only human worlds, but humans. (p. 19)

In other words, Gee claims we are constituted by our ideologies. Therefore, the manner in which we carry out, for example, our research or our teaching is intimately related to the particular ideological perspectives we hold. Our actions as well as our words are complicit with and representative of the ideologies we hold. To indicate, however, that ideology is something held is not to imply that an ideology is an "optional extra, deliberately adopted by self-conscious individuals ('conservative ideology,' for instance), but the very condition of our experience of the world, unconscious precisely in that it is unquestioned, taken for granted" (Belsey, 1980, p. 5). An ideological perspective recognizes, according to Goran Therborn in his discussion of Althusser in *The Ideology of Power and the Power of Ideology,* that "no position can lay claim to absolute, timeless truth, because finally all formulations are historically specific, arising out of the material conditions of a particular time and place" (quoted in Berlin, 1988, p. 478). Ideology is not an entity existing on its own, which can in time become easily codified into words. Rather, it is embedded implicitly, in many ways, in discourse. As Berlin writes in his discussion of Therborn's interpretation of Althusser: "The choice for Therborn is never between scientific truth and ideology, but between competing ideologies, competing discursive interpretations" (1988, p. 478). Since ideology is embedded in language use it enters all aspects of our experience (Berlin, 1988, p. 479). As a result, suggests Gee, it is incumbent that through discourse analysis linguists explicate ideologies. Gee goes so far as to suggest that "to the extent that ideologies are tacit, removed or deferred and self-advantaging they are the root of human evil and leave us complicit with, and thus responsible for, the evil that is in the world" (1989, p. 44). Stephen Jay Gould speaks of this ideological complicity with evil in the following: "We pass through this world but once. Few tragedies can be more extensive than the stunting of life, few injustices deeper than the denial of an opportunity to strive or even to hope, by a limit imposed from without, but falsely identified as lying within" (1981, p. 29). In seeking to uncover the tacit ideological implications of theories and practices associated with the teaching of writing, I seek to clarify the means by which the tragedies to which Gould alludes can, with hope, be prevented. This is my goal in writing this book. This has been my goal throughout my life.

The Centrality of Subjectivity: My Evolving/Revolving Position(s) in Context

It is perhaps fitting that I state at the outset my position in relationship to the context and issues that will be discussed in the chapters that follow. First, in reference to my relationship to rhetoric, composition studies, or writing: I do not have an academic background in any of the fields directly related to the teaching of writing. I am an applied linguist whose areas of study include literacy, discourse and narrative analysis, and cross-cultural communication. As editor of the *Journal of Education* at Boston University for ten years I found myself gladly immersed in readings in the sociology of education and critical pedagogy. My undergraduate degree is in political science, which no doubt contributes to my lifelong propensity for viewing the world through the lens of politics and language, not to mention the fact that my parents viewed the world through the very same lens. So I approach this book as an outsider of sorts, but one with a keen interest and driving commitment to the ideals of a democratic education and the untarnished hope that all children within our society should reap the benefits of these ideals. Now the reality: I know that the ideals of a democratic education are not being reached, and in good part, the failure to provide an egalitarian education—despite the fact that so many more members of non-middle-and-upper-middle-class backgrounds have gained entrance into college—is what I wish to address as well within this book. Perhaps Noam Chomsky captures best what I alluded to earlier in this chapter. In a discussion with Donaldo Macedo, Chomsky argues that "An education that yearns for a democratic world ought to provide students with critical tools to make linkages that would unveil the obvious hypocrisy. Instead of indoctrinating students with democratic myths, schools should engage them in the practice of democracy" (Chomsky & Macedo, 1999, p. 18).

As the book progresses I will make, I hope, my position clearer, but I will attempt now just to lay the groundwork for situating myself as represented within the text. In so doing, I draw justification from *Culture and Truth: The Remaking of Social Analysis* (1989), in which Renato Rosaldo argues "it is a mistake to urge social analysis to strive for a position of innocence designated by such adjectives as detached, neutral, or impartial" (p. 69). Rosaldo goes on to suggest that: "Because researchers are necessarily both somewhat impartial and somewhat partisan, somewhat innocent and somewhat complicit, their readers should be as informed as possible about what the observer was in a position to know and not know" (p. 69). I suggest, in line with Rosaldo, that it is only fair, therefore, that I present a brief synopsis of my position at the time of the classroom observations, writing conference observations, interviews with the writing instructor and the four students selected for the study, and the greater part of the on-site work that comprise a portion of this book. At the time I was a part-time faculty member in the English Department at the University of Massachusetts Boston (UMB) where I was responsible for teaching writing to nonnative speakers of English (either 101E, the first course in the sequence, and/or 102E, which focused on the writing of a research paper as the final project for the course) and a graduate course in the Bilingual/ESL Graduate Studies Program, which was at that time also in the English Department. I had been recruited to teach at the university after inviting Vivian Zamel, the director of the undergraduate ESL program at UMB, to speak at a weekly colloquium series that I was responsible for organizing at Boston University during the academic year 1983–84. After the talk it was generally the practice for the organizer, and whoever else was interested, to take the speaker to lunch. During lunch Vivian and I had an animated discussion on a myriad of creative ways in which writing courses could be structured. It was an enjoyable lunch and discussion.

Getting through the Gate

Interestingly, months before the after-colloquium lunch I had applied for a position teaching in the ESL program at UMB at the recommendation of a friend who taught linguistics there and who knew me as his teaching assistant during a summer linguistics program at Boston University. My friend had said he would speak to Vivian about me, so I had assumed that I would at least get an interview. I had eight years' experience teaching nonnative speakers at the high school level, had a master's in teaching English to speakers of other languages (TESOL), and was well on my way to a Ph.D. in applied linguistics—I was well qualified. I sent in my résumé and cover letter to Zamel, but never heard a word from anyone in the English Department. I told the individual who had recommended that I apply, but he had no idea what had happened, as he had spoken to Vivian as promised. A mystery, and one that shattered my self-esteem somewhat. But as I am not one to be deterred for long, I thought, why not invite Vivian to speak at a colloquium—because, so I have heard, it's not what you know, but who you know, that matters—and since that had not worked on my route to university employment thus far I thought it best that I get to know someone closer to where I wanted to be. So that's how the invitation came about.

After the successful lunch, I got an indirect communication from Vivian, through a fellow grad student who did teach at UMB in the ESL program. Melanie Schneider, to whom I will always be grateful for her kindness and support on my behalf at this point and at many others, told me the following: although Vivian liked me and my ideas, she thought my résumé was awful; in fact, Vivian said, "Who sends a résumé to a university? We expect a vita." Melanie communicated this to me in a very subdued tone, as if she were embarrassed to have learned that I, of all people, was capable of such a faux pas. I remember well the context of the communiqué: we ran into one another unexpectedly at the symphony. Thus hushed tones, even at intermission, were not suspect. Well, all I could say was: "Melanie, what's a vita?" And so she explained very clearly what a vita was and, moreover, graciously offered to give me a copy of hers to use as a model so that I could structure one of my own. I did. The form changed, although the past and present educational qualifications, work experience, and academic activities remained the same. But the new packaging landed me the position at UMB. Here I had thought that I was dripping with cultural capital, yet I had not a clue as to how one presented oneself for review at the university level. I was stuck back in the culture of the public schools, not fit to associate at the workplace, excuse me, the academy, with writers of vitas.

Oppressive Progressives

Imagine my shock then when I arrived at UMB to teach my first two ESL classes and was told that I was being oppressive when I required that my students hand in all work typed and double-spaced. Apparently, it was common practice in the ESL writing program to allow students to handwrite their work. Of course some— those who had already had greater exposure to the academic world, and money, I would imagine—typed their work anyway, but the uninitiated wrote by hand on notebook paper, and some even used pencil! I would argue that to consider requiring that a paper be typed to be an oppressive act represents the extreme of a laissez-faire pedagogy. Computer labs were available on campus. Students have friends who can type. And if all else failed, students could pay by the page for typing services. This is just one example of how form counted in one context—it was used as a gatekeeping device to exclude me from the university—while in the context of the writing program explicit practices that were promoted served to undermine students' chances of obtaining further access to the academic context. What was stunning was that this practice—allowing students to handwrite papers—was said to be in place to serve the best interests of the students. And when analyzed together, what is even more stunning is that neither had much to do with "the act of writing" but, rather, with the form in which the printed word was to be presented and, in turn, whether or not the purveyors of the context in which the printed word was presented for judgment would find it to be acceptable or not.

Some teachers valued length. In fact, I can remember a colleague exclaiming over the fact that a student who had formerly been silent during class discussions and seemingly blocked when asked to write had "acquired diarrhea of the mouth," which apparently poured forth in print. My colleague expressed her glee as she waved the penciled paper before me, spewing the tattered confetti endemic to the torn notebook page around the office. This instructor—now a full professor—was ecstatic; I was concerned for the student and not at all enamored with the scatological imagery used to describe this student writer's accomplishments. So clarity, content, cohesiveness, organization, and so forth were not at issue. The instructor was elated that the student had overcome a "blockage" that had heretofore prevented him from writing anything extensive. Even with the medical and scatological imagery aside, one still wonders why length was so highly valued. This instructor zealously assumed the role of savior in that she had served somehow to loosen the student's writer's block. This instructor's sensitive, nonauthoritarian, seemingly progressive approach to the teaching of writing supposedly allowed for an emotional release and a flood of words from this previously silent student. Perhaps I should not be so snide; it was at least a beginning for the novice writer, but where was he to go thereafter?

Writing for the academy, I argue, is therefore far more than the mere engagement with print; it involves a set of behaviors defined by a particular community whose members may or may not feel it necessary, or even appropriate, to explicitly reveal these behaviors to the novice. To allow students to handwrite papers and not to inform them explicitly that to do so in a discipline-based course would lead to a return of the paper without a grade, or perhaps a failing grade, is disingenuous and paternalistic. If these issues of form—typed, double-spaced with appropriate title page formatting—are not discussed and required, students are left in the dark as to one of the expected discursive practices in the academy. In my case, Zamel read my résumé as proof that I was an inappropriate fit for the academy. And here "read" should be understood as meaning solely a superficial reading, a taking-in of the fact of my nonmembership in the academy and the degree of distance between my professional community—public schools—and the exalted community—the university. In the case of the students, it was understood that they were not members of the academy, but certain members of the ESL faculty were not going to put any undue pressure upon them. I do not believe that any of the teachers engaged in these paternalistic pedagogical practices perceived them to be anything other than the best thing possible for the benefit of their students. My jaded side argues that there were in fact internal contradictions working to motivate these progressives to act as they did. The instructor who exclaimed joy at her student's "diarrhea of the mouth" taught for pennies while enjoying the luxuries that flow from a trust fund of great substance. There was indeed a great deal of post-1960s self-congratulatory back patting underlying the culture of UMB. This was particularly the case within contexts that were peripheral to the established, mainstream disciplines and departments that represented the core of the university, in particular, and academia, in general.

Methodology

Writing and Power brings together extensive secondary research necessary to provide the historical contexts and changing theoretical perspectives leading to the status of writing or composition in academia today. The more I researched writing and the history of higher education, the more I realized the importance of the profound manner in which the historical and social circumstances at the turn of the twentieth century affected not only the structure of academia but also the teaching of writing. Without an understanding of history, the social, political, and theoretical debates driving the teaching of writing today would seemingly exist in a vacuum, as if the present were a self-contained entity easily viewed through a lens. A microscopic, myopic approach to such a complex social activity as theorizing and teaching writing strikes me as far too simplistic, though many researchers approach the task in such a manner. I choose the far broader, deeper, and more complex approach by combining secondary historical and theoretical research with an in-depth ethnographic approach incorporating classroom observation, narrative analysis, discourse analysis, critical commentary, and a first-person accounting of my own experiences in the field. My involvement in writing and presence in academia provide a first-person accounting intended to support the themes raised in the discussion derived from secondary sources from on-site observation and text analysis. Further, I report on the primary research I undertook of a real teaching context at the University of Massachusetts Boston. The manner in which the research was conducted is explained in what follows and detailed more fully in the book's appendix.

I carried out the ethnographic component of this study during a seven-week summer ESL writing course. I chose to use UMB for the following reasons: As a large inner-city university, the institution has made an overt commitment to the education of minority students. However, despite the fact that the university has in many ways opened its doors to the often disenfranchised, nontraditional student, it nonetheless maintains a strict policy requiring students to pass a writing proficiency exam prior to continuing with upper-level course work. In order to pass the exam, students may submit a portfolio of their writing for evaluation or take a three-hour writing exam in which they are asked to write an essay in response to a question posed by the examiners. Students must respond to the question by calling upon a body of literature (readings are supplied to students prior to taking the exam) to support the student's assertion. In other words, students must argue a point and call upon an authoritative body of literature, not personal anecdote, to support their argument. The students must produce a logical essay—personal narrative, poetry, short stories, letters, or any other genre is considered inappropriate in this context. Although writing instructors are not explicitly required to "teach to the exam," implicit in the very structure of the university's writing proficiency requirement is the message that a writing instructor must prepare her students to pass the exam. In a certain sense writing instructors are being called upon, in the words of Terry Eagleton, to "train students in the effective deployment of certain techniques, in the efficient mastery of a certain discourse, as a means of certifying them as intellectually qualified recruits to the ruling class," that is, the academic community (1984, p. 91). The very nature of this institutional constraint, while overtly imposed on students, may have a covert impact on the classroom practices of writing instructors. Or the institutional constraint may not affect to any degree the practices of particular progressive instructors, as the examples noted above suggest. Many instructors overtly resisted the constraints of academic discourse and sought to engage students in writing personal narratives or journals rather than focusing on the logical essay. Progressives within writing sought to fracture the notion of what constituted appropriate academic discourse. It is this very issue—the relationship between beliefs regarding what constitutes good academic prose and the manner in which these beliefs translate into classroom practice—that I will focus on in this book.

Participants in the Primary Research Component

Prior to the onset of the ethnographic component of my primary research, I identified an ESL writing instructor who professed to adhere to a process approach to teaching writing. This instructor, Sarah, was observed and audiotaped daily as she taught a college writing class to ESL students. I attended each of Sarah's classes, took field notes as a nonparticipant observer, and audiotaped each class she taught. I also undertook a focused analysis of Sarah and her interactions with four students in the class and developed case studies of these four students. The methodology I used included ethnography (Erickson, 1975), case study (Emig, 1971; Zamel, 1983), interview and narrative analysis (Mishler, 1984, 1986), and discourse analysis (Gee, 1985, 1988; Gumperz, 1982; Michaels, 1981; Michaels & Collins, 1984) of written and oral texts.

The Writing Instructor: Kind, Organized, and So Generous with Her Time

Prior to the onset of the interviews and observations I had never spoken at any length to the instructor, Sarah, who agreed to participate in the study I envisioned. This was the case because we never shared an office or had overlapping schedules, not an unusual situation for part-time faculty members in the department. Our relationship before the observations and interviews began could be characterized as distant friendliness, a friendliness that called for a "How are you?" uttered each of the possibly three times a semester chance meetings occurred. These meetings generally happened once at the very beginning of a semester, perhaps midway through, and when final grades were due. Part-time teaching does not offer many avenues for collegial interaction. Sarah did not agree to participate in the study out of friendship, as we essentially did not know one another, but rather out of what, I believe, was both a concern for a colleague and fellow graduate student as well as a true support of and interest in scholarly research. Further, had Sarah not consented to participate in the study I would have been in a very difficult situation since she was the only ESL writing instructor whose schedule matched my needs. She was aware of this, and I believe her kind and empathetic nature would not have permitted her to refuse me. For this I am forever thankful, because I know that my presence throughout her course increased her already heavy workload tremendously.

An Important Disclaimer

A disclaimer is necessary at this point: nothing I have written herein is to be taken as a negative personal or professional critique of the instructor, Sarah, who participated in the study that makes up a portion of this book; I have nothing but the highest regard and deepest respect for her. She was one of the most organized, most committed, and hardest-working individuals I have ever met. This despite the fact that she was balancing a grueling teaching load with the pressures of graduate school, all of which she did with a calm and good humor I envied and enjoyed. Nonetheless, critique is central to this book. But critique is to be viewed here as part of a process of inquiry and is not to be seen as directed, by any means, at a single instructor. In fact, critique is not to be associated solely with negativity, but rather with the notion of the unveiling of ideologies informing practices. Essentially, what I am interested in conveying in this book is "how the structures of knowledge, the way courses are defined and structured, what is taught and what is absent, have strong ideological parameters" (Tierney, 1989, p. 19). I have sought to do so, once again, from a critical perspective, which takes as the underlying assumption the notion that knowledge can never be neutral.

Structure of the Book

In the first four chapters of the book I present a historical review of the changes in academia that led to the emergence of the teaching of writing at the college level. Further, I provide a critical analysis of four theoretical approaches to the teaching of writing. In chapter 1 I discuss historical conditions in academia that I argue led to the development of the traditional approach to the teaching of writing. Chapters 2 and 3 in turn address two schools of process writing theory: the cognitive approach and the expressive approach. Chapter 4 presents the social/cultural approach to conceptualizing and teaching writing. In establishing such a framework I am by no means implying that this is the only way to conceptualize writing theory; nor do I intend to imply that any teacher might necessarily engage in practices reflecting one theoretical perspective to the exclusion of the others. Certainly the classroom worlds writing instructors inhabit are infinitely more complex than the academic characterization of opposing theoretical perspectives would indicate. Nonetheless, I believe it is important both to characterize and attempt to uncover underlying ideologies embedded within the various perspectives noted above. To do so through theory leads with hope to a greater interrogation of practices. Once again, as noted above, I seek to steer clear of false dualities, though unfortunately the present constraints of language impinge on my efforts.

I argue in chapter 4 that the social/cultural perspective offers the most comprehensive theory to date of the complex issues underlying the teaching of writing. Further, I suggest that those who teach writing consider reflecting critically upon their own assumptions regarding how writing should be taught and, in turn, reconsider their practice in light of the discussion presented herein. I would hope that this critical reflection occur with the recognition that the very practices in which composition (or writing) instructors—note, not professors of writing—engage are affected not only by personal—at heart, socially produced—ideologies but also by the very contexts in which the teaching occurs. These site-specific issues are never neutral, nor are the historical conditions responsible for shaping the present contexts and practices. At this point I want to clarify that I do not want to fall into the trap of switching the perceived failure to acquire academic discourse or, referred to generically as the failure to learn to write very well (or at all), from the individual student to the teacher. Such an argument would be counterproductive and inherently in opposition to the support given at the outset to a social/cultural approach to understanding both writing theory and practice.

In chapter 5 I discuss the historical, educational, social, and practical conditions and contexts that lay the foundation for the development of Sarah's ideological perspective toward the teaching of writing. Chapter 6 turns to a discussion of Sarah's practice. Here I draw from my interviews, observations, and discussions with Sarah. In addition, I draw from my own extensive experience teaching and working with and observing teachers in contexts ranging from small private schools to public schools in inner-city and suburban contexts to diverse college and university settings. Throughout the discussion of the research my presence will be felt. I have not entered the scientific world of game playing that suggests the existence of a state of pure objectivity. In the words of Stephen Jay Gould:

> Science, since people must do it, is a socially embedded activity. It progresses by hunch, vision, and intuition. Much of its change through time does not record a closer approach to absolute truth, but the alteration of cultural contexts that influence it so strongly. Facts are not pure and unsullied bits of information; culture also influences what we see and how we see it. Theories, moreover, are not inexorable inductions from facts. The most creative theories are often imaginative visions imposed upon facts; the source of imagination is also strongly cultural. (1981, pp. 21–22)

Gould's perspective lies in stark contrast to the one held by those he characterizes as determinists who "have often invoked the traditional prestige of science as objective knowledge, free from social and political taint. They portray themselves as purveyors of harsh truth and their opponents as sentimentalists, ideologues, and wishful thinkers" (p. 20). As a sentimental ideologue filled with hope for a better tomorrow—though many have dubbed me a cynic—I gladly shed any effort to argue that what is presented in this book represents an ultimate truth about writing theory and practice. The issues are far too complex, and anyway I lack the arrogance. All I can hope for is that situating the discussion in a historical, cultural, and political context, while focusing on an analysis of the theoretical and methodological debates that have dominated the field, each in its turn, over the course of the past century, and, finally, examining a real context, might shed light on the myriad issues that play a role in what is so simply called the teaching of writing or composition. As author (authority), researcher, former writing instructor, now graduate professor quite happy to teach "Literacy and Culture," as well as other courses, I actively seek to insinuate myself in time and place and as an active, or at times acted upon, participant in the process.

Chapters 7 and 8 deal with the four students chosen for close attention throughout the study. Here I present each student's history (or, in academic language, each student's case study) so as to better understand how their lives—academic experiences, social contacts, class background, native language and proficiency with English, and so forth—might impact on their work in the research writing class I observed. As an aside, as I write this introduction after the fact of writing the book, I realize the subtle textual hierarchy I unconsciously established and only now noted: I have privileged the instructor over the students in the structural presentation of the book. By so doing, I reflect the reality of the institutional privileging that has existed through time. Teachers, even those writing teachers engaged as so-called facilitators, inhabit a space—both real and culturally understood—that sets them above, and apart from, students. Instructors have offices (shared or not), students do not; instructors are paid to be in class, students are not (they pay to be there); instructors have academic degrees, students, for the most part, do not; instructors have direct access to other instructors in their area, students generally do not even have direct access to their own instructor (except during office hours, or now through e-mail—not that the student will always receive a response). So the status is quite different.

Institutional Democracy

UMB is overtly a very democratic institution. Its imposing brick exterior blunts the horizon. One enters through an underground garage. Once inside, there is little access to the outside world other than to a concrete courtyard that is vacant always. Open, imposing, and harsh, the courtyard might better serve as a landing pad for space invaders inhabiting a Ray Bradbury short story. The university, founded in the 1960s with an urban mission to educate previously underserved populations, is a commuter school, though it never intended its students to arrive by flying saucer despite building the landing pad. Both instructors and students drive, or take public transportation, to and from school from home bases apart from the institution. Overnights are not allowed. Housing must be found elsewhere. Designed by an architect whose previous works had been in prison design, UMB is structured so that any uprising (the effects of the 1960s again) could be readily contained. Windows do not open, nor were they intended to. Air is truly appropriated democratically: we share the air, wondering always what harmful particles it might contain. Though situated on Boston Harbor, for some inexplicable reason (perhaps just to further emphasize containment) many classroom windows are at ceiling level, thus providing no view when spectacular vistas lie outside the university's walls. Many offices look out onto walled courtyards that serve no purpose. Cement blocks are the foundation upon which the university rests and the building blocks that form its walls, and in most areas no effort has been made to mask this hostile building material. The blocks are painted in tones that hinder a desire to congregate. As a graduate student of mine recently commented, UMB is the McDonald's of universities. One is compelled to enter only when required and to exit as rapidly as possible. I think of it as a housing project: a university that wishes to mirror the home spaces many of its students inhabit. Cozy it is not, but so well intended with its urban mission. Students are not lulled into thinking they have entered the hallowed halls of the ivy-covered elite spaces that have a history and power far exceeding that of the quite new, rapidly crumbling UMB. Yes, the university does open its doors to the previously underserved, offering hope in the process. Yet only 28 percent—calculated on a six-year basis; four-year graduation rate figures are unavailable—of those who enter its doors exit with a degree (University of Massachusetts Boston, 2003, p. 9). Why: students are working full time, often raising families, and have to pass the writing proficiency exam. But the university is truly an equal opportunity provider: for some inexplicable reason it maintains a policy whereby faculty do not have separate, reserved parking areas. This leads to the absurd situation of faculty left trolling the lots, often for forty-five minutes or more at peak times, seeking a parking place, often only to lose a space to a student. UMB is a democratic commuter school.

Analysis of the Discourse of the Writing Conferences

In chapters 9 through 12 I undertake a detailed analysis of selected—by me and reviewed by far more accomplished linguists than I—portions of exchanges between each of the four students and the instructor during two writing conference sessions each student attended as they revised first and then second drafts of their research papers. I focus on areas of the exchanges—key encounters (Erickson, 1975)—where communication is flowing in such a way that either the teacher, or more important, the student, achieves a perceived goal. Of equal interest were areas—more common—where communication broke down. Here I was interested in analyzing why the exchange failed and what impact that failure had on the student's revision process. In this chapter I describe in detail the linguistic framework—drawing from the work in discourse analysis focused principally on cross-cultural communication—I applied in my analysis (Erickson, 1975; Gee, 1985; Gumperz, 1982; Gumperz & Cook-Gumperz 1982; and Michaels, 1985).

Conclusions

Chapter 13 characterizes explicitly the expected behaviors in writing conference and summarizes Sarah's perceptions of the four students. Finally, as is required after much research and analysis, in chapter 14 I draw conclusions that I hope will have a positive impact on the field(s). These conclusions are grounded in the explicit recognition of a fundamental tension that exists in higher education today: the recognition that although mastery of academic prose is not the key to the entrance door to most colleges, especially community colleges, and universities, it remains, in most cases, the key to the exit door (Applebee, 1974; Baron, 1982; Finegan, 1980). In many ways, it is the institution itself that creates the atmosphere for the support and reproduction of dominant ideologies. This situation reflects what Althusser refers to as the Ideological State Apparatus. By this he means that certain institutions within society, in this case the educational institution, work to prepare individuals to "act consistently with the values of society by inculcating in them the dominant versions of appropriate behavior. . ." (Belsey, 1980, p. 58).

Who Might Want to Read This Book

I hope that *Writing and Power* will be of use to individuals presently teaching writing and to those professors—note the use of individuals versus professors—who teach undergraduates and graduate students who may someday have a class or two, or likely more, of their own, and maybe even an office to share. In the end I hope that the book will be not only instructive but also thought-provoking for the individual reader and/or for readers reading the book as part of an assignment for a course on writing theory and practice, literacy acquisition, or discourse analysis. For the general reader I offer an insider's, no-holds-barred view of academia. Most certainly, this book is not meant to answer all the questions one might pose about the teaching of writing; it would be absurd and pretentious for me to even imply that it does. It is meant, rather, to raise questions in the manner so provocatively posed by Paulo Freire:

> I think it important to note that there is an undeniable relationship between being surprised and asking questions, taking risks and existence. At root human existence involves surprise, questioning and risk. And, because of all this, it involves action and change. Bureaucratization, however, means adaptation with a minimum of risk, with no surprises, without asking questions. And so we have a pedagogy of answers, which is a pedagogy of adaptation, not a pedagogy of creativity. It does not encourage people to take the risk of inventing, or reinventing. (Freire & Faundez, 1992, p. 40)

Herein I engage in more than a bit of risk taking as I raise fundamental questions dealing with writing theory and practice, from a historical, political, ideological, educational, and personal perspective.

1

THE TRADITIONAL APPROACH

The first textbook on rhetoric, which still remains to us was written by Aristotle. He defines rhetoric as the art of writing effectively, viewing it primarily as the art of persuasion in public speaking, but making it include all the devices for convincing or moving the mind of the hearer or reader.

Aristotle's treatise is profound and scholarly, and every textbook since written is little more than a restatement of some part of his comprehensive work. It is a scientific analysis of the subject, prepared for critics and men of a highly cultured and investigating turn of mind, and was not originally intended to instruct ordinary persons in the management of words and sentences for practical purposes. —Sherwin Cody, *The Art of Writing and Speaking the English Language*

Sherwin Cody's analysis of Aristotle's original intent in the writing of his rhetoric ironically highlights the dilemma faced by teachers of writing in the early twentieth century: at that time young men, and a few women, were entering colleges and universities needing to learn to write in a manner deemed appropriate by the academy. As institutions of higher learning opened their doors a bit—expanding to 12 percent of the population of eighteen-to-twenty-year-olds before World War II (Herzberg, 1991, p. 111)—to those who were not entirely of "a highly cultured and investigating turn of mind," it became obvious and necessary to create the means by which "to instruct ordinary persons in the management of words and sentences for practical purposes" (Cody, 1903a, p. 1). Sherwin Cody is but one of a number of men schooled in rhetoric who sought to construct the means by which the instructional goal—

learning to write for the academy—could be reached. However, Sherwin Cody's goal was not solely to instruct for the academy, but to reach those whose interest was in the business world. The expanding role of education, which had heretofore served solely the ruling class, shifts at this time to accommodate the need to instruct members of the bourgeoisie, and it marks a dramatic shift in the culture of academia. This radical shift put language and culture at the forefront of the enterprise of education. As Cody writes, "While language as the medium of thought may be compared to air as the medium of the sun's influence, in other respects it is like the skin of the body; a scurvy skin shows bad blood within, and a scurvy language shows inaccurate thought and a confused mind" (Cody, 1903b, p. 9).

The Social Construction of the New Rhetoric

The radical social, cultural, and educational conditions affecting higher education and subsequently the teaching of rhetoric as the nineteenth century ended and the twentieth began is the subject of this chapter. In the nineteenth century rhetoric—now generally known as teaching writing or composition—held a very esteemed position within the academy, which it had maintained for more than two thousand years. For the most part, teaching rhetoric during the early portion of the nineteenth century and throughout history involved the teaching of persuasive oral discourse. "The professor of rhetoric," argues Robert Connors, "was in 1800 a respected figure on his campus. His courses were subscribed, his opinions listened to, his guidance sought out by both students and administrators. A chair of rhetoric was a chair of power and honor, as it had been for 2500 years" (1991, p. 55). At the turn of the century, around 1900, this situation had completely changed. By this time, rhetoric, rather than focusing on oral discourse as it had in the past, turned out of necessity to a focus on the written word. This change in focus came about for a variety of reasons related to cultural, political, and economic shifts in emphasis in the academy that occurred subtly and at times radically over the course of the previous century. Globally, the shift served to wrench the focus of academic study out of the hands of clerics and into the hands of scientifically trained specialists. With this shift came a change in focus to "an education that prepared students for work in this life, not for rewards in the next" (Berlin, 1984, pp. 58–59). Public institutions in particular sought to develop a practical curriculum, restructure institutionally, and find new ways to define the student whose membership was increasingly from the middle class, so that higher education could meet the needs of the burgeoning economy. Berlin notes that

> At some schools, especially at state universities, this meant abandoning classical studies, complete with the cancellation of entrance requirements that insisted on an elementary knowledge of Greek and Latin. At most institutions, however, the new scientific courses were offered alongside the old classical offerings. The crucial difference was that an elective system enabled the student to choose the courses he wanted. (1984, p. 59)

What did this all mean for rhetoric? First, in the United States Hugh Blair's *Lectures* (1783) had gained tremendous popularity within universities, maintaining dominance as a text until about 1825 (Connors, Ede, & Lundsford, 1984, p. 2). Blair's text elevated attention to literary style and an aesthetic appreciation of the literary, particularly poetry, while diminishing the classical emphasis rhetoric had traditionally placed on oratory. This movement away from public discourse represented the beginnings of a mounting support for English studies, or for what was considered at that time to be the "vernacular" as opposed to the revered classical orientation toward the study of Latin and Greek. Second, concomitant to the move toward support for the "belles lettres" and English studies came organizational specialization within other disciplines in the academy. Thus emerged the further development of departments and the separation of the academy into specialized fields. Prior to this movement, rhetoric was firmly situated within the academy; "its goal was the discovery and sharing of knowledge" (Connors, Ede, & Lundsford, 1984, p. 3). Rhetoric was not conducive to specialization as it had always played a role in bringing members of the academy with diverse interests together for debate, and those with positions in rhetoric were known and respected as generalists (Connors, Ede, & Lundsford, 1984, p. 3). Third, by the last quarter of the nineteenth century enrollments in higher education had doubled. This factor in and of itself demanded a restructuring of the academy. The possibility for oral interaction and debate and the emphasis on public discourse required of rhetoric was no longer suitable with such large numbers of students. A more standardized mode of evaluation was needed; thus professors turned to writing and other modes of evaluation assumed to be more uniform and away from oral discourse. Fourth, the advancement of scientific knowledge proceeded at such a rapid pace during this period of time that the academy struggled to keep up with it.

Finally, in the nineteenth century there was little or no opportunity for advancement beyond the level of a bachelor's degree in the United States. Thus the development of German graduate programs of high quality attracted American scholars in pursuit of advanced degrees in the social sciences, chemistry, psychology, mathematics, and philology (Connors, 1991, p. 62). As a result, rhetoric quickly lost credibility, as it had no foundation in empirical study—despite Sherwin Cody's claim to the contrary—and no advanced degrees in the area were offered either in the United States or in Germany. Without graduate students, rhetoric had no means by which to replicate itself in the traditional academic manner that was fast developing in the other more empirically oriented fields of study. Rather, rhetoric, with its emphasis on persuasion, was viewed as an emotional enterprise, which further contributed to its rapid decline in status. Without advanced degrees in rhetoric, the discipline ultimately lost the ability to sustain itself with any status. As Connors argues,

> It was this demand for doctorates that truly spelled the end for rhetoric as a discipline, because, as Graff and Veysey point out, English Departments after 1885 were not equipped to reproduce any sort of nonliterary or nonphilological

PhD candidates. Rhetoric after 1870 tended to be left in the hands of that curious transitional generation of non-PhDs that arrived at universities in the 1870s and 1880s and came to be especially associated with Harvard's English Department. (1991, p. 64)

The Institutionalization of Comp I and II

It was Harvard College, in fact, that instituted entrance exams in written English as a result of a concurrent "cultural preoccupation in America with the onset of the great usage debates between Henry Alford, G. W. Moon, Richard Gould, and others" (Connors, p. 66, quote in Finegan, 1980, pp. 62–74). When these exams were introduced in 1874, "to the horror of professors, parents, and the intellectual culture as a whole, more than half the students" failed (p. 66). These results precipitated a focus on writing for all students upon entering Harvard. The practice of requiring entering students to take one or most often two semesters of writing that was established at Harvard was replicated throughout colleges and universities in the United States and remains in practice to this day.

It was at Harvard, as well, that the final blow to classical rhetoric was struck. As English departments developed, battles were fought to include the study of English literature—the vernacular elevated in status to the belles lettres—in the curriculum. At Harvard, the battle for literature was won by none other than the university's esteemed James Francis Child, Boylston Professor of Rhetoric, who held the post from 1851 to 1876, at which time he was offered a position at Johns Hopkins University. Child promptly turned the offer down once Harvard created a new position for him as the college's first chair of English literature. Gone was the chair of rhetoric and gone as well was rhetoric's status within the Department of English that Child subsequently developed: one based primarily on literary scholarship, that is, a focus on the belles lettres, not rhetoric. Child was perhaps the first to live every writing instructor's fantasy: life without entry-level student themes to be read, commented on, and evaluated . . . over and over again, seemingly without end. The new life Child structured for himself and members of his department, which became the model for English departments around the country, was one of great fulfillment. Central to the curriculum of the English department was the reading and discussing of the great works, with upper-level students, smaller classes, and far fewer papers to read. Thus the teaching of rhetoric was institutionally diminished by a distinguished professor of rhetoric: could there be no greater irony?

Shaping Writing Instruction and the Expansion of English Studies

This new academic system did recognize writing as a necessary skill; courses in writing were required, as noted above, and were not part of the elective system.

Unfortunately, despite this new emphasis on writing in the academy, it appears that the results, in terms of students' perceived ability to master academic writing, were quite poor. James Berlin reports that the situation "came to a head at Harvard in 1891" (1984, p. 60). Harvard's board of overseers appointed a committee of three: Charles Francis Adams, E. L. Godkin, and Josiah Quincy, none of whom had any experience teaching writing but were destined because of their status to shape the future course of writing instruction. As is often the case, the committee members found fault not at the universities, where writing courses were overenrolled and instructors overworked (at Harvard there were twenty instructors responsible for two thousand students), but, rather, at the high schools. The committee recommended that writing become more of a focus at the high school level and that universities tighten their admissions requirements—close those gates even more tightly. Though unfortunate in some regards, the committee's recommendations did serve to bring the study of English to the forefront at the high school level. Unfortunately, since not one of the members knew a thing about writing, their recommendations regarding instruction were abysmal: they focused on spelling, grammar, and handwriting—the most superficial of features that have, as Berlin notes, "haunted writing classes ever since" (1984, pp. 60–61).

The Transformation of Rhetoric

So within less than a century, rhetoric was completely transformed. First, its focus was no longer on oral discourse but, rather, on the written word. Second, its esteemed professors were no longer viewed with high regard; quite the contrary, they were more often than not disdained. Third, rhetoric's newly semi-acquired position as a discipline within departments of English was now amorphous, because there was no way to obtain a higher degree in the subject, other than for a short period of time from 1903 to 1927 at the University of Michigan, under the leadership of Fred Newton Scott (Connors, 1991, p. 65). Fourth, the workload associated with the teaching of rhetoric, increasingly referred to as writing or composition, was such that those who taught it were left with energy for no other intellectual pursuits. This is the case because "writing is an interior activity, and although techniques can be used to share writing among students, a primary transaction in any serious composition course came to be seen as between the student and the teacher. Each student came to be seen as deserving a measurable individual chunk of the teacher's time and energy" (Connors, 1991, p. 68). It is no wonder the five-paragraph essay emerged as the ideal form in the traditional approach. Had no limits been set, teachers would never have had time to sleep, let alone eat, given the need to read, correct, and comment on student papers.

The reconfiguration of rhetoric from an orally based, persuasive discourse in the classical tradition—which did not set outrageous demands on the highly regarded men who taught it—to a course of study designed to teach entry-level students to write for the academic community and the world of business established its low status. In turn, the reconfiguration of rhetoric placed an enormous workload on instructors ill-prepared to teach in the void that had once been filled by an esteemed area of study.

A Last-Ditch Effort for Status and Control: The Traditional Approach

With no foundation in theory or research, those involved in this now poorly regarded nondiscipline of rhetoric turned, I argue, to pedagogy for structure, if not for solace. This led in turn, I argue, to the emergence of what is referred to as the traditional approach to teaching writing. "The traditional approach, which dominated writing pedagogy in American education from the nineteenth century to the 1960's" (Bizzell, 1986, p. 60), views, in its strongest form, the "successful writer as one who can systematically produce a 500-word theme of five paragraphs, each with a topic sentence" (Hairston, 1982, p. 78). Richard Young more fully delineates the traditional approach: "The overt features . . . are obvious enough: the emphasis on the composed product rather than the composing process; the analysis of discourse into description, narration, exposition, and argument; the strong concern with usage . . . and with style; the preoccupation with the informal essay and research paper; and so on" (1978, p. 31). More specifically, the traditional approach stresses expository writing to the virtual exclusion of all other forms, elevates style to a position of utmost importance, subsumes invention almost entirely, and posits an unchanging reality independent of the writer and that all writers are expected to describe in the same way regardless of the rhetorical situation (Berlin & Inkster, 1980). The traditional approach "embodies . . . the aura of technical neutrality or objectivity," thus privileging elite modes of discourse—literary and belletristic essays—that carry with them the implicit assumption that these forms represent an embodiment of "ideal types of psychological universals" (Herzberg, 1991, p. 110).

Adherents of the traditional approach maintain that "competent writers know what they are going to say before they begin to write; thus their most important task when they are preparing to write is finding a form into which to organize their content" (Hairston, 1982, p. 78). The traditional approach presupposes that all students are organically connected with the reading of their world, which motivates them to critically and reflectively express their world reading in a written form that has been a priori proposed. This view is not only naive but also abjures the complexity, tensions, and contradictions involved in the reading of the world that precedes the writing of the world that was read. As Paulo Freire argues, writing constitutes a postliteracy phase that should "contribute to the people so that by taking more and more history into their own hands, they can shape their history. To shape history is to be present in it, not merely represented in it" (Freire & Macedo, 1987, p. 65). In this sense, the traditional approach to writing ignores the obvious: having something to say is intimately related to one's presence in history. To be merely represented and yet not present leads writing students to a silenced culture that leaves them with very little to say that would be found acceptable within the academic context. While this is the case to a greater degree for students from outside of the middle and upper classes, initiation into academic discourse is by no means unproblematic for those students as well. The example from earlier in this chapter of the introduction of a writing entrance exam at Harvard in the late nineteenth century illustrates this point.

Moreover, the divergence in style and expectations between entering students and the academy is finely illustrated in the comments of a turn-of-the-century instructor (a graduate student) on a student paper: "You should develop a grace of style and depth of comprehension. You need, too, to understand the aesthetic and spiritual values of the great masterpieces of the world's art, literary and pictorial" (Thayer, 1926, p. 773, as cited in Connors, 1991, p. 75). If the instructor assumes that all of this is to be known, understood, and clearly written about upon entrance to college, one wonders what this instructor assumes his role to be. Clearly, he is not engaged in assisting this poor undergraduate in gaining access to any of this knowledge that he, the graduate student, and the academy so value. Quite the contrary, his sole purpose seems to be to point out that the undergraduate neither knows nor understands anything of what his instructor values. Unfortunately pomposity is often displayed by those who lack the humility to comprehend how little it is that they do in fact know. Remember, Socrates felt no shame in admitting that he knew nothing.

Remediation and Fragmentation

Perhaps in an effort to avoid such pretentious pitfalls, the traditional approach set about to define a methodology, a set of strategies, instructors could uniformly follow. These strategies include a focus on a writing technique that calls for paper outlining, writing, and then rewriting to correct sentence-level features and grammar (Knoblauch & Brannon, 1984). The traditional approach reflects the assumption that writing is a linear process and that the intent behind the process is the creation of a final product modeled on the logical essay. In the traditional approach the role of the writing instructor is authoritarian as well as authoritative: he or she is responsible for providing models of good prose (provided in the assigned rhetoric, now a textbook, for the class) and for evaluating student papers. Often students, especially those considered less-proficient writers, are presented with a series of textbook tasks that break the essay into fragmented, unrelated components that students are expected to master piece by piece. Working with models, students are asked, for example, to find the topic sentence in a paragraph decontextualized from its original source.

Jan Nespor (1991, p. 179) discusses the manner in which "authentic" texts become "inauthentic" and uses as an example a paragraph about Francis Bacon (or it could be Roger, this is not made clear in the exercise the textbook provides) taken from a book about chemistry. Asked to find the topic sentence from the paragraph, the students flounder, pointing out sentence after sentence, until one fits the instructor's notion of main idea. What Nespor argues is that the main idea (topic sentence) that is finally elicited remains meaningless when placed in the thematic context of Bacon's book. More important, argues Nespor, the notion that each component of a larger text holds its own "main idea" serves only to distort "the nature and coherence of naturally occurring texts and sends ambiguous messages about how the latter are to be read" (pp. 179–180) or, for that matter, written.

Unfortunately, it is the least-proficient student writers who are asked in the traditional approach—and in other approaches as well—to focus on fragmented components of language. Correct grammar is stressed. Exercises dealing with sentence-level production, often with no cohesion between sentences required, are the norm. Once the sentence is "mastered," students move on to the paragraph, as if learning to write were a matter of building language blocks one upon the other until the five-paragraph essay would most magically appear. Of course, lower-track students—students of color, of the working class and underclass, and those new to the United States with little background experience in school settings—will not master the five-paragraph essay, and the more "remediated" they are the farther they are distanced from real, contextualized, meaningful language (Collins, 1991).

A Space and Place in the Academy

What the traditional approach did, I argue, was attempt to reestablish a sense of belonging—a defined, bureaucratically privileged space and place in the academy—to a once esteemed area of study within the classical academy of the eighteenth and nineteenth centuries. By focusing on pedagogy, those left teaching writing were at least able to refer to the rhetoric (textbook) in an effort to reassume a semblance of authority in a context in which there really was little power to be had. Through the association with a clearly defined methodology, the traditional approach, powerless instructors had at least not only the authoritarian stance allowed the teacher but also an authoritative reference in published rhetorics that would soon come to define the new, diminished field of rhetoric or writing instruction. In all, a series of circumstances leading to a major reconfiguration of colleges and universities in the United States transformed rhetoric into a labor-intensive, devalued, and dreaded nonsubject area with only those most powerless in the academy charged with teaching it: most generally next year's crop of teaching assistants bound for servitude. Not all those who taught writing were teaching assistants, of course. Some were part-timers, forever destined to remain on the fringes of the academy, most often without a Ph.D., or if the Ph.D. were in hand, perhaps a full-time position leading to tenure review was not.

What role does traditional rhetoric play today? James Berlin captures its essence quite nicely:

Rhetoric's sole appeal is to the understanding and reason, with its highest manifestation to be found in exposition and argument. The distinction between argument—the bringing about of conviction through appeals to reason—and persuasion—appealing to the will through emotion in order to bring about action—is accepted. Persuasion, however, is made the province of oratory and is relegated to speech departments. The appeals to imagination and emotion found in poetry are consigned to the literature section of the English department. The business of the composition teacher is to train the remaining faculties, and despite the attention paid to argument, this effort focuses primarily on the understanding, the faculty involved in scientific investigation. Exposition, "setting forth" what is inductively discovered (narration and description are similarly conceived), becomes the central concern of writing classes. This is also, of course, the kind of writing most valued by the technologically oriented business community. Freshman English becomes a course in technical writing. (1984, p. 63)

Berlin's argument is clear. Writing instruction has become the province of skills acquisition; the first required set of courses students must take and pass in order to not only maintain their place within the academy but also ensure acceptance into the workplace. Clear writing, in other words, is deemed a necessity for entrance into the technocratic class, that is, the business community. High schools prepare students for the world of work (Bowles & Gintis, 1976), and so too do universities. Even Berlin's choice of the terminology "business of writing instructors" serves to situate the pedagogical process outside of the central notion of the academy as site for the "production" of ideas and the advancement of knowledge. In the end, the traditional approach represents a concerted effort on the part of its creators and supporters to ensure the maintenance of a precariously obtained status quo for writing pulled from the rubble of classical rhetoric.

To conclude, I quote again from Sherwin Cody, who argues:

The right kind of language-teaching will also give us power, a kind of eloquence, a skill in the use of words, which will enable us to frame advertisements which will draw business, letters which will win customers, and to speak in that elegant and forceful way so effective in selling goods. When all advertisements are couched in very imperfect language, and all business letters are carelessly written, of course no one has an advantage over another, and a good knowledge and command of language would not be much of a recommendation to a business man who wants a good assistant. But when a few have come in and by their superior command of language gained a distinct advantage over rivals, then the power inherent in language comes into universal demand—the business standard is raised. (Cody, 1903b, p. 13)

2

THE COGNITIVE APPROACH

Method is not innocent or neutral. It not only presupposes an understanding of what constitutes social and political life; it has also become a powerful factor in shaping (or rather misshaping) human life in the modern world. — Richard J. Bernstein, *Beyond Objectivism and Relativism: Science, Heurmenutics and Praxis*

Beginning in the 1960s, writing teaching and research shifted from a focus on product to a focus on process (Graves, 1983; Murray, 1976; Raimes,1983; Zamel, 1976). Essentially this shift to a focus on process was a revolutionary plan born of a progressivism that sought opportunity and inclusion for those previously denied access to education and academic literacy. This paradigm shift (Kuhn, 1970) emerged initially as a result of a critique of the premises underlying the traditional approach to teaching writing, which found its roots (among the rubble) in classical rhetoric. Eventually many within the field of composition teaching and from education in general came to question the fundamentally authoritarian and hierarchical assumptions underlying the traditional approach (Graves, 1983, 1990; Murray, 1985; Zamel, 1976). Researchers and teachers, many of whom were associated with the progressive educational movement of the 1960s, questioned the primacy of the logical essay as a model for good writing, the premise that writing was a linear process, and the role of the instructor as authority figure. A revolution was born. And it had a plan.

Noam Chomsky versus B. F. Skinner: The Primacy of Cognition

The whole notion of an approach to writing based upon cognition gained credibility through its tertiary association (see appendix for a discussion of tertiary
association) with Noam Chomsky's argument against B. F. Skinner's behaviorist
notion of language and language acquisition as encapsulated in Skinner's book
Verbal Behavior (1957). In short, Skinner argued that humans are born tabulae
rasae—blank slates—and acquire language solely through a process of mimicry,
memorization, and analogy. Skinner argued further that humans are shaped by
their environment through a process of operant conditioning, never once uttering
a phrase or word that has not before been heard in the environment. Grounded in
the teachings of logical positivism, Skinner's theory places great emphasis on the
power of the teacher or caregiver to shape the learning of the student or child.
Skinner himself was known to spend considerable time actively working to shape
the development of his own children, not just the mice, parrots, and other crea-
tures he experimented with in his Harvard labs (Bjork, 1993).

In sharp contrast to Skinner, Noam Chomsky's thinking harks back in time
to the philosophical notions put forth by René Descartes, considered the father of
modern philosophy, who placed at the forefront of his views the notion of the
primacy of the mind. Chomsky's review of Skinner's *Verbal Behavior,* published in
the journal *Language* in 1957, not only launched Chomsky's career but also sent
linguistics and the teaching of language in all its guises into upheaval. Chomsky's
linguistic argument—which he himself referred to as Cartesian linguistics—led
to an increasing interest in linguistics and language acquisition and to the emergence of departments of cognitive science and linguistics, thus situating cognition
and language at the forefront in many an academic debate. In stark contrast to
Skinner, Chomsky argues that humans are born with an innate capacity or faculty
for language acquisition. This faculty, which he calls the Language Acquisition
Device (LAD), is said to be located in the brain and provides all humans with the
universal foundation (Universal Grammar) upon which to acquire language with
rapidity and ease. All children, Chomsky maintains, once exposed to their linguistic environment, begin to sort through the vast linguistic input available to
them. This leads to the eventual formulation of internalized linguistic rules of
their own, as children find their way into the language of their community through
a process of hypothesis testing and creative construction. Thus, from a Chomskian
perspective we have not the Skinnerian passive and pliable learner but, rather, an
active, engaged acquirer. The Chomskian acquirer/learner fits the progressive educators' notion of a model student: one prepared to interact with a nonauthoritarian
instructor, mutually engaging in the process of written language acquisition.

Jerome Bruner and Process

Jerome Bruner, a Harvard psychologist, no doubt drew from Chomsky's theory in
his 1960 report published after a ten-day conference at Woods Hole, Massachu-

setts, sponsored by the National Academy of Sciences. Orchestrated in response to Sputnik, the "meeting was intended to examine the teaching of science in the schools" (Berlin 1987, p. 122), but Bruner included in his final report—*The Process of Education*—many references to literature teaching. Due to the influence of Bruner's report and his other work, specifically "The Act of Discovery" and "The Conditions of Creativity" published in *On Knowing: Essays for the Left Hand,* money for studies in English became available (Berlin, 1987, p. 122). Bruner, I argue, draws heavily on the arguments and terminology used by Chomsky. Bruner incorporates Chomsky's notion of the primacy of cognition and the theory that the child language acquirer/learner comes to know his or her native language through an inductive process allowing for the internalization of the rules of one's language. Important here are the notions and terms: cognition and process. Bruner's theory of education situates cognition and process as central to learning (Bruner, 1960). For Bruner, as was the case for Chomsky, the learner/acquirer comes to know through an inductive process, which involves an engagement with the discipline/ language. Where Chomsky wrote of creative construction, a process by which children came to internalize the rules of their language, Bruner wrote of "creative guesses" that would lead the learner to "verification in the more orthodox manner" (Berlin, 1987, p. 123). And while teachers of language argued for a methodology that would have students using language in real communicative contexts as a means to acquire language, in the manner described by Chomsky in his theory of first language acquisition, so too did Bruner argue that students would learn physics or math by doing physics or math. In both cases, the argument was against relying on the learning of rules dictated by experts in a particular area, whether language, math, physics, or any other discipline, including writing (not a discipline), for that matter.

Product versus Process

Once again, through tertiary association writing theorists and teachers incorporate first Bruner's notion of process, leading to "process writing," and many, I argue, further incorporate cognition leading to the "hot-off-the-press" cognitive approach to process writing. For instructors of writing, Berlin argues, the implications were clear: "Students should engage in the process of composing, not in the study of someone else's process of composing. Teachers may supply information about writing or direct students in its structural stages, but their main job is to create an environment in which students can learn for themselves the behaviors appropriate to successful writing. The product of student writing, moreover, is not as important as the process of writing" (1987, p. 123). Writing theorists and practitioners without a thorough and detailed understanding of the theoretical underpinnings of the Skinner–Chomsky debate, or of Bruner's influence on educational theory and practice, were nonetheless affected, I would imagine, by the whole tenor of the times—it was the 1960s. Further, if they were at all progressive in ideological perspective, writing theorists and practitioners would certainly have been affected as well by a desire to appear nonauthoritarian. After all, the 1960s, which culturally extended into the early 1970s, was an era of challenging authority. Not all writing theorists or practitioners would have had a background in linguistics or psychology, or political theory for that matter. Much of what was formulated as theoretical foundations for changes in practice may have come about more through attachment, as argued above, to tertiary knowledge, than to an in-depth understanding of the historical and ongoing tensions between empiricism and rationalism and evolving notions of how learning occurred. Nonetheless, what became important now to those who followed—through a tertiary association—a Chomskian perspective, or a cognitive approach, were the internal workings of the mind, not external behaviors. Though, ironically, the notion was that external processes would replicate the internal processes of the mind. It was getting it all to work together that became problematic.

John Locke, the Empiricist, versus René Descartes, the Rationalist

In like manner, the logical essay, itself a social construct that emerged in the seventeenth century, no longer retained the revered status it held in the eyes of an empiricist. It was John Locke, it must be remembered, who argued that knowledge itself resided within the logic, the argument put forth in the essay. Thus, Locke argued, firmly grounded in his empiricist perspective and entirely counter to the teachings of Descartes, that knowledge existed out in the real world, in the world of the text. Based on Locke's argument, this Enlightenment notion—fueled by the emergence of print culture and shaped by the linearity of the argument as put forth in the logical essay, led to the establishment of the logical essay as the preeminent form denoting appropriate scholarship and, in turn, the acceptable discourse of the academy. The logical essay's textual form and underlying premises retained exalted status from the seventeenth century on, and they still vie for, and more often than not win as, the favored and thus most valued of academic forms to this day. This is the case despite the tensions created beginning in the 1960s by progressives, feminists, and many multiculturalists, who have argued for the valuing and use of multiple forms of discourse within the academic context.

Writing Research: Cognition and Process

Researchers, both in reaction to the tenets of the traditional approach and the revolutionary work in education and linguistics in the late 1960s and early 1970s, began to focus on the act of composing in an attempt to understand the cognitive processes successful writers engage in as papers are developed. This change in focus emerged in response to the discomfort with the primacy given the logical essay, the emphasis on linearity, and the unquestioned authority granted the writing instructor within the traditional approach.

Writing researchers advocating the cognitive approach came to insist that in order to teach students to write one must also understand "what goes on during the internal act of writing" (Hairston, 1982, p. 84). James Berlin notes that "for cognitive rhetoric, the structures of the mind correspond in perfect harmony with the structures of the material world, the minds of the audience, and the units of language" (1988, p. 480). The assumption was that if this process could be identified, then writing instructors could have students emulate the process in the classroom, thus providing avenues to success where they had previously been blocked. Adherents of the cognitive approach rejected the notion that an outline—as required in the traditional approach—necessarily preceded the writing of a paper and that the subsequent correction of surface-level features represented techniques employed by successful writers. The very tenets of the traditional approach were not only being questioned but also were assumed to be an erroneous reflection of the manner in which the human mind works during the process of composing. The traditional approach was under attack because it did not appropriately replicate human thought processes. It was assumed, instead, that within the mind existed yet-to-be-discovered mental processes employed by successful writers. It was further assumed that these processes, once understood, could be taught to emergent writers, thus ensuring that they would be trained to think, and thus act, like successful writers.

Through a research methodology incorporating case study, ethnography, and protocol analysis (Flower & Hayes, 1981), researchers began not only to understand but also to delineate more fully the strategies successful writers, student as well as professional, make use of in the creative process. Those identified with the cognitive school of process writing focused on both successful and less-successful writers. Sondra Perl (1979), for example, found that poor writers accord inordinate importance and time to editing for errors in grammar, spelling, and mechanics, while successful writers allow for the recursive quality of composing by rereading the text throughout the process of production. Perl argued further that the successful writer waits for a felt sense of structure to emerge and allows this to guide planning, rather than approaching the writing task with a preconceived plan.

In response to Perl's findings and other studies, proponents of the cognitive approach argued that writing instructors needed to provide adequate time to student writers for brainstorming, note taking, talking about the planned paper, writing and rewriting, global restructuring, and, finally, editing and proofreading. Research revealed that early attention to surface features such as grammar, punctuation, and spelling in fact served to block the writing process (Zamel, 1983, p. 169).

As a result, composition classrooms were structured to create opportunities for students to engage actively in this process, a process that reflected the model of the production of texts within the academic community. The process was designed to begin with the individual germination of an idea for a paper and end, in some cases, with publication. For the most part this meant providing opportunities for students to write multiple drafts of papers, all the while emphasizing that students need not attend to surface linguistic features until required to hand in the final version of the paper. In other words, in order to become better writers, students must write and rewrite freely without attention initially to surface concerns.

Basically, the cognitive approach supports the belief that individuals will become better writers if they learn to think and act like good writers. In other words, cognitivists support the notion that students will become competent, if not successful, writers if they make use of these imparted strategies, techniques, or practices. While purportedly nonmechanistic in philosophy, those within the cognitive school do suggest that learning to write means acquiring a particular set of skills and strategies: those skills and strategies associated with how successful writers approach and carry out the writing task. And while claiming a mentalistic framework—perhaps as linkage to an academic buzzword, "cognition," of the day—process writing from the cognitivist perspective emphasized technique. Gone was the expectation that student writers could produce a text by starting at the beginning and working straight through, with an outline as guide, to the end. Instructors and researchers knew, or assumed they knew, that they did not in fact write that way, and they made every effort to impart the strategies they employed to their students. (I will argue in the next chapter, however, that in some contexts academic writing emerges from an imposed structure that precedes the writing of the text.) In the end, the effort to develop a cognitive approach to process writing was and is naively egalitarian.

Teaching Writing: The Cognitive Approach

As noted earlier in this chapter, inherent within the cognitive perspective is this notion of technique. The belief was that once successful techniques were delineated through the study of successful writers, these strategies could then be imparted to students. These very strategies in many ways began to represent, or in fact constitute, a body of knowledge, one easily codified into a set of techniques or rules for carrying out the writer's task. Thus writing is reduced to a subset of skills: becoming a writer means acquiring and carrying out these skills. Implicit within this assumption is the belief that if one does not become a good writer, that is, fulfill the expectations of the academy, it is the individual, not the institution, who is at fault. Embedded also within the assumption is the notion that failure stems from the misapplication of the skills, such as continued overattention to surface features when writing, or from failure to work hard enough throughout the process.

The cognitive approach in many ways incorporates, as well as reflects, the perspective of the meritocratic university (Berlin, 1988, p. 483). While egalitarian in essence, this egalitarianism is most superficial. For now the assumption is that the instructor has held back no secrets all that she knows and does has been imparted and often modeled in practice for the student. Teachers, in an effort to impart full disclosure, would often write at the same time students wrote in class, thus emphasizing again that students were as much writers as were teachers of writing. But still many students continued to fail to access the forms required of the academy. Now, failure surely resided within individuals who did not take it upon themselves to fully engage in the practices and techniques that the instructor has so benevolently shared, usually while sitting in a circle on seemingly "equal footing" with the students.

Teacher and Student: Equal in Status?

This notion of supposed or assumed equality between instructor and student appears also in the subtle change that occurred in the naming of the instructional period. The writing class became a writing workshop, and students met with instructors for writing conferences. The use of the terms "workshop" and "conference" elevates the status of the students—now generally referred to as "writers"—as participants in the process of learning to write, though this elevation is false and exists in name only. The instructor still, in the end, evaluates. The reconstituted status and role of the student vis-à-vis the instructor exists within the domain of linguistics only, for the reality is that the institutional constraints and structures have in no way been altered.

Further, the cognitive view of writing incorporates much of what Brian Street refers to as the autonomous model of literacy. In arguing against the autonomous model, Street contends that "what the particular practices and concepts of reading and writing are for a given society depends upon the context; that they are already embedded in an ideology and cannot be isolated or treated as 'neutral' or merely 'technical'" (Street, 1984, p. 1). Though focused on skills and procedure, the cognitive approach is not divorced from ideology. In fact it is this very focus that reveals its ideological orientation. In his discussion of the cognitive perspective, James Berlin asserts that the "pursuit of self-evident and unquestioned goals in the composing process parallels the pursuit of self-evident and unquestioned profit-making goals in the corporate market place" (1988, p. 483). Berlin argues also that cognitivists regard language "as a system of rational signs that is compatible with the mind and the external world, enabling the 'translating' or 'trans-forming' of the non-verbal intellectual operations into the verbal" (1988, p. 483). As such, language is tied entirely to the individual and is not seen as a social entity.

Establishing a Niche in the Academy

Once again, as had been the case with the traditional approach (though in this instance with adherents of the cognitive approach it is far more blatant), what is also occurring throughout this shift in focus in teaching approach is the effort on the part of academics to define a niche: a more clearly defined role for themselves within the academy. I will not go so far as to argue that concern for students was not a driving force in some instances for support of this approach to teaching writing. For clearly, many supporters of the cognitive approach did see that the traditional approach was not working and that what it did appear to do was nicely replicate the status quo. Those who entered traditional writing classes knowing how to write left those classes with an A. Those who entered the classes with grammatical or other language "problems"—nonnative speakers of English or nonstandard speakers, those with "scurvy" and "bad blood" as Cody put it—were not so successful. So perhaps advocates of the cognitive perspective felt that imparting the strategies that they had uncovered would somehow change this inequality. What everyone in academia does know, however, is that the real action for many on the cognitive bandwagon was no different from what I have argued were the motivations behind the initial effort to establish the traditional approach: an effort to move up the academic hierarchy. By the 1960s this was not possible for teachers, even with a Ph.D. in hand, unless one published original research, which is far better than the publication of a textbook or the development of a methodology, for that matter (though textbooks and methodologies, if successful, can surely make one much more money than a scholarly text can). Further, association with cognition—the thinking brain—is highly regarded because it contains an aura of pure science, yet these researchers were essentially watching behaviors. I have no problem with observing behaviors. What I do have a problem with is the misleading name: observing behaviors is not brain research. It is unproblematized, untheorized, reactive methodology development with a tertiary attachment to Chomsky's quite revolutionary work in linguistics, which was so important that it led to the reshaping of the academy.

Making It in Academia

One truly has made it in academia when departments are born as a result of the groundbreaking, revolutionary work one has done; this is what Chomsky did. And this is what writing theorists and practitioners struggle with to this day. We still seek a place of our own within the academy. For the reality is that many writing teachers are paid very little, have no status, and share an office with a number of others in the same sordid position. The few who have obtained tenure-track positions direct writing programs or centers, which means overseeing part-timers and scheduling the numerous sections of Comp I and II taught within English departments or in separate writing centers. And we must remember that programs and centers, while "places" and "spaces" in the academy, are not departments, and they do not have the institutional status and bureaucratic constraints that protect them from being arbitrarily eliminated. Tenure-track or tenured writing theorists and practitioners are often second-class citizens, unable to even speak the same language as their colleagues unless the writing teachers have expertise in other areas in addition to composition, such as Shakespeare, the Romantics, or some other accepted domain of the English department. With the latter expertise in hand, composition faculty can communicate with others in the department. The fact that writing faculty are expected to have dual areas of expertise highlights their diminished status in relation to literature faculty. In much the same way, linguistic minority students are expected to master English in order to maneuver in the United States. In contrast, native English speakers assume that their monolingual status is above critique to the degree that even when abroad, no matter where, English is privileged above all other languages. Who must obtain competency in more than one academic area, or in more than one language? It is members of subordinate groups who are expected to do so. It is always those with the least power who are asked to do the most.

3

THE EXPRESSIVE APPROACH

Once we recognize the extent to which we are constituted as reading subjects by the social and interpretive communities we inhabit, we ought to be able to deal directly with the lingering fear that subjectivity leads to chaos; to unstructured, incoherent responses; or to the expression of idiosyncratic biases.—Robert A. Schwegler, "The Politics of Reading Student Papers"

In the 1960s, personal writing revived as an expression of the political movements for civil rights, against the Bomb, and then against the Vietnam War. . . . People made meaning, and claims to the contrary were regarded as the means of oppression. Students in personal-writing courses would try to find their own voices, their own ways of seeing and understanding the world. To promote this search for authenticity was considered subversive teaching. It questioned authority, including the teacher's, even suggesting that students could learn to write without teachers. —Bruce Herzberg, "Composition and the Politics of the Curriculum"

In contrast to the cognitive perspective, some process-oriented instructors and researchers suggest that while the techniques, in particular the recursive aspects of the writing process, are important, it is equally important to focus on the expressive aspects of writing. Essentially, the "expressive view" (Faigley, 1986) emphasizes the development of the self. In Lester Faigley's words, the three principal ingredients of the "expressive" approach to process writing are "sincerity, spontaneity, and originality." These ingredients emanate from the Romantic tradition that views writing as "the act of a private consciousness" (p. 535). Fundamental to

41

the expressive view is the belief that writing teachers should work as facilitators to draw students out so that student writers can pursue their true intentions (Knoblauch & Brannon, 1984, p. 162). Further, advocates of the expressive view suggest it is the writing teacher's responsibility to come to understand the student's writing. This understanding can be enhanced by commenting on papers in a non-directive and nonauthoritarian manner while seeking to engage interactively with the writer. Thus, expressivists do recognize the social aspect of language, but they nonetheless focus essentially on the individual's search for meaning and, as is the case with the cognitivists, they abhor a traditional, authoritarian approach that emphasizes models and outlining, and other such components of writing instruction that they consider to be restrictive.

Discovery of Meaning

Fundamental to the expressive view is the assumption that individuals are capable of making sense of the world. Philosophically this view is rooted in the Kantian notion that knowledge resides in, and emerges from, the individual. Adherents of the expressive approach believe that if student writers engage actively, imaginatively in the making of meaning, if they allow the writing process to reveal to them that which they know and will come to know, they will become good writers. Ann Berthoff, a leading process writing theorist, argues that in order to understand composing researchers must look at the dialectical relationship between the writer and his or her world in order to comprehend the intended meaning of the writer. Fundamental to Berthoff's conception of the writer is her notion of imagination. Imagination to Berthoff is form-finding and form-creating on the part of the writer. "My guiding philosophical principle," writes Berthoff in *Forming, Thinking, Writing*, "is that form-finding and form-creating is a natural activity" (1982, p. 2). Berthoff calls for a method of teaching that "recognizes the human need and ability to shape, discriminate, select: the mind's power to form" (p. 290). In other words, she maintains that form emerges as meaning becomes clear as knowledge is sorted out. From this perspective, writing allows the writer to come to know. Here we have, in the words of James Paul Gee, the representation of a "bourgeois individualism that desires a free individual creation of meaning apart from culture and history," a task Gee argues is impossible (1984, p. 29).

Like Berthoff, Donald Murray, an early proponent of process writing, suggests that the process of revision will lead to the discovery of what the writer has to say as well as to the natural discovery of form and structure (Murray, 1976). The message is, again, that form will emerge naturally as long as opportunities to engage in the "process" are provided. No explicit statement about what constitutes good form is needed, because the assumption is that students will come to uncover the implicit expectations of the academy. Somehow, out of the search for and the subsequent finding of meaning, a coherent form will emerge.

The Social Construction of Form

Form-finding and form-creating may in fact be natural abilities. Coherence may in fact emerge in the act of writing. The point remains, however, that the form to emerge may not be the form anticipated by the academy (Gee, 1989, 1996; Gumperz, 1982; Michaels, 1981; Shaugnessy, 1977). What Berthoff and others of the expressive school do not address is the issue of the varieties of structures and ways of coherently ordering reality through text both in oral and written forms that exist across cultures and discourse communities (Gee, 1985; Michaels, 1981). We do find order out of the supposed incoherence of chaos (Roskelly, 1988). And, as Gee writes, "all humans are masters of making sense of experience and the world" (1985, p. 27). This natural ability emerges in the production of the stories we tell, the narratives told in an effort to make sense of the ever-unfolding events of our daily lives. The forms most generally expected within the academy, however, are not narrative but, rather, the logical essay and research paper. Neither the logical essay (Ong, 1982) nor the research paper (Coleman & Tyler, 1987) is a natural linguistic form; they are socially produced. Student writers have a proclivity to order, as do we all, but this proclivity may not find its form in the logical essay or research paper. Instead, students may find themselves drawn to narrative or poetry, genres that are respected in English departments as worthy of analysis and critique, and whose production is encouraged in the creative writing class but not, for the most part, in the academy. In fact, even those who produce and publish in these genres remain marginal in academia (Hatlen, 1988, p. 791).

Nonetheless, the curriculum emerging from the cognitive and, in particular, from the expressive view of writing process does tend, at least in the first paper assignments in courses, to focus on personal writing rather than on the logical essay or any of the other more academically oriented forms, such as the compare/contrast essay. This is the case because expressive-writing adherents believe that individuals have a natural desire to write (I would say communicate) and that this desire would be constrained if student writers were given assignments they were not interested in (Graves, 1983). Thus, they believe that writing that is acceptable to the academy will emerge from the individual. Facilitators within the academy should work interactively with writers to enhance this assumed-to-be-natural process that is, in reality, socially produced. We are not born writers, we are just born with an innate ability to acquire language (Chomsky, 1967). However, what this approach fails to acknowledge is that teachers read a text with a particular set of culturally determined expectations about how the text should be structured (Gumperz, 1982; Michaels, 1985). If there is a mismatch between teacher expectation and the student's own culturally based schema, the interactive process will most likely break down. The possibility of a mismatch in structure and other devices associated with the making of meaning is more likely to occur when the student writer is from a background that differs from that of the mainstream (Gee, 1987, 1996; Gumperz, 1982; Michaels, 1985). This is the case because individuals from outside mainstream homes and communities—such as working- and lower-class students, immigrants and refugees, speakers of Black English Vernacular (BEV), women even—have been socialized into language use in ways that may differ considerably from those expected in institutional contexts, especially schools (Heath, 1982; Scollon & Scollon, 1981). Further, not only may this mismatch deny subordinated students access to middle-class–based schema but also the fact that such schema require blind assimilation of these nonmainstream students often produces in them the experience of subordination in the very task of learning to write (Macedo, 1994b).

The Privileging of "Appropriate" Forms

While the assumptions inherent in the expressive process model are certainly nonauthoritarian—in that form is not imposed on student writers as it is in the traditional approach, which relies on a constrained set of textual models for "good prose"—the perspective is, nonetheless, problematic. Even though no ideal model for form is presented, at least explicitly, as is the case with the traditional approach, it is implicit in the expressive approach that the ideal form to emerge will be that of academic literacy. By this I mean that the expressivist assumes and expects that the form to emerge will be a form acceptable within the academic context. It is not always the case, however, that forms consistent with academic literacy do emerge. Few nonmainstream students, for example, successfully complete writing courses, and not all students become proficient writers. Therefore, one is left wondering who is to judge, in the final analysis, when meaning is created, when the writer has come to know, and when form has emerged. And, in turn, one wonders what bases, in terms of meaning, knowledge, and form, are used to reach these judgments.

It is no secret that within the academic context there are certain expectations about what constitutes well-organized, well-written prose. Linda Brodkey (1987) makes this point clear:

> All writers use the language of a community, and all must write in ways deemed appropriate to and by a community. In this sense, then, scientists and poets are subject to similar constraints. Scientists write to those who read and write science, poets to those who read and write poetry. And while it will not be the case that all the readers of science and poetry are actually writing science and poetry, reading an article in a scientific journal or a particular poem relies as much on one's knowledge and experience of science or poetry as on one's knowledge of the language in which it is written. (pp. 1–2)

So too must student writers write in the forms deemed appropriate by the members of the academic community: first their writing instructors and then, perhaps, the readers of their writing proficiency exams. Thus it is the community, the academic community, that ultimately has the power as well as the "knowledge" to assess whether or not initiates into the community also have come to possess this knowledge. As Myron Tuman argues, we must recognize that "while academic writing does take on the appearance of communication, its real goal is often a public demonstration for the purpose of being judged, perhaps akin to figure skating or gymnastics, what Bartholomae labels, in a memorable epigram, as 'an act of aggression disguised as an act of charity'" (1988, pp. 47–48). Neither cognitive nor expressive theorists or practitioners deal with the issue of the hegemony of their practice or the hegemony of their assumptions regarding the value or necessity of acquiring academic literacy. The cognitivists remain constrained, in particular, by the assumption that literacy is an entity that can be packaged and handed along from teacher to student as a clearly defined body of knowledge related to ways of acting. The expressivists are dually constrained: both by their emphasis on process as technique and by their assumption that form will emerge as writers engage in the process of meaning making. The expressivists fail to recognize that the accepted, anticipated forms in the academic context are not natural but are socially, culturally, and historically produced.

Research on Teacher Response to Student Writing

As noted earlier in this chapter, expressivists focus to a considerable degree on communication between student-writer and teacher-facilitator. This focus led to research on teacher comments and analyses of how responses to students' texts affect a writer's development. One such researcher, Vivian Zamel, a recognized authority on second-language writing theory and practice, suggests this emphasis allows students not only to understand the intent of their writing but also to make discoveries about their use of language and ideas. The instructor, argues Zamel, should intervene in the writing process in a nonauthoritarian, nonjudgmental manner in order to affect the outcome, all while attending to each student's search for meaning, thus making every effort not to appropriate students' work.

As student and instructor interact, Zamel maintains, they participate dialectically in the making of meaning. Zamel suggests further, based on research I will discuss below, that it is preferable that these interactions occur orally in conference situations because students are often confused by written teacher comments they perceive to be vague. This conclusion is based on a study Zamel undertook of fifteen teachers' written comments, reactions, and markings on ESL student papers, the results of which were first presented at the Eighteenth Annual TESOL Convention in 1984 and later published in *TESOL Quarterly* (Zamel, 1985) and reprinted in *Writing in a Second Language* (Leeds, 1996). In her study, Zamel did not analyze oral responses to written work, nor had she done so in any previous research; nonetheless she concludes that

> we should set up collaborative sessions and conferences during which important discoveries can be made by both reader and writer. The reader can discover

the underlying meaning and logic of what may appear to be an incoherent text and instruct the writer how to reshape, modify, and transform the text; the writer can simultaneously discover what lies behind and motivates the complex reactions of the reader and help the reader understand a text that up to this point may have been ambiguous, elusive, or unintelligible. (1996, pp. 169–170)

To suggest, as Zamel does, that oral comments allow teachers to act as "consultants, assistants, and facilitators" rather than as obtuse authorities begs the obvious question of what evidence there is that suggests that this is the case (Zamel, 1996, p. 96). For example, I would argue that it is naive to assume that just because the instructor and student are face-to-face speaking English, they are speaking with shared background assumptions and mutual cultural understandings of, for example, how arguments are to be structured, stories to be told, essays to be written, or even how a writing conference is to proceed. The list of possible divergences goes on and on the further the instructor and student—Zamel's reader and writer—are from one another in terms of shared history and membership in discourse communities.

The Rubric of Facilitator

The assumption that ESL students, or other writing students for that matter, share similar backgrounds with their instructors fails to acknowledge that considerable numbers of students come from a lower-class background and share little cultural capital with the writing teacher who is, more often than not, middle class and white. In failing to acknowledge the power and cultural asymmetries that inform face-to-face teacher-student conferences, the white middle-class teacher may hide behind the rubric of facilitator, creating a false student-teacher equality assumption that not only is disingenuous but also reproduces the very dominant values that relegate most ESL and other minority students to a subjugated position in society and in school in the first place.

In addition, the teacher turned facilitator may confuse the distinction between authoritarianism (often associated with traditional teachers who overcorrect and overimpose) and authority, which is inherent in the very position of the teacher. In other words, the teacher has the final say about curriculum and materials selection, grading, and so forth. While it is important to critique any and all forms of teacher authoritarianism, it is academically dishonest to adopt a facilitator posture that hides the inherent authority of the teacher. As Paulo Freire succinctly argues,

I consider myself a teacher and always a teacher. I have never pretended to be a facilitator. What I want to make clear also is in being a teacher, I always teach to facilitate. I cannot accept the notion of a facilitator who facilitates so as not to teach.

The true comprehension of dialogue must differentiate the role that only facilitates from the role that teaches. When teachers call themselves facilitators and not teachers, they become involved in a distortion of reality. To begin with, in de-emphasizing the teacher's power by claiming to be a facilitator, one is being less than truthful to the extent that the teacher turned facilitator maintains the power institutionally created in the position. That is, while facilitators may veil their power, at any moment they can exercise power as they wish. The facilitator still grades, still has certain control over the curriculum, and to deny these facts is to be disingenuous. I think what creates this need to be a facilitator is the confusion between authoritarianism and authority. What one cannot do in trying to divest of authoritarianism is relinquish one's authority as teacher. In fact, this does not really happen. Teachers maintain a certain level of authority through the depth and breadth of knowledge of the subject matter that they teach. The teacher who claims to be a facilitator and not a teacher is renouncing, for reasons unbeknownst to us, the task of teaching and, hence, the task of dialogue. (Freire & Macedo, 1995, p. 201)

Many writing teachers—in ESL and in mainstream contexts—who uncritically embrace process writing at the same time create a laissez-faire structure where little or no teaching takes place. Through their overemphasizing and pop-psychologizing the need for self-worth and personal expression, a comfort zone is created in which pedagogical conditions that would help students apprentice into academic discourse are lost. For the vast majority of learners, the nuances of meaning making in a middle-class-based curriculum must be taught explicitly (Freire & Macedo, 1995).

Meaning Making

The issue of the student's level of English oral/aural proficiency arises, especially with ESL students. In addition, one might assume when working with students in an ESL program that shared histories will be far from the norm and that students who are struggling with the written word are most likely struggling with the oral word in English as well. The shared meaning making Zamel assumes will result from the oral interactions between instructor and student is by no means guaranteed, and communication difficulties may prevent the instructor from further understanding the underlying logic of the text, thus frustrating both the instructor and student. It is quite likely that the logic embedded in the student's text may not conform to constructs determining the logical construction of texts in the academy, the very constructs that would implicitly guide instructors in their search for meaning within student texts.

Are we to assume that the mutual construction of meaning making romantically implied in Zamel's closing arguments quoted earlier will in turn lead the student—Zamel's writer—to an understanding of the expected text structure?

When and how are issues of textual form supposed to enter the discussion? Or is it assumed that meaning drives structure and these structures have universal foundations across cultures? I will attend to these questions directly in chapters 9 through 12, which are devoted to the analysis of the discourse of the writing conferences I observed. I pose these questions here in order to highlight the complexity of the relationship between meaning and structure and to suggest that arguing that oral interactions between student and instructor-facilitator will solve—or even begin to solve—the myriad problems nonnative and also nonstandard speakers of English face in the writing classroom, and in other contexts in which they must display knowledge in written and/or oral form, does a disservice to both students and teachers.

"Responding to Student Writing": An Analysis of Context, Motive, and Form

I turn now to a closer examination of the context in which Zamel's study "Responding to Student Writing" emerges. I follow with an analysis of the article, in which Zamel draws conclusions regarding the privileging of oral conferences over instructors' written comments. I do so to highlight the inherent contradictions underlying the process approach to teaching writing and, in particular, the conflicting array of naive and ethnocentric assumptions central to the expressive approach. While I focus here for the most part on one article and one context, I do so with the recognition that the article and context are representative of many other articles and contexts in which writing is discussed and taught. I have chosen to focus on the context in which Zamel works because I worked as a part-timer in the program she directs and am intimately aware of the conditions under which I and other part-timers were expected to teach writing. The institutional practices at the University of Massachusetts Boston (UMB)that determined part-timers' status and pay, once again a context that is representative of many others in academia where writing is taught, were determined not by Zamel, the program's director, but by administrators in far more powerful positions at the university. Further, I choose to analyze the article "Responding to Student Writing," briefly discussed earlier in this chapter, because it directly relates to the primary research I discuss in this book. As will become clear in my discussion of the text of the article, Zamel's views of writing pedagogy and the goals she sets for students clearly differ from the writing she engages in and the goals she establishes for herself in the process and act of research. These contradictions highlight profoundly the overall arguments I present against the process approach to the teaching of writing. My analysis is driven by the critical desire that readers of research attend closely to the manner in which the research was undertaken and to the connection (or lack thereof) of the research findings to the conclusions drawn from the study.

Research Context and Textual Form

Zamel directs the undergraduate ESL program at UMB, where she has unlimited access to student writing that she collects regularly from instructors to maintain files both for assessment and for purposes of her research. In general her work—especially when published in *TESOL Quarterly,* the journal associated with the organization Teaching English to Speakers of Other Languages—is academic in tone and structure, research-based, and often contains an implications section where she draws conclusions that are ostensibly logically related to her research results. In "Responding to Student Writing," in particular, the academic style and tone is that of a scientific report describing an experiment, its results, and its implications. The experiment or research component is grounded in the work of others in the field, in this case the field of writing or composition.

In "Responding to Student Writing," even Zamel's title was used previously as the title of an article by Nancy Sommers, former director of Harvard's expository writing program. Sommers's article was first published in 1982, in volume 33 of *College Composition and Communication,* a major journal in composition studies supported by the National Council of Teachers of English. There are several important things to note here. First, Sommers's work on responding behaviors preceded Zamel's. Thus it is odd that Zamel, while referencing Sommers extensively in her article, never mentions that she has drawn even the title for her article from Sommers. Second, Sommers wrote and worked from an academic context of great prestige: Harvard. Third, Sommers's analysis of teachers' responding behaviors draws from the written work of students whose first language was English and, thus, represents "mainstream" writing. Fourth, Sommers's conclusions, which negatively characterize teachers' written responding behaviors, were published and well received within the community of composition and writing research.

Finally, all of Sommers's conclusions are replicated in Zamel's observations of second-language instructors' comments on students' work. Sommers argues that teachers appropriate student work, attend too closely to surface error when meaning should be the focus, fail to direct genuine revision, and collapse the processes of revising, editing, and proofreading, and comment in a non-text-specific manner. Sommers even goes so far as to accuse teachers of "commanding"—a word used repeatedly in the article—students to correct errors and of expressing "hostility and mean-spiritedness" in their comments (1996, p. 149) quite in contrast to what she describes as the "calm and reasonable language of the computer" programmed with "Writers Workbench" that she and her fellow researchers, Lil Brannon and Cyril Knoblauch, employed to analyze some of the student texts under study (Sommers, 1996, p. 149). Sommers concludes that the challenge teachers face is

> to develop comments which will provide an inherent reason for students to
> revise; it is a sense of revision as discovery, as a repeated process of beginning

again, as starting out anew, that our students have not learned. We need to show our students how to seek, in the possibility of revision, the dissonances of discovery—to show them through our comments why new choices would positively change their texts, and thus to show them the potential for development implicit in their own writing. (p. 154)

To a great extent, Zamel situates her own research in an academic context that ensures acceptance: Zamel did not set out to go against a dominant perspective. Instead, she replicated a previous study with only a slight variation from the original work; this nicely insinuates Zamel's work into the scientific–medical research model, gaining for the researcher even more status and stature. Zamel goes one step further, however: she concludes, as Sommers had not, that since teachers' written response behaviors are inappropriate, changing to oral responses would strongly enhance students' chances of improving as writers. This leap is made without evidence and with no substantive argument to support Zamel's assertion.

I turn now to a specific discussion of Zamel's "Responding to Student Writing." The article-cum-chapter consists of five sections: an introduction; a review of the literature addressing teachers' written responding behaviors in contexts in which student and teacher alike speak English; a review of the literature of responding behaviors in second-language contexts; a section in which Zamel reports on her research; and an implications section. When the article was reprinted as a chapter in a book, it contained a short acknowledgments section that addresses the context in which the chapter first appeared, as an article in *TESOL Quarterly*. Almost three pages of references follow the chapter; sixty-five works are listed, all of which deal directly with composition studies in first- and second-language contexts, and most of the works are specifically directed to responding behaviors. There is not one reference—except, perhaps, to Stephen Krashen, whose work deals more directly with language acquisition than it does with writing, though his work addresses the issue of error correction that is central to Zamel's study—that steps out of the very narrow confines of the field or of the specific concerns of Zamel's study. In contrast, Sommers's article references seven sources, one of which she authored and another of which she co-authored.

Doing Science

What does structure tell us about Zamel's "Responding to Student Writing"? First, it is logically ordered in the manner of scientific research articles. The work is placed into a preordered structure; it follows an outline, if you will. The very notion of following an outline and model falls far outside the confines of process writing theory, whose adherents argue forcefully, as noted at the beginning of this chapter, against the practice of outlining prior to writing a paper and against providing for students models upon which their writing could be structured, practices that are common in the traditional approach to teaching writing. The structure of Zamel's article also serves to demonstrate the author's expertise and her engagement in the field. This demonstration is necessary not only to position the author within a very small community of scholars but also to legitimize her research and the conclusions she draws. Only a deep and very careful reading of the text would lead to the questions I have raised regarding the validity of her implications. I deal with what I consider to be major flaws in her study in the section below entitled "The Study."

Though logically ordered from an academic perspective, Zamel's article is difficult to follow at times because it is so often interrupted by long lists of references to the work of others. For example, in one sentence chosen at random, but representative of many in the article, I counted eighteen words, while in parentheses—the American Psychological Association (APA) referencing system was used in Zamel's chapter—there were sixteen words, including dates. Clearly the writer has set out to impress her readership with the intertextual complexity of her article. However, none of the other work cited is dealt with in any depth; there is no analysis, just a listing of associated works that ostensibly support her ideological perspective regarding responding to student writing or, in a rare instance, to note a divergence of perspective., By failing to discuss the existing literature in her field, Zamel narrows considerably her audience to a very limited set of readers, those who are acquainted with the work Zamel cites. This article speaks from and to a very specific discourse community, much in the same manner as does Sommers's piece.

Further, Zamel's decision to reference the work of researchers who discuss English-speaking students serves to legitimize the research in second-language writing. Zamel does not put herself in a position of standing in opposition to assumptions held by other academics who write in support of the mainstream student but, instead, embeds herself within a narrow and, one could argue, supportive context. The work she cites from research with writers whose first language is English argues conclusively that teachers fail to respond appropriately to student writing. Essentially, Zamel reiterates all the characteristics of responding behavior Sommers noted (which I have summarized earlier in this chapter). Zamel's work justifies not only her own perspectives but also, for the most part, those of all the other researchers—both in "regular," that is, English-only, contexts and in second-language writing research—referenced in her article.

Zamel's research and implications are characterized implicitly as objective. The objectivity is demonstrated in the very structure of the text, one that is modeled on experimental research emerging from "pure" science, such as biology, physics, chemistry, and so forth. Berl Lang describes the appeal of, but ultimate impossibility of, neutral or objective writing.

> Writers, we know, are moved by interests, at least in part their own; they are speaking about themselves even when the writing by means of which they speak denies it. The ideal of detachment, neutrality, thus becomes an occasion for mystification: the bystander is invited by the writer-magician to watch him

jump out of his skin. Admittedly, the allure of the prospect is understandable, both for writer and for reader: Who would not wish to see things, one's self, clearly, without affect—and then to fix a description so artless that a reader might also see through it to the thing itself? But constraints on expression, like constraints on any action, are inherent in the agent. The conceptions of the self that have turned out to be most revealing, that have come closest to realizing for human affairs the scientific ideal of disclosure have openly—flagrantly—violated the diplomatic principles of neutrality and non-belligerence now assumed to be self-evident for rhetoric. (1991, p. 64)

What Lang describes fits perfectly the model of scientific reporting of research in Zamel's "Responding to Student Writing," except that Zamel has not "violated the diplomatic principles of neutrality and non-belligerence now assumed to be self-evident for rhetoric"; instead she has engaged those principles.

Zamel appropriates what Lang refers to as "the rhetorical model of science" (p. 57). In so doing, she reports an objective (her own) analysis of a series of partial texts (which she chose for analysis) written by ESL students, samples of which are shown in the article with teacher comments and markings. The author assures the reader that "these compositions were originally collected to establish files of student writing, not to study teachers' responses. Thus, it is unlikely that the teachers' responses were influenced by the artificial conditions prevailing in an experimental situation" (p. 159). And further, Zamel seems to want the best of both worlds: the objective, scientific world and the untainted, real world of data collected in context.

Zamel drew her examples from files of student work and then analyzes but a small (and self-selected) sample of partial texts, each of which she uses to illustrate, from her perspective, how poorly teachers deal with students' written work in much the same manner as did Sommers. Zamel includes portions of student texts with teacher comments directed toward error correction and a list of what she describes as typical teacher comments addressing student content and organization. Overall, Zamel provides a negative assessment of teachers' comments and markings. In fact, there is but one example illustrating what would be characterized as positive comments: those, for example, encouraging students to provide more detail to support a point by asking questions that would lead to development of this point or assertion. This example is followed up with the student revision of the small portion of the text under review. The student chose to ignore the teacher's efforts to elicit more detail and focused instead on the grammatical features, which the instructor had noted also needed attention. On the revised text the teacher praises the student for the lack of error. Zamel faults the teacher for this. In addition, Zamel repeatedly argues that teachers should not attend to surface features, that is, grammar and spelling, when responding to students' texts but, rather, to meaning. She makes this point often, as do others adhering to a process approach. I agree, but more needs to be said and attended to.

The Study

None of the texts Zamel analyzes are contextualized fully. Readers do not know what the assignment was, whether or not the teacher responses are to a first or second draft, or even if other drafts were expected; nor do readers know whether they are viewing a complete student text or a portion of one, and if a portion, what portion. We are assured, however, that the samples used in the reported research are representative of each teacher's responding behavior. But without context, the reader is left to image the size of the classes from which the writing samples were drawn, the proficiency levels of the student writers, the backgrounds of the teachers whose comments are reviewed and harshly criticized, and at what point in the semester the writing occurred. These are but a few of the contextual factors that would have influenced each teacher's choices of written comments.

Nor do we know as readers whether any of these teachers who are so severely criticized spent time with each student discussing the student writing Zamel reviews. When I taught at UMB, it was often the case that students would come to instructors' offices to meet to discuss a paper after written comments were made. Often instructors established in-class conferencing as well. The reader knows nothing of the possibility of other contexts in which the teacher and student may have discussed an assignment. The only teacher readers are introduced to—albeit superficially—is one said to be a graduate student of Zamel's who is quoted perhaps from a journal entry required in Zamel's course on writing or ESL methods. The graduate student's comment relates to her difficulties with and concerns about responding to her students' writing, specifically the trouble she has ignoring surface-level errors. However, we do not know definitively whether this graduate student is one of the teachers whose comments have been analyzed in the article. And, oddly, Zamel makes no note of the fact that her student/instructor laments the fact that she attends too closely to surface errors and makes no reference to revision or the number of drafts she requires of her writing students. In fact, from the quote provided, it appears that the student/instructor required in the instance she comments on only one draft of a paper. And it appears also that this is her practice in general. Zamel does not comment on this practice, a practice that is considered to be inappropriate by process-oriented theorists and instructors.

So, How Do Students Fare?

How do students fare? Not well at all. At UMB, the failure rate among ESL students and other minorities of the required Writing Proficiency Exam is extremely high. In fact, in the late 1980s the university was cited by the U.S. Office of Civil Rights for the disproportionate failure rate of minority students taking the writing proficiency exam. Failure rates today are analyzed not by ethnic background but in relation to the freshman seminar students were enrolled in. This new analytical structure serves to mask the relationship between minority status and failure rate and places the onus on instructors and professors participating in the seminar program, a component of the curricular framework of general education at UMB. Students do not take the exam immediately after completing their general education requirement, or the writing requirement, but at a point when they are nearly halfway through their university studies. At this point a student must pass the exam in order to continue with upper-level courses and move on to graduation. To this day, UMB, which serves primarily an urban, nontraditional student body, has a graduation rate of only 28 percent. Nonetheless, nonauthoritarian, facilitative writing instructors are often inclined to grade students for effort, leading to many high grades and thus leading in turn to a false sense of competence on the part of students. What advocates of a cognitive and/or expressive process approach to teaching writing have succeeded in communicating to instructors is that correcting grammar is inappropriate—though it is still done even by those staunchly opposed to the practice—and that paternalism is an appropriate attitude to express toward those who are less fortunate than you, such as nonmainstream students, refugees, and immigrants.

The ideological perspectives of process-oriented theorists, researchers, and practitioners discussed in chapters 2 and 3 fail to confront the contradictions inherent in their narrowly conceived proposed problem-solving suggestions intended to increase the writing proficiency of students. Increased proficiency cannot be reduced, for example, to a change from written responses to student writing to oral responses, by diminishing the status of instructor to that of facilitator, or by allowing students to practice the behaviors—as in writing and rewriting—"real writers" engage in. In the end, a cognitive and/or expressive approach to process writing fails to address openly the problematic practices that operate in academia's social and political realms that place undue constraints on marginalized students and faculty. In chapter 4 my discussion of the social/cultural approach addresses the lapses noted thus far in process writing theory and practice and I offer a more comprehensive, though admittedly ideologically, politically, and socially driven, theory of writing instruction.

4

THE SOCIAL/CULTURAL APPROACH

> A spoken language, in terms of an ability both to speak and to understand, comes as part of the normal process of growing up in a particular society, unless there are some individual physical disabilities. Writing, by contrast, has been from the beginning a systematic skill that has to be taught and learned. Thus the introduction of writing, and all the subsequent stages of its development, are intrinsically new forms of social relationships.—Raymond Williams, *Writing in Society*

While the cognitivist focuses on the writer's thought processes and the external manifestations of these processes, and the expressivist focuses on the writer's search for meaning, a third perspective focuses on the social and cultural aspects of writing and how these factors influence a writer's performance (Bizzell, 1986, 1992; Faigley, 1986). The fundamental distinction between the cognitive and expressive approaches and the social/cultural approach is the distinction between the notions, on the one hand, that writing is an individual act and, on the other hand, that writing is a social act. In other words, for the adherents of the expressive and cognitive approaches, language is used primarily to communicate ideas generated in the individual's mind to the minds of others in the social context (Bruffee, 1986). In contrast, the social/cultural approach—or what Bruce Herzberg (1991, p. 115) refers to as the academic-discourse approach—assumes that the writer's language emanates from the community to which he or she belongs (Bruffee, 1986, p. 784). Language within the social/cultural perspective—the terminology I will continue to use because I believe it more accurately delineates the necessity for understanding language in its full complexity—is viewed, in the Marxian sense, as an ensemble of social relationships (Arthur, 1970, p. 122). As Valentin Volosinov writes,

> Even though we sometimes have pretensions to experiencing and saying things urbi et orbi, actually, of course, we envision this "world at large" through the prism of the concrete social milieu surrounding us. In the majority of cases, we presuppose a certain typical and stabilized social purview toward which the ideological creativity of our own social group and time is oriented, i.e., we assume as our addressee a contemporary of our literature, our science, our moral and legal codes. (1973, pp. 85–86)

Writing as Social Practice(s)

This reorientation in perspective not only places writing in a larger social context, thus highlighting it as a social activity, but also provides the conceptual basis for the recognition of the hegemony of particular forms of language use and the recognition of the ideological foundations of language practices. Knowledge and authority from this admittedly ideological, social/cultural perspective are understood as being community-generated. The social/cultural approach is, in many ways, comparable to what Brian Street (1984) refers to as the ideological model of literacy, a model that seeks to understand literacy in terms of social practices and in terms of the ideologies in which different literacies are embedded. I use the word *literacies* (Gee, 1996) instead of the more generally applied *literacy* to highlight the notion that the attainment of control over particular and multiple language and literacy practices implies intense variability across discourse communities. There is no singular literacy as is implied in the use of its negative counterpart, illiteracy. To discuss literacy as if it were a unified, universalized, ideal form is to negate the social and cultural reality of the forms in which oral and written language occur and the varying degrees of competence individuals in particular communities demonstrate within their own communities. Even more problematic is the possibility of demonstrating competence to an individual who is outside of one's community. For example, many students from inner-city contexts, in particular, are well versed in rap, and for those who are most adept at controlling the genre the words flow with an ease and often a power that is both threatening to the outsider and commanding to the insider. Others, from mainstream contexts, are well versed, prior to schooling, in speaking about and through literary and nonliterary texts, which gives them an an advantage in academic contexts. Most mainstream upper- and middle-class young people do not have the ability to rap, and this is not a problem for them. But those who do have the ability to rap find that it is not an advantage in the academic context. Of course this is just one simple, concrete example; there are many other inequalities and many other forms that manifest these inequalities. But for the moment I will continue to discuss rap.

Rap (and a Black Man's Poetry) in the Classroom

A man I admire and know well, Leor Alcalay, while working in the 1990s as a substitute teacher in the Boston public schools, attempted to use this poetic form—rap—to encourage his students to write. First students would present orally, then put words to paper. Once this pedagogical approach was discovered by the administration, this teacher who had been able to engage previously silenced, bored, and sometimes hostile students was fired from his long-term substitute position. It is far safer for those in control of dominant literacies to paternalistically attempt to remediate those who do not have control of dominant forms. Remediation seeks to ensure continued silence and maintenance of the status quo, as do the romanticism of the expressivists and the technical orientation of the cognitivists. As Mike Rose writes in *Lives on the Boundary*, "The designation *remedial* has powerful implications in education—to be remedial is to be substandard, inadequate—and, because of the origins of the term, the inadequacy is metaphorically connected to disease and mental defectiveness" (1989, p. 209).

Much like Leor Alcalay, Jonathan Kozol was fired from his provisional position as a fourth-grade teacher in Boston during the 1960s for teaching his Black students—a number of whom were designated as remedial—the poetry of Langston Hughes. The explicit reason: Hughes was not included in the required curriculum. Yet, as Kozol writes:

> Of all the poems of Langston Hughes that I read to my Fourth Graders, the one that the children liked most was a poem that has the title "Ballad of the Landlord.". . . The reason this poem did have so much value and meaning for me and, I believe, for many of my students, is that it not only seems moving in an obvious and immediate human way but that it *finds* its emotion in something ordinary. It is a poem which really does allow both heroism and pathos to poor people, sees strength in awkwardness and attributes to a poor person standing on the stoop of his slum house every bit as much significance as William Wordsworth saw in daffodils, waterfalls and clouds. (1967, p. 190)

Kozol's students were enthralled with the poetry of Hughes. They were enthralled that Hughes's poems together comprised a book with a green jacket that Kozol held before them as he read from it. The young people in Kozol's class were enamored, shocked, and intrigued by the fact that a Black man's picture was on the back cover of the book: this man was the author of the book, the poet whose words resonated with their lives. Kozol copied poems for the children so they could take them home to read over and over again themselves—for of course the school had not provided copies of the Langston Hughes book of poetry to the students. Kozol had purchased the copy he read from in class himself. Students memorized poems, though Kozol had not required this of them. Many asked to recite Hughes's poetry and, as Kozol writes, "before long, almost every child in the room had asked to have a turn" (1967, p. 191).

What Jonathan Kozol and Leor Alcalay were able to do was invite, excite, and engage their students in language—both written and oral. The forms employed—rap and poetry—opened for the students previously closed doors to literate forms of language that emanated from their home communities. Both teachers opened the first of many gates one must pass through in order to acquire the discourse(s) of schooling. The success both experienced as teachers was startling, as was the success the students in turn experienced, as engagement, joy, and an emerging sense of belonging to a previously alien environment became a tenuous reality, a possibility previously unconsidered. But opening the gates to poor, marginalized immigrant and Black students was and is not acceptable. Just think of the threat these teachers' successes portended: the possibility that students might access even more forms of academic discourse that would make it more likely that they would find their way through the system. Thus the implicit reason for the firings: both teachers' work with students threatened the status quo and, in so doing, threatened as well the privileged positions of those whose "ways with words" and skin color matched those of the administrators. These administrators needed to act quickly to stem the trickle that might sluice through those first gates marking the pathways through academia.

Discourse Communities

By reorienting the focus of discussion from differences in individual performance to a concern for the social/cultural context of writing, the social/cultural approach allows for movement away from the assumption that individual performance is related to individual talent and turns instead to the recognition that success or failure in the writing classroom may be more directly related to the distance the writer's own discourse community is from the discourse of the academy. Gee characterizes discourse as "a socially accepted association among ways of using language, other symbolic expressions, and 'artifacts,' of thinking, feeling, believing, valuing, and acting that can be used to identify oneself as a member of a socially meaningful group or 'social network,' or to signal (that one is playing) a socially meaningful 'role'" (1996, p. 131). In fact, it has been argued that learning socially significant forms—and understanding how they function, how to use them appropriately—is a key to success (and sometimes survival) in a discourse community (Coe, 1987, p. 21). Likewise, understanding the discourse conventions of the academic community is the key to success in school. In an analysis of texts written by poor writers, Mina Shaugnessy (1977), for example, found meaning and structure where at first there appeared to be none. According to Shaugnessy, what differentiates a poor writer from the successful writer in the academic context is the understanding, or lack thereof, of academic discourse conventions, which are, of course, class-based and thus inherently hierarchical in nature. In this light, learning to write within the academic context can be viewed as a socialization process. As writers come to share conventions they also come to incorporate values, ways of thinking, and the worldview of those in the academy, which may in turn begin to isolate them from the very communities from which they have emerged. Assuming a new discourse involves the acquisition of a new identity as well—at best, a fractured, yet hopefully successful border-crosser, at worst, an individual who has lost his or her true identity and association with his or her primary community.

Richard Rodriguez poignantly discusses this disassociation from one's roots in his autobiography *Hunger of Memory*. His powerful book, co-opted by political conservatives as a testament to the virtues of English Only, begins as follows:

> I have taken Caliban's advice. I have stolen their books. I will have some run of this isle.
>
> Once upon a time, I was a "socially disadvantaged" child. An enchantedly happy child. Mine was a childhood of intense family closeness. And extreme public alienation.
>
> Thirty years later I write this book as a middle-class American man. Assimilated. (1983, p. 1)

Richard Rodriguez embraced the books of the dominant culture, but it was the dominant culture that first embraced him. He and his family chose no longer to speak Spanish at home when urged by his school-teaching nuns to speak only English. This initial "choice," the monies that followed, and the positive impact of affirmative action—which he no longer supports—led Rodriguez to a literary life. Eventually he became a professor at Berkeley, but he now lives a life apart from academia. Why was he successful? Rodriguez explains: "A primary reason for my success in the classroom was that I couldn't forget that schooling was changing me and separating me from the life I enjoyed before becoming a student" (p. 45), a prior life he could never recapture. Rodriguez embraces Richard Hoggart's definition: "scholarship boy: good student, troubled son" (p. 48). Rodriguez argues that "education is not an inevitable or natural step in growing up" and characterizes himself as "a child who cannot forget that his academic success distances him from a life he loved, even from his own memory of himself" (p. 48).

Must the acquisition of dominant, secondary discourses entail the absolute abandonment of one's primary discourse? I think not. I hope not. For I wish to imagine students seeking and being allowed to gain access to education and all the hope and possibility this implies without the painful, near total absence of the language and the culture of family, home, and community that Rodriguez allowed or, more aptly put, abandoned. For this he suffers; because of this others gain. Rodriguez is the darling of the right, the starling of his life. So sad.

Success or Failure

Success or failure in writing class correlates closely with social group. Students from middle-class backgrounds come to schools already well versed in the discourse structures expected in schools, whereas students from nonmainstream backgrounds, Black and White working- and lower-class students and many nonnative speakers of English, for example, enter educational institutions well versed in the discourse structures of their communities. These structures have been found to differ in fundamental ways from those of the mainstream (Heath, 1982, 1983; Michaels, 1981). Those who fail in schools are those who fail to master the genres of schooling; that is, they fail to master the ways of structuring and dealing with experience that schools value in varying ways (Heath, 1982).

Though now supported by ethnographic research and careful linguistic analysis (Gee, 1985; Gumperz, 1982; Michaels, 1981), this notion of mismatch, and the ramifications of the mismatch, is not a new conception. Antonio Gramsci, for example, wrote early in the twentieth century, "In a whole series of families, especially in the intellectual strata, the children find in their family life a preparation, a prolongation and a completion of school life; they breathe in, as the expression goes, a whole quantity of notions and attitudes which facilitate the educational process properly speaking" (1971, p. 31). Pierre Bourdieu's notion of cultural capital speaks to the same issue:

> Indeed, one can put forward the hypothesis that the specific productivity of all pedagogic work other than the pedagogic work accomplished by the family is a function of the distance between the habitus it tends to inculcate (in this context, scholarly mastery of scholarly language) and the habitus inculcated by all previous forms of pedagogic work and, ultimately, by the family (i.e. in this case, practical mastery of the mother tongue). (1977, p. 72)

Unfortunately, this mismatch often leads to the erroneous reaction on the part of individuals in authority in educational institutions that students from nonmainstream backgrounds are not making sense, when, in fact, they are. What is occurring is that the sense making is embodied in structures alien to individuals outside the student's ethnic or cultural group. The fact that these structures are perhaps alien does not mean, however, that they are impenetrable (Gee, 1985; Gumperz, 1982; Michaels, 1981). Although the structures (both oral and written) may be negatively evaluated by instructors who hear and read them as lacking coherence, the language forms are, in fact, coherent and senseful. What occurs over and over is that linguistic minority students are negatively evaluated for producing language that conforms to structures deemed appropriate and meaningful to members of their own communities.

The Social Construction of Form(s)

In many ways the writing process approach recommended by proponents of the cognitive and expressive approaches is an attempt to democratize education through a process of personal liberation. Despite these attempts, however, certain groups of students, those from the middle and upper classes, are still more likely to succeed in school than those who come from lower- and working-class homes and from linguistic and cultural backgrounds that differ from the mainstream. A central question remains, then: How is it that students from nonmainstream backgrounds will come to know the discourse structures of the academy, particularly if these structures are not articulated? This very issue has become the center of a spirited debate within the community of writing and literacy theorists (Bizzell, 1986, 1992; Coe, 1987; Delpit, 1995; Tuman, 1988). It has been suggested that possibly a process classroom focus, as characterized by the cognitivists and expressivists, could do a disservice to students by not explicitly stating what the expectations are regarding use of language in the academic context, particularly in terms of text structure. Although they may not be explicitly stated, the discourse communities of the academy do have very specific constraints on form. These constraints are embedded in beliefs about what constitutes good writing and what does not, what genres are appropriate in what context, what behaviors are appropriate in relation to texts in particular contexts, and even what can be discussed in the process of text production, and so forth.

The level of complexity surrounding particular discourse communities within and outside the academy is enormous. Further, these beliefs, or, more specifically, the ideologies surrounding language use and structure in the academic community, are socially constructed and therefore without universal foundation. John Clifford explicates this notion in his discussion of literary theorist Kenneth Burke's views on form:

> To raise our political consciousness, then, Burke would have us interrogate our received ideas about rhetoric, problematizing such notions as form, intention, and identification. Form, for example, still appears in our rhetorics and handbooks as merely a problem in organizing our thinking. We are still inheritors of the formalist attempt to objectify structure by decontextualizing it, removing it from a historically situated writer and an ideologically interested audience. (1988, p. 35)

Clifford goes on to assert that Burke maintains form cannot be decontextualized. As Clifford writes, "for Burke, form is far more problematic. For him it is the embodiment of the writer's attitude toward reality and toward an audience. As such, it helps to create a certain relationship between a text and its reception. Form is rhetorical power, a way to shape reality and manipulate audiences. The forms we inherit from our rhetorical past gather an aura of tradition around them, making them seem natural, commonsensical" (p. 36).

Clifford further suggests that "to see academic writing in this way, as a kind of anthropological behavior, is to demystify and make it more accessible to our discursive formations" (p. 35). To assume, as many writing theorists and teachers do, that these structures will emerge naturally in the meaning-making process they propose is disingenuous. This disingenuousness has particular impact on those students who must seek to uncover, or decode, implicit expectations of rhetorical models that they do not, in fact, share (Inghilleri, 1989). While given no explicit models, students are nonetheless expected to create texts accepted in a community whose ways with words are unfamiliar to them.

Explicit Teaching of Form: Anathema to Process Approach Adherents

This shift to an emphasis on discourse communities has brought with it the revisionist argument that students need to be explicitly taught the conventions of the academic community in order to learn them. In other words, social/culturalists argue that in order for students to gain access to the academic community these forms need to be made explicit to initiates to the community. David Bartholomae, for example, calls for direct teaching of the forms and uses of academic discourse so students may come "to speak in the voice and through the codes of those of us with power and wisdom . . . before they know what they are doing, before they have a project to participate in, and before, at least in terms of our disciplines, they have anything to say" (1985, p. 156).

Social/culturalists maintain that the demystification and explication of writing forms and functions to writing students will facilitate student access to the academic community. As John Clifford articulates, "Armed with an awareness of the multiple and rather arbitrary ways different discourses privilege certain rhetorical strategies against others, writers can decide more knowingly which of these conflicting discourses to align themselves with. If these writers are students, they should be aware that acceptance into interpretive communities depends on one's ability first to master the conventions of that discourse" (1988, p. 38). These conventions include, in the words of David Bartholomae, "such commonplaces, set phrases, rituals, gestures, habits of mind, tricks of persuasion, obligatory conclusions and necessary connections that determine the 'what might be said' and constitute knowledge within the university" (1986, p. 11 as cited in Clifford, 1988, p. 36).

At this point it is important to clarify that in arguing for the adoption of a rhetorical approach to teaching writing, social/culturalists are not arguing (nor am I) for a return to the basic tenets of the traditional approach to teaching writing. In other words, while the social/cultural approach recognizes the fundamental importance of form and calls for the explicit teaching of form, it must not be confused with the traditional approach. The social/cultural approach in many ways seeks to incorporate the teaching of form within the context of the cognitive and expressive approaches to teaching writing. In doing so, adherents of the social/cultural approach in no way accept the authoritarian and hierarchical assumptions that lie at the core of the traditional approach to teaching writing. Rather, social/culturalists recognize the importance of form and its variability across discourse communities and, as a result, the need to make explicit to students the required forms of the academy—especially to those students whose ways with words differ from the ways with words of the academy. Therefore the social/cultural approach should not be seen as a simplistic rehashing of the traditional approach to teaching writing but, rather, as an approach that seeks to highlight and problematize the hegemony of particular forms of language while in turn providing all students, regardless of background, access to these forms.

While social/cultural writing process theorists argue that writing teachers "adopt a rhetorical approach to the study of writing in the disciplines" (Faigley & Hansen, 1985) many argue even further that politically oppressed students need to master academic discourse so that they will become linguistically empowered to engage in dialogue with the various sectors of the wider society (Bizzell, 1986; Freire and Macedo, 1987; Giroux, 1983) and that process pedagogy has failed to accomplish this goal (Delpit, 1995; Tuman, 1988). It has also been argued that rather than functioning as a liberating influence, process pedagogy as exemplified by the cognitive and expressive approaches has instead subjected students to new forms of domination while at the same time weakening their ability to resist them (Tuman, 1988).

Lisa Delpit argues forcefully and eloquently in *Other People's Children* that adherents of process writing, while having good intentions (as I have argued) have failed to grasp the fundamental problem inherent in the approach: the failure to teach explicitly the textual forms and skills needed for success in schools further ensures that students who do not already possess these forms through accident of birth will continue to fail or do poorly in school. Delpit defines "skills" as "useful and usable knowledge which contributes to a student's ability to communicate effectively in standard, generally accepted literacy forms" (Delpit, 1995, pp. 18–19). Delpit argues, further, that teaching form is not enough: "students must be critically and creatively able to participate in meaningful and potentially liberating work inside those doors" once they are opened to those who have accessed the conventions of the dominant class (p. 19).

This is worth repeating: "students must be critically and creatively able to participate in meaningful and potentially liberating work inside those doors." For this to occur, the doors must first be opened. This is the first premise. The second premise: the rules dictating the work that occurs inside these doors must be made explicit. Nothing can be intuited; all must be made explicit. And not only must the rules be explicit but also opportunities to practice these rules must be provided the newcomers, the apprentices to the dominant discourse(s). To do otherwise suggests noncompliance with a commitment to equal access to a democratic society and, further, even negates a commitment to a democratic society.

In sum, while well intended in the manner associated with many liberal reform movements, cognitive and expressive process writing theory and pedagogy is nonetheless replete with contradictions. These contradictions point to a fundamental tension within individual teachers and institutions regarding the expectations surrounding what a student needs to master in order to begin to gain access to the academic community. This tension points, as well, to the inherent conflict that exists in higher education today: recognition that although mastery of academic prose is not the key to the entrance door to most colleges and universities, it remains, in most cases, the key to the exit door (Applebee, 1974; Baron, 1982; Finegan, 1980). Writing teachers, as gatekeepers, need to consider seriously the implications inherent in their ideological stance toward the teaching of writing. Teachers need to recognize that they, in fact, make theoretical choices even if they have yet to explicitly articulate them or even bring them to a metacognitive level.

Border Patrol in the Academy

Often we cannot see outside the constructs and constraints of our own belief systems, and often efforts to do so are discomforting, disquieting, and unsettling. For academics, in particular, seeing and thinking in different ways present the possibility of loss of status and authority. There is nothing as powerless in academia as a theoretical model that is passé or one that has been debunked. Previous adherents, or those who still cling to this now debunked theory, know that in reality they face being sent to pasture. Students will no longer register in great numbers for their courses, articles will no longer be sought for publication, and adherents will move into the shadow world inhabited by misguided, wrongful thinkers.

I write these words with compassion as I recall the kind, elderly Jesuit with whom I spent a day of intense interviewing at Georgetown University. This priest, an academic, a linguistic, was soon to retire. He seemed very tired, yet he was attentive to my needs. Interviewing for an academic position is grueling for interviewee, interviewers, and all participating in the process. As this elderly priest accompanied me from dean to provost to faculty luncheon, we spoke. I learned that he had begun his career as an adherent of the contrastive analysis approach to the study of language, a teacher/professor of linguistics who advocated an audiolingual approach to teaching language. Now an anachronism, his ideological perspective toward language learning and teaching had been submerged completely by Chomskian linguistics and now, in part, by a social approach. He was so kind, despite the fact that I was in many ways a symbolic representation of the theoretical perspectives that had displaced him. I remember that, after having spent more than an hour with the provost, who was very much in agreement with my perspective toward language, I left the office to be met by this kind priest who had waited for my return. He asked if I needed anything, and I replied that I was thirsty. He approached a bank of vending machines and attempted to insert coins to buy a bottle of water for me, but nothing came out. He was persistent; I was pained. "It doesn't matter. I'm fine," I said. But he replied, "It's the least I can do for you who will follow in the path that I and others have constructed, and that has now been demolished." And he laughed ironically. I said, as is my way, "I'm sorry." (Such a typical response from a woman!) He said, "It's not your fault."

This battle with technology, marked by a failure to elicit a bottle of water, left me parched and the priest defeated. But off we went to a gathering of faculty and students I was to address as part of the interview process. Some sat eagerly awaiting what I had to say, others appeared to begrudge having been called to campus for this special lecture. I was dry-mouthed, exhausted from talking in an effort to sell myself and from traveling and being worried sick about my dying mother, whom I had left in northern New York State just thirty-six hours before so that I could drive to Boston to teach a graduate course, return home to pack, and then drive to the airport to fly to Washington, D.C. Yet I was expected to project enthusiastic brilliance, and I was determined to make this talk work.

I discussed an analysis of a written text produced by an eighteen-year-old Puerto Rican student, Oswaldo, who had been in the United States for only three years, during which time he spent more days out of school than in. My intention was to illustrate the narrative's powerful rendering of the conflicts and contradictions this young man had faced and resolved during the three-year period of time it chronicled, arguing that the text was intricately complex and logical, though its features superficially did not conform to academic prose. In fact, it read superficially as one big, run-on sentence, replete with misspellings and grammatical errors. But I argued that the text's underlying structure—lines and stanzas—harked back to oral renderings as contained in the Bible, poetry, and just plain talk unaffected by print culture.

Initially response to the lecture was extremely positive, and questions raised issues central to the arguments and concerns I had posed in my talk. Then, from the back of the room, from a single individual came an onslaught of verbal attack. The man nearly flew out of his seat as he asked question after question, and made assertion after assertion, assumption after assumption. I was not prepared for this hostility. At first I thought that a crazy person—how readily we determine that those who do not think and behave as we do are irrational—had found his way into the lecture by mistake. At the heart of this individual's unrelenting attack was the assertion that what I had to say did not belong in the discipline of linguistics but should be situated within literary theory. I was aghast. Others looked pained. After the long attack, another faculty member, with whom I had spoken at length at lunch, asked a question that sought to bring my discussion back into the realm of social linguistics and literacy, and I know in retrospect it was thoughtful and well intended. This member of the linguistics faculty asked how one could begin to identify lines and stanzas other than focusing on thematic issues that bound the structures together. Now even though I had discussed ways to do so in the talk—syntactic parallelism, rhyme, echoing, and so forth—I could no longer find these answers, or the many others I knew, because my mind had gone blank. I was a novice. I responded, "I don't know." This is not accepted at an academic lecture. I had been thoroughly defeated by an arrogant theoretical linguist, a member of the faculty who knew that opening the department to yet another socially oriented applied linguist would further diminish his stature in the department.

After the talk another faculty member with whom I had also had lunch told me that this sort of thing happened to Deborah Tannen all the time, and that I should just have said, "I'm a linguist because my degree is in linguistics." What I wish I had said is the following: "You (to the obnoxious syntactician) need time in arrogance-detox. Let's move on to others who have questions related to what I have just said, its implications for marginalized students and for the acquisition of academic literacy. Let's consider more fully how texts such as the one I have just analyzed are perceived within schools. This paper would receive a failing grade. The writer might be evaluated for special education placement and remediation begun. A death sentence. I speak as a concerned linguist, not as one who wishes to privilege my discourse over that of others." Oh, so much to say in hindsight! But I was just starting out, I was exhausted, famished, and thirsty, and I was not yet truly aware of how vile individuals can be when threatened (though I should have been). The college dean subsequently canceled funding for the new position. Apparently the dean, a well-known, very out-of-date, teaching English as a second language (TESL) academic, felt the position the department had requested fell too far outside of the domain of language (as in teaching French, English, Spanish) acquisition and methodology, thus he revoked the promised resources. Territorial battles were being fought on all fronts.

All teaching is grounded in theoretical and ideological assumptions; whether they are implicit or explicit, they exist. Teachers, researchers, and theorists need to realize that the choices they make, the arguments to which they adhere, and their subsequent actions are never neutral but remain ensconced in ideological perspectives, which may inadvertently serve to inhibit rather than enhance students' access into the academic context. To ignore these issues almost ensures that subordinated students will be entrapped by the revolving doors of the academy. Thus entrapped, these students may never have the opportunity to critically engage the ideological constructs that serve to enable their entrapment and to work to change the very institutional structures, actions, and beliefs that function to enhance the continued status quo readily accepted by the dominant class.

In his time, the kind Jesuit I met at Georgetown adhered to an approach to linguistic analysis referred to as contrastive analysis. This analytical approach argued that a contrastive approach, comparing English to Spanish, for example, would point to areas—be they in pronunciation, grammar, vocabulary, or syntax—that would highlight differences between languages, thus isolating points that would prove to be difficult for language learners to acquire. Focused attention on these points of difference was the basis upon which a whole new scientific approach to language teaching was developed. The audiolingual method, or army method as it was also known, dominated language teaching from the early 1950s to the early 1970s. Developed in the context of a Cold War mentality, the method focuses on oral language and served to train many a foreign service employee, and many a high school student, who after studying a language for four years would be lucky to be able to find their way to a bathroom when traveling abroad. The audiolingual method is now defunct; theories come and go, profoundly emerging from the ideological locus dominating the eras of their emergence until a new perspective seeks to undermine the old.

Maintaining the Status Quo: An Academic Accolade

Faculty also find themselves entrapped by these revolving theoretical doors. This is the case not only for those who find themselves identified with a defunct theory, as was the soon-to-retire linguist at Georgetown, but also particularly for women, minorities, faculty from working-class backgrounds, and others who enter the academy not fully conversant in the discourse(s) deemed appropriate in the various contexts of the academy. (I clearly demonstrated this nonmembership during the question-and-answer period after my talk at Georgetown.) It is particularly perilous for those who critique dominant discourses and whose radical words threaten change. These often critical, nondominant discourses themselves—minority, feminist, radical, and so on—vary considerably across disciplines. In fact, the variation is so extreme in some instances that even among members of the same department who do not share specialties communication is nearly impossible.

This was made abundantly clear to me when I served on the English Department Curriculum Committee at UMB during the 1994–95 academic year. The committee, at least the active members, consisted of junior faculty with a shared interest in discourse communities. As an applied linguist, I was most removed from the mainstream members of the department, but I was able to converse, negotiate, and assist in the writing of recommendations for curricular changes within the department that would bring us in line with the college's proposed move toward a model of general education. I also served on the university-wide general education committee, thus I was conversant in the "discourse of general education" and aware of the university's goals for curricular change at the departmental level.

After a year of work and three committee chairs, a report to the department was finally ready for presentation. Though we were nervous, I must admit, knowing the conservative nature of the academy in general and the proposed threat that any change in the department would imply to tenured, entrenched faculty, I was still not prepared for the reaction the report received at the department meeting. Prior to the meeting, the committee chair, a friend and colleague whom I greatly respect, asked that I please back her up if an attack were to occur. I begged forgiveness, but noted the obvious: I was untenured and already in a high-profile university-wide position working for major changes in the foreign language curriculum that had thus far gained me more enemies than friends. I told my friend that I felt that I needed to take the advice given all untenured faculty: attend all meetings, but say nothing—though this would be the first time I truly adhered to the advice. On a personal level I felt terrible, because the assault was without mercy. It began with the most senior and most arrogant member of the department and continued for some time. The report was characterized as unreadable, incomprehensible, filled with jargon, unrelated to anything remotely connected to the concerns of the English Department, and so forth. What I found most amazing was that although the attacks centered on language and our—the committee members'—supposed inability to manipulate it in a manner acceptable to the department, the real agenda was, in fact, an all-out effort to ensure that change did not occur. For if this were to happen, it would have marked a point of disequilibrium, a shift in power that the literature professors knew must be avoided at all costs.

It was turf that was being defended, but no one said, "I will not give up my privileged position teaching a seminar in Shakespeare each semester in order to ensure that our students can manipulate the discursive structures required of the discipline we call English Studies." Instead the focus was redirected onto us and specifically the chair of the committee, as acknowledged author of the report—though the report was socially produced, that is, it represented a compilation of the work that had been done over the course of the last semester in committee. As the chair of the curriculum committee argued that the department needed to incorporate new courses addressing explicitly the discursive practices of English, she was in turn attacked for engaging in discursive practices seen as alien, thus threatening to the power structure of the department. Further, those on the attack knew that the courses that we were proposing be required (focusing on the discourse of English studies and a capstone experience) would mean fewer students would enroll in the entrenched faculties' favored authors' courses and more work with newly declared majors and at the completion of the major with the capstone experience. It would have also meant a renewed focus on rhetoric—and they thought the battle had been won at the turn of the century—within the academy.

It was a bloody awful battle. We lost. A new program in applied linguistics (formerly bilingual/ESL graduate studies) was formed and removed from the English Department, though the linguists already tenured in English retained their tenure. I had been hired by the English Department but was now scuttled to applied linguistics, and I will be a test case of sorts when I become the first to be reviewed for tenure in a program (note: not a department) that deals so openly, critically, and politically with discursive practices. As of this writing, general education is in place at UMB, though not as originally perceived and often without a required capstone experience.

Reaching Toward the Not Yet

Many writing theorists and instructors, though certainly not all, are presently advocating and practicing in one form or another a process approach to teaching writing, an approach that abhors the explicit teaching of form because doing so brings to life visions of authoritarian models of teaching as exemplified in the traditional approach. Perhaps we need to reconsider the facilitator's abhorrence of teaching form and recognize the possibility that facilitators may serve to facilitate failure, not success. In the words of Paulo Freire,

> Authoritarian educators are correct, even though they are not always theoretically explicit, when they say that there is no education that is non-directive. I

would not disagree with these educators; but, I would say that to claim to be a facilitator is authoritarian to the extent that the facilitators make their own objectives and dreams the directives that they give to learners in their education practice. Facilitators are authoritarian because, as subjects of the educational practice, they reduce learners to objects of the directives they impose. (Freire & Macedo, 1995, p. 378)

Similarly, Donaldo Macedo argues "that to renounce the task of teaching under the guise of facilitating is part and parcel of a paternalistic ideology" (Freire & Macedo, 1995, p. 379). The liberal progressivism inherent in process writing pedagogy leads to contexts in which students are placated in a "vacuous, feel-comfort zone" (p. 379) where personal experience is celebrated and process elevated above style.

In order to counter the disservice process pedagogy does to the nonmainstream student, we need to seek to create contexts in which forms are explicitly taught as well as interrogated. In other words, I argue it is not enough just to make textual forms explicit. We must also recognize that the choice of which forms count in particular contexts speaks to the issue of the relationship between language and power. Clearly, some forms count more than others, and nowhere is this more obvious than in the context of the academy. Though, as William Labov (1972) made abundantly clear in his groundbreaking research on Black English Vernacular, to be known as a "Lame," one who speaks standard English and adheres to the imposed practices of schools, is to be designated as an outsider in one's own community. Thus not only do the forms that count need to be made explicit but also an explicit recognition of the disparity between various discourses is needed. This practice portends the possibility of enticing the "Jets"— those (Labov, 1972) who resist the discourse practices of dominant culture—into beginning to perceive the possibilities inherent in coming to master the language of the master, as Leor Alcalay and Jonathan Kozol sought to do. Language teaching is, in other words, never a neutral enterprise.

Finally, the question remains: How can we articulate forms and structures students need to know while at the same time providing opportunities and contexts in which students may voice their own experiences of the world within the structures and forms of their own discourse communities as well as within those required of the academy? To begin to do so, I suggest that we move the field of writing away from a myopic view of the mind, beyond a limited focus on expressive desires, and into social, cultural, and political contexts. This is not to say, however, that we negate the mind and emotions but, rather, that we incorporate discussions of cognitive strategies and expressive drives within a larger context. In other words, we need to move writing into the world we inhabit. As Maxine Greene suggests,

> the world we inhabit is palpably deficient: there are unwarranted inequities, shattered communities, and unfulfilled lives. We can not help but hunger for traces of utopian visions, of critical or dialectical engagements with social and

economic realities. And yet, when we reach out, we experience a kind of blankness. . . . How are we to . . . break with the given, the taken for granted—to move towards what might be, what is not yet? (1986, p. 440)

Greene comments not only on inequity in society but also on the need to break, as she writes, "with the given, the taken for granted" in order to "move towards what might be, what is not yet." For teachers of writing in nonmainstream contexts to do the same we need to consider seriously the implications of the theoretical underpinnings that inform our practice and to reevaluate how these affect our students and our own hoped-for "move towards what might be, what is not yet." To do so necessitates, in Peter McLaren's words, "engaging in a critical praxis that addresses the transformation of dreams and desires in the search for what we might already be and in the struggle for what we might become" (1991, p. 25).

5

THE SOCIAL CONSTRUCTION OF A WRITING INSTRUCTOR: SARAH'S IDEOLOGY

> To invoke the importance of pedagogy is to raise questions not simply about how students learn but also how educators (in the broad sense of the term) construct the ideological and political positions from which they speak. At issue here is a discourse that both situates human beings within history and makes visible the limits of their ideologies and values.—Henry Giroux, *Border Crossings*

And What Do You Want to Be When You Grow Up?

Sarah Thomas did not spend her adolescence dreaming of the days when she would teach writing. As she says, "You know, ten years ago I never would have thought I would be doing what I'm doing . . . I had thought of myself teaching English, but I thought I was going to go on in English literature, so I guess I didn't think of myself as being a writing teacher." Sarah did not, in other words, plan for the position she was in in the manner in which a doctor, for example, may have dreamed as a young child of healing others or perhaps of becoming financially secure. Rather, Sarah came to her position through a circuitous route, in much the way many do who teach writing.

I know I never gave the possibility of teaching writing a thought when I was young. In fact, I never knew that writing instructors existed; I considered college an institution defined by disciplines and I considered many future possibilities for myself to be open: the possibility of studying and then finally choosing the particular discipline I wished to pursue was for me a given. My mother was a mathematical engineer with two undergraduate degrees, one from Cornell and the other from Rensselaer Polytechnic Institute (RPI), each completed in two years rather than the traditional four. In fact, I was proud, though sometimes overly awestruck, to be the daughter of a mother who was a member of the first small group of women to be admitted to RPI in response to the needs of the historical contexts surrounding World War II. Later, in the mid-1960s my mother became one of the first to complete a master's in communications in the newly developed program at RPI. She never completed her dissertation because her career, and her need for financial security, became a priority. My mother's true love was writing, and she published fiction and technical articles in her field. My mother's mother had graduated from Syracuse University with a degree in music in 1916 and had spent a number of years in Manhattan working in publishing, which she maintained involved doing all her boss's writing and reading and deftly avoiding physical encounters with him whenever he approached her in the office. So my grandmother did a lot of writing too, as did the men in my family.

I spent my childhood knowing what I would not be: a housewife considering the positive properties of a newly marketed detergent; instead I would be "Something." The fact that my journey to becoming "Something" would include a foray into language teaching, and eventually a number of years teaching writing, garnered not a moment's thought from me during my teens. Sarah, in considering teaching literature, was closer to the field of writing in forethought than I ever was, because when I was younger I thought of teaching as a death sentence meted out to those housewives whose households would benefit from a supplementary salary.

I do not hold this ideological perspective today. I taught in an inner-city public high school working with refugees and immigrants for eight years. I have to admit that by my third year I did decide never to enter a teachers' room (a space provided for "free" periods") ever again. I had tired of colleagues commenting for my benefit that my students "should get back on the boat that brought them here and head back to where they came from" and on and on. The final blow came when a retired army officer teaching industrial arts, Mr. Paddles (a pseudonym, of course), started a diatribe including the phrase "those damn niggers." I blew— first verbally in response to Paddles's blatantly racist comments, and then physically from this contaminated space called a teachers' room, seeking refuge in any quiet corner I could find within the locked-door confines of this public high school. This same man had severely chastised a student of mine, Bartolo, the previous year for arriving in class without a pencil. The next day Bartolo made sure he had a pencil in hand for industrial arts, but before entering the class he stopped for a drink from the bubbler—New England for drinking fountain. When Bartolo raised his head from the fountain, Paddles was by his side in the hall. Bartolo took this opportunity to display his pencil and announce, "Look, Mr. Paddles, I have a pencil with me today." Paddles promptly snatched the pencil from Bartolo's hand, snapped it in half, and replied, "Now you don't." These examples could be expanded upon extensively, though this is not the place to do so. They are presented to illustrate the tensions that exist within educational institutions faced with educating individuals whose home languages and cultures differ from those of the dominant culture. Having taught in the public schools, I now hold the profession of teaching in high esteem, and the arrogance born of the ignorance of youth has been replaced by a deep respect that I wish was shared, in particular, by those in control of establishing teacher salaries and working environments. Having taught in the public schools, I know too that for every Mr. Paddles there is a Norma Audy, Christine Tunstall, Wendy Tsapatsaris, Sheryl Norris, Jane Cooper, and so many more who battle daily to seek to ensure access to those from outside mainstream contexts.

Part-Timers: Servitude and the Creation of an Underclass

Becoming a writing teacher is generally not a specific career goal; in fact, the teaching of writing is often viewed as a temporary position, one held by graduate students as teaching assistants en route to the Ph.D. James F. Slevin writes in "Depoliticizing and Politicizing Composition Studies" of his experience as an outside evaluator of a writing program where he found:

> A cadre of 59 graduate students, teaching two composition courses per semester, for a stipend (now taxable) of about $7,500. In addition to poverty-level wages, they were systematically prevented by these teaching duties from advancing toward their degrees; as a result, many of them had become permanent part-timers, in their seventh, eighth, and even ninth years of the graduate program. In some ways, by virtue of their temporal distance from their course work and from their dissertation director (who could help them find real jobs), they were moving backwards on a treadmill. (1991, p. 1)

At the same institution, Slevin "found a part-time faculty of 75, teaching a 3–2 load" while the full-time faculty in the department taught a 2–2 load. These part-timers were housed in a basement that was "at least a quarter of a mile away from their full-time 'colleagues.'" The highest paid of this cadre of part-timers made "30 percent less per course" than an assistant professor who had just begun teaching at the university (p. 1).

Life beyond Teaching Writing: Just a Glimpse

Both Sarah and I have moved beyond teaching composition, we each earned a Ph.D., and we each sought, and obtained, positions that did not include teaching freshman comp. The route to the Ph.D. was not without bumps and detours, however. I found, especially, that my increasing responsibilities as a part-timer hampered considerably my ability to attend to my own work. It is interesting that

I impose the distinction here, prevalent in academia, between one's own work—research and writing initially for the degree and eventually for publication—and the work entailed in teaching and evaluating students. Most privilege "their own work" over teaching, for it is the degree and publication that lead first to a tenure-track position and eventually to tenure. Part-time writing instructors are well out of the academic track. In many ways, so too are untenured faculty, like I am at this writing. I have prepared and taught more than fourteen very different courses at UMB alone. In all I have prepped and taught more than twenty-five distinctly different courses since entering higher education.

Without a real job offer from the University of New Hampshire as a visiting lecturer—a position not designed to lead to tenure review, but one in my field of linguistics, at least—I would not have finished my Ph.D. I could not face the embarrassment of beginning a position in September without my degree in hand. Thus with the continued support of the most generous and brilliant advisor any student could have, James Paul Gee, I frantically wrote the final three chapters of my dissertation the summer before my job began, and I mailed each chapter to him for comment and feedback, which was done over the phone because he was in California and I in Massachusetts.

Hierarchical Structures

For others in English departments, writing is but one of the assigned courses for which they are responsible. I can still remember an assistant professor (whose field and name will remain unacknowledged) approaching me in the early 1990s in a state of distress with multiple complaints about his need to teach writing in the department at UMB. He felt safe venting to me (after all, I was just a part-timer and held no power over him, and we did get on together collegially). "Why do I have to teach writing? My degree's in literature!" "I know nothing about teaching writing." "No one helps here, they all hate it too." "What am I left with?" "I teach the way I was taught, and I hated that." "All those errors and the need to correct, correct, correct." "God, this place is just too democratic."

My colleague had not slept the night before, he explained, because he had to plow through multiple assignments, long overdue for return to his students, all due to the fact that "I couldn't face having to read another one of those god-awful papers, but I know that if I didn't finally do it, I'd be cooked in the evaluations." This is the most agitated I had ever seen this particular faculty member, whom I always liked because he made eye contact and didn't act like it was beneath him to speak to those outside the "official" department. In this instance he was over the edge; his venting occurred in the hall, not even in the privacy of an office. Luckily, no one passed by, so the conversation was not used against him. But in hindsight, I realize, if the conversation had been overheard by a senior member of the department, there is the strong possibility that his comments might have elevated his status, not diminished it. And what could I say? I told him, "I know exactly what you mean. It is really difficult." I could have added more, but I chose not to. I actually liked teaching writing, found it to be an adventure and sought each semester to try harder to engage students in active, productive, creative ways to access the discourse of the academy while at the same time learning to assess what these forms demanded of them as individuals from distinctive historical, linguistic, and cultural communities. Teaching writing had allowed me access to the academic environment that I coveted; how could I approach it with disdain? At the same time, teaching writing placed considerable constraints on my time and thus hindered my ability to complete my dissertation.

Writing is but one of the assigned courses for which English Department faculty are responsible, as was the case for my venting friend described above. Full-time faculty members also taught other courses in their fields of interest and areas of expertise, such as Shakespeare, Hemingway, Medieval studies, the Romantics, and so forth. Although writing—also called composition studies or rhetoric, depending on the school; it seems a single name cannot be agreed upon to label this endeavor—is increasingly recognized as an area (as opposed to a discipline), as of this writing only two full-time writing positions exist in the English Department at UMB. These professors are responsible for teaching not only undergraduate writing classes but also courses in writing theory and practice to undergraduates and graduate students seeking an M.A. in English. Many of the other sections of undergraduate writing are taught by half-timers and part-timers.

The Colonization of Writing

Drawing from Modern Language Association (MLA) figures gathered and presented in an in-house report by Bettina Huber and from subsequent publications and reports based on the figures compiled by Huber, James Slevin concludes that the conditions he witnessed within the English department he was charged with evaluating were not representative of an isolated instance but were, rather, entrenched practices central to English studies (1991, p. 4). And, argues Slevin, despite the move to hire full-time faculty in composition, most writing teachers are still part-timers. A number of historical, political, and profoundly economic conditions have made composition into a subdiscipline and its faculty members into a powerless underclass. Harsh in his analysis of the reality of the status of composition studies and faculty, Slevin argues that English departments have recognized, like the French in the running of their colonies, that "composition programs function more harmoniously when headed by fairly secure colleagues whose complexion matches that of the staff" (p. 4).

The situation at the University of Massachusetts Boston in the ESL program provides significant anecdotal evidence supporting this claim; the MLA figures gathered by Bettina Huber supply the data that proves this practice is not limited to the named and unnamed institutions of higher learning discussed here. Further, in chapter 3 I discussed the general responsibilities of Vivian Zamel, the head of UMB's ESL writing program. They are not heavy in terms of teaching load: she taught an undergraduate seminar in tutoring that may draw up to ten students and a composition course followed by a semester teaching one graduate course. A staff member with nonfaculty status is responsible for hiring and scheduling the ESL institute courses—noncredit courses designed for nonnative speakers to acquire oral and written skills in English. The "running of the program" means hiring instructors out of the M.A. in Applied Linguistics Program at UMB for the most part—part-timers "whose complexion matches" that of the director, though part-time status requires little in the way of staff meetings, discussions of curriculum development, direct advocacy for more full-time positions, and so forth.

Part-Timers: Maintenance of an Underclass

When Sarah and I were teaching writing, the pool of applicants for the part-time positions came primarily from Boston University (BU), where Steve Molinsky ran a very successful TESOL master's program and where Ph.D. candidates studied psycholinguistics in the School of Education or applied linguistics in the College of Arts and Sciences. In the early 1980s the Bilingual/ESL Graduate Studies Program was just establishing itself at UMB; it had moved to UMB from the defunct Boston State College and was plunked unceremoniously into the English Department. It thus took over a decade for Vivian Zamel to begin drawing more directly from UMB's M.A. program for instructors rather than from BU.

With her own graduate students as future writing instructors, Zamel acquired additional power that had not been available to her with the BU group. Now she gained status not only as director of the program but also as a member of the graduate faculty who taught courses in ESL theories and methods and, most especially, a course called Writing in a Second Language. While her currency increased among the part-timers, their overall status remained the same. Positioning among the part-time instructors was dependent on maintaining favor with Zamel; if they were allowed to teach three consecutive semesters, they gained access to the faculty union, higher wages, and benefits, and if Zamel assigned them to teach coveted summer courses they would see an increase in their annual income. I suppose it was not much different than when Sarah and I had taught at UMB with master's degrees from BU, except the faculty teaching part-time were much more entrenched because they had terminal master's degrees and were not being drawn from Ph.D. programs. These part-timers were more likely to stay around for far longer, which was much better for the director.

Back to Sarah's Story

Sarah viewed her position at UMB as interim, as do many adjunct writing faculty, and not as her life's work. Since 1984 Sarah had taught two sections of composition per semester while at the same time teaching two sections at BU. Thus she taught four writing classes each semester and four sections at UMB during the two summer sessions, to create a total of twelve courses a year! Even if Sarah had only fifteen students per class (this is a low estimate—she had had up to twenty-nine in a course) Sarah would have read approximately 60 papers per course for a total of 720 by mid-August when the second summer session was completed. Many of those 720 papers would have been ten pages in length, thus bringing the total number of pages read per year into the thousands. In order to read so many pages of student writing one would need, if nothing else, good eyesight, a considerable number of waking hours, lots of coffee, and undying patience. When I asked Sarah whether she felt teaching writing was exhausting, she replied, "Yes, I think it's exhausting just because of the piles of papers. You still have to read all those papers. . . . There are ways to cut down on the work, but when push comes to shove, you still have to read all of those papers."

Why would anyone do this? And by what route would one travel to come to read, comment on, and evaluate 720 student papers a year? For Sarah, much contributed to her present professional status as writing instructor: educational preparation, previous job experience, economic necessity, and present status as a graduate student in a Ph.D. program in applied linguistics. In order to understand her practice one needs to consider the various components of her past and those concurrent to the time she taught at UMB.

Sarah, a name I chose, was called "professor" by her students but was nameless and without a title other than part-timer in the department. I choose to use her first name (a pseudonym) not only to provide "a face" to her story—I could have chosen, for example, to refer to her as "the instructor"—but also to emphasize her lack of status within the institution. My choice of Sarah is meant as well to illuminate the personal regard I held for her. We interacted on a first-name basis and came to respect and like one another as we learned together throughout the course of the study of each other's history, goals, and dreams. I have the highest regard for Sarah; the choice of first name as a referent should by no means imply a lack of respect on my part.

Anyone Can Teach ESL

Sarah received her undergraduate degree in what she referred to as "teaching regular old English." Her student teaching experience as an undergraduate major in English education was what led her directly into ESL. This happened to be the case because the supervising teacher she worked with taught an ESL class in addition to her other sections of "regular English." This was in 1980, at the end of Sarah's senior year in undergraduate school, a period of time in which many Indochinese (as they were referred to at the time) were coming into the United States, creating a need for ESL instruction in the public schools in areas where focused resettlement was occurring. Many who had no previous training in teaching

ESL were called upon to teach these newcomers English. Sarah describes the time period: "And people were just saying, 'Well, here is this group of students. I don't know what to do with them. You're an English teacher. You do something with them.' So that the teacher I was working with was teaching a class of ESL English, but she had no training in ESL and she really didn't know what she was doing, and some of the things she did kind of upset me. I thought they were kind of demeaning."

This early experience with ESL spurred Sarah's interest in teaching nonnative students and served to solidify some of her notions as to what constituted appropriate teaching. The fact that she felt that the English teacher she worked with treated the nonnative students in a demeaning manner was particularly influential. The ESL students were mainstreamed into other academic subjects while at the same time learning English. The fact that Sarah's supervising teacher did not present English in the same manner that (Sarah assumed) subject matter was presented in other classes disturbed her. When I asked what Sarah found demeaning about the ESL class she responded, "Well, like she would show them cartoons and here they are, you know, they've been mainstreamed—they're trying to take, you know, freshman biology with everybody else, or whatever, and then they come into the English class and then they're shown Walt Disney cartoons."

I do know, and did when I was talking with Sarah, because I had seen the same approach used over and over with nonnative speakers. On the one hand, the system would place outlandish demands upon them, expecting that newly arrived students with no background in English would be able to follow the curriculum of a class like biology while, on the other hand, paternalistically feeding them the English language and culture as if it were pabulum for an infant. With a firm grasp of this contradiction, Sarah determined that professionalism in ESL meant creating a classroom environment that mirrored that of the other academic subjects, such as biology. It also meant not stepping out of the role of teacher. This is revealed implicitly in Sarah's description of her supervising teacher's behavior with her students: "And she was also an Avon lady and so she sold all the girls Avon products . . . it's just my personal opinion, but I thought it was a little unprofessional."

On to a Master's Degree

As a result of this student teaching experience, Sarah decided to pursue a master's degree in teaching ESL at a major university in the Great Lakes Region. Her rationale: "I did want to go into ESL because I really liked the students and I liked working with them." If I were asked the same question, my answer would not differ. After completing a B.A. in political science, I decided, once I realized what working in the foreign service really required, that I would not enter the foreign service. Instead, without a plan or money, I ended up in a city with a large immigrant population working as a substitute teacher—engaging in the very activity that I had earlier sworn with disdain to avoid. What happened, however, is that I found myself being called on repeatedly to substitute in the ESL program. I loved it, and the program loved me. Apparently few who substitute taught agreed to assignments in ESL or special education. So, somewhat serendipitously, I found myself abroad without having left the United States. Neither Sarah nor I planned to teach ESL, but by chance we were both exposed to the wonder of working with such eager students from whom we had so much to learn.

Developing an Ideology of Teaching: Graduate Study and Practical Experience

During the first year of her master's program, Sarah taught junior high school— regular English—in order to support her graduate studies. The experience was "awful, it was terrible." A number of factors contributed to her stress. She had just married, just started graduate school, and just started teaching full-time in the public school system. The marriage endured and her graduate studies continued, but after that one year, Sarah would never return to the public schools to teach. She recalled that throughout the year she would often wake from a sound sleep, sit up in bed while still dreaming, and say, "Get back in your seat." To Sarah's horror, one of her most troublesome students was returned to her class after being arrested for assault with a deadly weapon. Sarah worked with a principal she describes as "unsupportive" because he insisted she teach exactly what was mandated as ninth-grade curriculum despite her objections. Thus she had to teach *Romeo and Juliet* to ninth-graders she insisted should have been placed in individualized programs.

Out of the Public School System and on to Composition

Determined not to teach in the public schools again, Sarah applied for a teaching fellowship for her second year of graduate studies. She received a teaching assistantship and became a composition instructor in the ESL program. It was this teaching experience that further solidified her perspective toward teaching nonnative students. In addition, during her second year of graduate school, Sarah took a course in teaching writing to ESL students, a course she described as a historical survey of teaching writing that ended with what was characterized by her professor as a presentation of the process approach. Sarah said the course was, overall, "a pretty objective presentation" of a number of approaches to teaching writing, and she felt that it had not influenced her practice much. What was influential was her teaching experience, an experience she describes as "mostly difficult" because she had one professor for transformational grammar and he was a grammarian, and he believed anything could be solved grammatically. He had decided that he wanted to teach writing that semester, so he and I and another teacher were the three people teaching this one writing course (but different sections) which is like our 101 [the first composition course for entering students at UMB] here. And so since he had never taught writing he wanted for us to meet together and plan because he didn't know what he was doing and he wanted us to give the same midterm and the same assignments and the same final. And that was really bad.

This situation was particularly problematic for Sarah because while the grammarian was her colleague at meetings, he was her professor in the transformational grammar class she was taking as a requirement for the master's in ESL. And to make matters worse, the professor was also, according to Sarah, prejudiced against women. Sarah describes his practice as follows:

> And it wasn't teaching writing. It was analyzing every sentence and looking at their grammar. And it was a lot of very prescriptive assignments. You know, "we want you to do this." . . . When he taught introductions he wrote a whole essay and then told the students to compose the introduction for it. I mean, that's really hard to do, for one thing, and for another thing, I thought it was a strange writing assignment.

From Sarah's description of her grammar-oriented instructor it is apparent that he was influenced by the work of Francis Christensen, including his articles "A Generative Rhetoric of the Sentence" (1963), "Notes toward a New Rhetoric: I. Sentence Openers; II. A Lesson from Hemingway" (1963), and "A Generative Rhetoric of the Paragraph" (1965). Christensen, drawing on Chomsky's work, urged writing instructors to combine "an empirical approach that considered the way writers actually compose sentences with lessons from the new linguistics" (cited in Berlin, 1965, p. 136). In addition to suggesting a new research methodology, according to Berlin, Christensen claimed that he had developed "the new rhetoric," one that focused on sentence and paragraph formation. Berlin argues that Christensen did teach writing teachers "something about the relation of form to meaning, especially the ways in which linguistic forms can themselves generate meaning"(p. 136). I agree with Berlin, but would argue further that Christensen's hyperbolic claim for a "new rhetoric" was in many ways a marketing strategy.

This marketing of the "new rhetoric" is so very American; new is always better and seems to appear magically without influence from history or culture. In the academic environment it is a useful construct, because new ideas garner attention and, the scholar hopes, publication, which is necessary for tenure and promotion. The scholar also hopes that his or her new approach will be purchased as packaged-in-book-form by as many school systems and institutions of higher learning as possible. This all reminds me of the dramatic yearly unveiling of the new model Chevrolet I witnessed with glee as a child in front of the old black-and-white TV in our den. America's sweetheart, Dinah Shore, introduced with dramatic flourish each new year's model promising its prospective buyers a greater ride, a more panoramic view—the wrap-around window was a real innovation—and the pure joy of riding a horseless carriage uncontaminated by previous wear and tear, not to mention the scent of use. "See the USA in your Chevrolet"—preferably in one fresh off the assembly line—characterizes a cultural maxim that has permeated our society and shapes academia to this day.

Once the semester ended the grammarian decided not to teach writing again—perhaps his article based on the experience was completed (only a guess)—and Sarah was on her own. To Sarah being on her own meant "I had input into what book I wanted to use, and then I was able to begin developing my own teaching style."

Here is the first insight into Sarah's reliance on a textbook (rhetoric) for teaching writing. The importance for Sarah of the choice of what book to use also emerges in her comments on the class of English-speaking athletes she taught during what was now her third year in the master's program. Sarah said of the athletes, "With the athletes I couldn't choose my own book, and that upset me 'cause I didn't like the text we were using." She did not like the book because it "was like reading, grammar exercises." At the same time she was dealing with a book she did not like she also had the athletes keep journals, which she describes as "kind of a riot to read." The use of journals represents a break from a primarily traditional approach to teaching. Though she was able, at this time, to begin to have more control over the direction her teaching would take, she also felt situational constraints over and above the imposition of a text for the course. Sarah describes these constraints in the following: "It was an interesting class to teach. It was a difficult class because it had a lot of constraints on it because these were athletes and they were horrible writers and they were supposed to make the grade so that they could be eligible to play. . . . I had one student, a coach called me, you know, and said, 'Look, can he do some extra work?' So it was sort of a weird kind of situation." Thus, Sarah experienced not only the imposition of a text chosen by someone in the program with far more authority than she had but also further constraints from the institution in the form of pressure from coaches to pass certain students in her course. At this point in her career, however, Sarah was free from the very close supervision she encountered under the watchful eye of the grammarian, and she is able to describe her teaching as "interesting." Certainly this description is more positive than her descriptions of public school teaching as "awful" and "terrible" or of working as a teaching assistant as "mostly difficult."

After two and a half years of teaching Sarah had yet to experience a situation in which she felt she had control over the direction her writing courses would take. Through her own practice, as well as through a critical view of the practice of others who had authority over her, Sarah began to develop her own theories of the appropriate manner in which writing should be taught. She had not yet found, however, a position as writing instructor where she could establish her own course and where she could be truly autonomous in teaching—though true autonomy may be a manufactured, ideal state, fabricated by faculty to assist in dealing with the overpowering institutional constraints that we come to know the longer we experience academia. Nonetheless, at this point in her life, Sarah truly felt that she would find such a position, no doubt when her master's was completed.

During the second semester of her third year in the master's program, Sarah taught "regular" students from the Educational Opportunities Program (EOP), a federal program developed as an outgrowth of 1960s progressivism designed to provide access to higher education to underprepared individuals—most generally people of color, members of the working class, immigrants and refugees, and others whose families and communities had not yet had access to a college education. Sarah really enjoyed working in this program:

> The second half of that year I taught the regular EOP students and I had a wonderful experience with them. And that was a really neat teaching position because the course was a three-credit course and then they also got a credit for their tutorial, so you worked with them three hours a week in class, and then for every student you did an hour of tutorial a week. So it was pretty much a full-time job, but you were able to do so much with their writing and to know them and their writing so well . . . I really enjoyed teaching in that program.

It was in the EOP program that Sarah first encountered working with multiple drafts of a student paper, because the program required students to write two drafts of their research paper. Sarah came to believe in the importance of writing multiple drafts as a result of this experience. In reflecting on teaching in the EOP program and the impact she felt the experience had on her present-day practice, Sarah notes, "I got their final drafts and I kind of thought: Well, geez, it could have been so much better if they could just do it one more time. And a lot of them, especially when I do the three drafts now, the first time around I only look at the content and the organization and then the second time I start to mark the other things, because in the beginning I want them to really focus on what they're saying and how they're saying it." The EOP program was Sarah's first exposure to applying, albeit to a limited extent, aspects of the process approach to teaching writing—student conferencing and multiple drafts of papers, the components of teaching practice that correspond most directly to the cognitive perspective.

Sarah's Emergent Ideology

In spring 1984, Sarah was awarded a master's in ESL and was free to leave for Boston to begin as a doctoral student in the Program in Applied Linguistics at

Boston University. Her goals now were far more clearly defined: she hoped to obtain a position in a third-world country dealing with issues and policy related to language planning and literacy development. Her husband's goal was to study for the ministry in the Boston area and to eventually do missionary work abroad as well. Upon her completion of the course work and comprehensive exam requirements for the Ph.D., Sarah and her husband, now a minister, moved to Bangladesh to fulfill their chosen paths in life. Sarah planned to combine her professional work with the research and writing of her dissertation. She doubted that she would ever return to UMB.

But I will return to UMB, in order to trace Sarah's developing ideology of writing and the manner in which it was expressed in her responsibilities at the university. Sarah enjoyed working at UMB. It was here, as well as at Boston University where she also taught writing, that she felt a true sense of autonomy in the classroom. This was possible, Sarah believed, because the directors of the two undergraduate writing programs were "very free." By this Sarah means that neither was in any way an interventionist; essentially their policy was to hire instructors and remain aloof until student evaluations came in. If the evaluations were fine, the instructor was ensured another semester of work. As a result, Sarah maintained, "You know it's your course; you design it the way you want."

How then did Sarah design her courses once given the perceived autonomy to do so? In chapter 6 I respond to this question in detail. Before dealing with an analysis of Sarah's actual practice, however, it is helpful to recapitulate here the major beliefs Sarah held regarding the teaching of writing. First, Sarah found it important to present the teaching of ESL or of writing to ESL students (or to others from nonmainstream backgrounds) as courses that have the same status as classes in other disciplines. Second, Sarah was shaped as a teacher by working with an individual who was a strict grammarian, by teaching in a program that incorporated components of the process approach to writing (EOP), and by her desire to resist the imposition of texts chosen by others for use in her classes. To Sarah autonomy meant being free to choose one's own text for writing class; resisting overemphasis on the teaching of grammar; creating a context within the classroom that communicated to students that this was a class with equal bearing as courses in the sciences; and establishing a program that allowed for the writing of multiple drafts of students' papers.

How did Sarah now situate herself as a writing instructor? Did she feel philosophically associated with adherents of the process approach—perhaps due to her association with Vivian Zamel? Did she have clear notions about how, or whether, her perspective on the teaching of writing had changed over time? If so, who or what did she feel influenced her beliefs regarding writing instruction? When I first approached Sarah to ask her to consider participating in the study I planned to undertake at UMB, she said she was a process-oriented instructor. I was quickly inclined to categorize her as adhering totally to a process approach because I was familiar, as an instructor of writing in the same department as Sarah, with the strong emphasis on process writing verbalized frequently by Zamel. Through the course of the interview process, when Sarah began to reflect more critically on her practice, she modified her self-characterization. In addition, I came to view Sarah quite differently as the interviews progressed and as the observation process unfolded.

When asked, after classroom observations had begun, to categorize her perspective toward the teaching of writing, Sarah responded as follows:

> I would probably put myself definitely not totally in either camp. I would put myself somewhere in the middle but leaning towards the process end of it, because in my 101 course I spend time on some points of grammar. I spend time on sentence-combining things because I feel that even when students are going through the process, a lot of times they don't yet have the sophistication in sentence structure and things like that, and so I think some things like that belong to a more traditional approach.

Sarah did feel she had changed in her approach to teaching over time. Here is how she characterizes this progression: "I've come to change it a lot. When I began I was really a traditionalist, and everything was very structured and a lot of writing was grammar and I did a lot of controlled writing. I don't know how much of it I did, but the people that I worked with were doing it a lot. . . . Give a student a paragraph and tell him to write a topic sentence for it, exercises like that." This change from an overriding focus on grammar was not easy for Sarah. As she explains: "The first time I graded a bunch of papers that way [without correcting grammar] it was almost as though I had to physically pull my arm away from the paper, but now I've gotten quite good at it." She went on to explain what she now believed was more important in terms of teaching students:

> I think that it's [teaching grammar] very, I don't want to say, deceiving students, because that doesn't sound very good, but it's not giving students an appropriate view of what goes on in real life, of how people really write. You know, if on a midterm you hand them a sheet of paper and say write this, yes they have to do that in some situations, but in a lot of writing situations they don't, and I think that if your courses only teach those kinds of things then students really aren't learning; and they're learning nothing about revising because revising isn't part of that framework.

Sarah, in her tempered and most polite way, skirts the issue of grammar teaching in the writing classroom in mitigating her comments with "I don't want to say, deceiving students, because that doesn't sound very good," and goes on to restructure her critique in "but it's not giving students an appropriate view of what goes on in real life, of how people really write." Essentially, what Sarah is getting at here, though she couches her comments in hedges and mitigation, is that strictly focusing on grammar, or overemphasizing grammar to the exclusion of having students engage in the real behaviors of "how people really write," promulgates an insidious and truly deceitful pedagogy. Teaching points of grammar can be pretty straightforward. Students can be given exercises to do. Tests can be administered. Objective outcomes can be obtained. This is all to the benefit of the instructor and is superficially appealing, perhaps, to the student who wishes to see the acquisition of language as the accumulation of correct grammatical forms. Structured exercises, sentence-level grammatical exercises, and even work at the level of the paragraph keep those piles of dreaded student papers under control. Finally, successful writers don't consciously attend to grammar because they don't need to, having acquired the necessary grammatical forms from home and through advancement academically. And most academic writing that is accepted for publication goes through copyediting, during which the grammatical and spelling errors and much more are corrected. Therefore, Sarah maintained that students needed to know about process writing because "that's the way most writers who write, write."

What else influenced Sarah? Clearly she was affected not only by her past teaching experiences but also by her present professional environment. As Sarah noted:

> When you work under someone like Vivian Zamel you think about what she has to say, and I think that you think about process a lot more. I think that if I had gone into a university where everyone taught in a traditional approach, I'm not saying I would be totally influenced that way, but maybe that would come out more in my writing courses 'cause I think even though we don't have a lot of gatherings and we don't have a lot of talking together here as teachers among ourselves, I think that just being in a certain environment and knowing people think about things a certain way, I think that that influences you. I really, really do.

6

FROM IDEOLOGY TO PRACTICE: SARAH TEACHING

> We may admit that practice always implies a process of knowledge far removed from any passive recording, without thereby presenting it as a purely intellectual construction. Practical knowledge is an operation of construction which sets up systems of classifications (taxonomies) in terms of practical functions. These systems organize perception and appreciation, and provide a structure for practice.—Pierre Bourdieu, *Homo Academicus*

Establishing Status as a Discipline

Sarah's course began with a determined effort on her part to present to the students her belief that writing and learning to write constitute the acquisition of a body of knowledge much like the demands of learning physics or computer science. Sarah spoke initially of English, seldom using the term "writing" despite the fact that the course is regarded informally among the composition-writing-underclass faculty at the university as a research writing course. However, its official designation is ESL Freshman English II. Sarah's discussion of English as a discipline emerged as a result of her announcement at the beginning of the first class that there would be a quiz and a midterm exam in the course. This announcement prompted a question from Zola, a student in the course, who asked whether the quiz would cover grammar. Sarah quickly dismissed the possibility of testing grammar: "No, no, no, it's not, no, it's not grammatical." This strong response reflects her professed support of a process approach to writing that sees grammar as anathema and her resistance to the imposed methodology of her trans-formational grammar professor. (Sarah has, however, maintained the grammarian's practice of examining students in writing class, a practice not common among process-oriented instructors.)

Sarah deflected the concern about grammar to a discussion of her beliefs concerning English as a discipline. Her discussion did not hint at the problem-atic, nonuniform manner in which the discipline of English is perceived (Graff, 1987). English, she maintained, had terms that those who study the discipline should know. In making this distinction Sarah very clearly set the agenda in the context of her notions of writing. Sarah distinguished between writing itself, the act of engagement and creativity, on the one hand, and the metalanguage used by those who evaluate and analyze texts. The distinction is revealed in her justifica-tion for establishing a quiz and midterm in the course: "The first quiz will be over things like probably things that you have already had in some of your other courses. I say to you, in your research paper, 'this paragraph isn't unified.' Well, if you don't know what a unified paragraph is or you don't know what unity is in a paragraph, then my comment doesn't mean anything. OK?"

This reveals much about Sarah's perspectives regarding writing. First, she established the fact that she is the evaluator in her comment, "I say this paragraph isn't unified." Sarah is in a position to judge student writing. Second, she con-veyed her assumption that knowing the meaning of a term used in the discourse of composition textbooks and by instructors—*unity*, for example—has, in some way, an implicit relationship to being able to meet this goal in one's writing. If a paragraph is judged to lack unity, the implied task of the student is to establish unity. This assumes that if a student writer is notified, for example, that her paper lacks coherence, the "fact of notification" in and of itself will lead the writer to the proper path—a coherent paper. But what if the student believes that her paper already is coherent? How is she then to enact changes that will lead her instructor to read her paper as coherent? Further, how is the student to know what the instructor's notion of coherence or unity entails, when she herself has not felt that either was lacking in her paper? Third, Sarah assumed that items included on the quiz would be information or knowledge the students already possess. She stated that the quiz will cover things "you probably have already had in your other courses." Thus she assumed a continuity of methodological approach and emphasis in pre-vious courses in English or English as a Second Language, an assumed conformity to curriculum that may or may not exist. Finally, Sarah suggested that giving quizzes would somehow establish how much a student knows about writing in much the same simplistic way one might seek to establish a student's knowledge of periodic tables in chemistry as a reflection of what a student knows or under-stands about chemistry. Sarah established her association—as instructor of writ-ing—between English and other disciplines in the following: "So this first part of the course is a review of some of the terms that we use in English to talk about writing—because English is just like any other discipline; it has terms. If you take a biology course you have to learn these certain terms that they call parts of the body. If you take a psychology course you have to learn terms that they call different mental illnesses. If you take a writing course you have to know the different terms we use to talk about writing. OK?"

Clearly Sarah sought, by drawing analogies to the teaching of terminology in other introductory courses, to establish that students need to know the terminology—jargon—associated with English. However, unity, clarity, and coherence are not terms one would necessarily associate with English, as are the terms critique, voice, literary, mood, and metaphor, to name just a few. Sarah did not, however, explicitly discuss how this knowledge of the vocabulary of the discipline would assist a student in becoming a better writer. Implicit within Sarah's discussion of terminology with her students was the message that ESL Freshman English II is as important a course as introductory courses in psychology and biology, to cite her examples.

Writing Classes Are Serious Classes

In the initial interview I conducted with Sarah she voiced a concern that students in writing courses did not take the writing courses as seriously as they did their other courses. Sarah maintained:

> I feel that even when students are going through the process, a lot of times they don't yet have the sophistication in sentence structure and things like that, and so I think some things like that belong to a more traditional approach. Like in this 102 yesterday I went over terms, and I really feel that I want the students to know what unity is and what coherent—what they mean. Some people would say, "Well, you don't need to do that." But I want to be able to look at that, to be able to look at a paragraph in a research paper and be able to say, "this paragraph isn't unified. It has too many ideas in it." And I want the students to be able to know that.

Sarah further justified her teaching of terminology:

> And I guess I do it too because I think that sometimes writing courses in students' minds and in—I don't know if it's the mind of the university or what—they get shortchanged. I don't think students always take them [writing courses] very seriously, and I think that sometimes if students know that there is a vocabulary to go along with writing and there is a way to talk about writing using some words that may mean something in another setting but that they have a particular meaning in a writing course, then I think that maybe students can see writing as a discipline in its own right. And even though it carries over into all their different courses, this course is a course to work on your writing, and it is as important as your psychology course.

In presenting English—though she is speaking of writing/composition/rhetoric—as a discipline with a clearly defined terminology and with a connection to other introductory courses, Sarah tried to secure a status for her course, and other writing courses, equal to that presumably held by introductory courses in other established disciplines within academia. Like those who taught rhetoric at the turn of the century, Sarah sought for her course equal status in academia.

Academic Writing

During this first class meeting Sarah further established her beliefs regarding writing. Sarah did so as she explained to students her expectations for the in-class writing sample students would be responsible for in her course. Sarah needed the in-class writing sample from students in order to assess whether or not students were appropriately placed in the course. The in-class writing sample was required by the director, Vivian Zamel, as a means of screening out underprepared students who may have registered for the course without having taken the first writing course in the series of two that are required. After instructors read the writing samples they were handed in to Zamel's office, where they were kept on file. Any questions regarding placement of students emerging as a result of the sample were taken up with the director.

After being asked to write a three-to-five-paragraph essay, one student in the class asked how many words the essay should have in it. Sarah responded in a tone of mock horror at the thought that she might even consider the counting of words and assured the student that this would not be the case. Sarah reiterated that she would be counting paragraphs, perhaps to emphasize that this practice amounted to a loftier pursuit than the mere counting of words, a task usually associated with elementary and secondary school assignments in composition, such as the 250-word essay that was a staple when I was in elementary school.

Once Sarah established the fact that she counts paragraphs, she proceeded to clarify her notion of the paragraph. "A paragraph, a good paragraph, has about seven to fifteen sentences. OK. All right. Yes, OK. We'll get into one-sentence paragraphs. They don't exist. All right." Sarah placed great emphasis on "don't exist," which reflected, in many ways, the overall manner in which she conveyed information to students. Here, writing represents a world, which designates an absolute. This is entirely incongruent with a process approach. At the outset, Sarah established a framework for students to view academic writing as a uniform, clearly definable entity, taught under the rubric of English. The implications: First, in order to produce good writing, students need to learn the rules and the vocabulary of writing. Second, learning to write will be accomplished by listening carefully to the instructor impart the rules of the discipline, by reading the textbook for the class, and by working closely with the assigned tutor on the grammar and cohesion exercises from the textbook.

In many ways, Sarah saw writing, which she often euphemistically referred to as English, as a body of knowledge defined through a set of explicitly stated rules, primarily rules of text structure. Clearly, the rule that says that a paragraph has seven to fifteen sentences excludes paragraphs of much lesser or greater length. In fact, Sarah taught students that one-sentence paragraphs do not exist, even though one-sentence paragraphs do, in fact, exist in all genres of writing. Sarah did not acknowledge, or perhaps accept, this existence as appropriate in academic writing. Sarah's notion of academic writing is captured in the following: "The kind of writing that we will be talking about in here is academic writing. We're not talking about the kinds of writing that you see in magazines and journals, in newspapers, in letters that you write home to your parents. The kind of writing we are talking about is academic writing, and that's the kind of writing that we find in textbooks."

In this explanation of academic writing Sarah, rather than speaking from her own personal perspective, which she often did, turned to the academic voice, the distant "we" that conjures the weight of a discipline imparting its wisdom and beliefs. Further Sarah's use of the inclusive "we" was misrepresentative of what had occurred thus far in class and what would continue to occur: Sarah talked and students listened, only rarely initiated questions, and just as rarely responded to questions posed by Sarah. The "we" used here is truly the authoritative "we" of the academic paper, not the inclusive "we" of a community discussion. Here, Sarah spoke with an objectivity implied in the depersonalized pronoun of choice among academics.

The Academic "We"

I recently (October 2002) observed this tendency to use the academic "we" as I reviewed my son's essay written for his sophomore Honors English teacher. Each use of "I" was circled in red, and Darien was directed to state his examples directly. In effect he was being asked to obliterate his voice and any reference of direct authorship of the essay. The work Darien created was to stand alone, representing asserted truths, in this instance truths emerging from Victor Hugo's *The Hunchback of Notre Dame.* Asked to link the theme—appearances may be deceiving—to Hugo's work, my son was directed to a form of writing that denied his direct association with the analysis. The text was to stand on its own merit, representative of the logical essay, an embodiment of truth and knowledge that already exist in the text, the final authority. When Darien revised the paper, his elimination of the use of "I" and corrected spelling, along with appropriate quotations from Hugo, supporting descriptive details, and a fine linearity to the five-paragraph essay earned my son a grade of 94 (this was after three drafts). At this point Darien refused to revise further, because a 94 was just fine by him.

Darien's English teacher requested, really insisted, that Darien not insert himself into the text through use of the personal pronoun "I," but the teacher also insisted that Darien work to insert his own "voice" into the text. This request befuddled my son. I explained to Darien that voice could be interpreted as the use of examples or turns of phrase that would catch the reader's attention and would help to differentiate his essay from others written by his classmates. Darien understood, but he remained frustrated by the fact that he is prohibited from using "I." As he said of his teacher, "Who does she think writes these essays anyway?"

I can remember clearly as a new graduate student sitting in my first seminar feeling a creeping disquiet each time the professor, a sociologist, used the academic "we": "We have determined from the research to date," or "we maintain that . . . ." Throughout his lectures I had to restrain myself from looking to see whether, in fact, the "we" of his presentation might be seated behind him. I knew that was not the case, of course, yet I could not shed the discomfort I felt each time this man, whom I admired, called upon the authority of the field to assert claims, assertions, and often speculations as if they existed out in the world as objectified truths. I felt as well an emotional discomfort that emanated from being in a communicative context that was so alien to me.

The first academic conference I attended evoked feelings of discomfort even greater than those I had experienced in my first seminar, as I listened to speakers refer to themselves in the third person. One speaker said, "(Heath, 1984) argues . . .", and it was Shirley Brice Heath herself who was speaking, yet not once did she utter the word "I." I use Heath as an example, though the collective voices of the academy—at this particular conference, scholars from the fields of linguistics and anthropology—spoke in the same voice, except for a very few who seemed to be cutting-edge renegades (I remember clearly that Deborah Tannen used the personal pronoun "I" when addressing the conference attendees). What I find most ironic in each of the examples drawn from the seminar and conference is the fact that all the speakers involved were seeking through their research to document everyday speech—the vernacular of previously ignored communities of speakers—yet they chose to do so through the objectified, distanced "voice of academia." So academics were in a position to "give voice" to the previously ignored, through the "voice of academia." But these linguists and anthropologists were assuming an audience who shared the discourse strategies they were displaying in their talks. As an initiate to the community, I was taken aback. As a renegade, Deborah Tannen spoke as if to a room full of friends. In my writing and teaching I do not hide behind "we," and I never will.

Essentially Sarah's assertions using the academic "we" sought the same end. She wanted her students to become aware that they were going to produce a valued form: academic writing. And while she attempted to differentiate the sort of writing required in the academy from writing done outside the academy, she did not attempt to differentiate between different forms of academic writing. Academic writing was presented to students as a uniform entity, which implied to Sarah's students that the writing discussed and produced in her class would be representative of all other writing produced in the academy. Later when I asked Sarah whether she, in fact, ever wrote using the format she required of students, she replied that she did not. Her use of the example of the "language used in textbooks" was odd as well in that textbook language, while a truly unique linguistic form, is not what I would choose as an example of academic writing.

Sarah's explanation to her students also reveals in part her notion of how her class was to be structured. Twice she mentioned the "kind of writing we're talking about here." Writing was talked about in Sarah's class a lot, and only four times was it produced during class: first, as the in-class writing sample; second, as short answers to quiz questions; third, as a summary on the midterm exam; and finally, as a list of pros and cons done as a part of an in-class exercise to highlight the notion of argument that was to be developed in the research paper. In each instance the language produced was in written form because there was no verbal give and take in this course, and although the linguistic forms produced were varied, they were fragmented and not representative of the particular form of academic discourse required in the class.

The Paragraph

A clearer definition of academic writing is embedded in a larger stretch of discourse in which Sarah established the expected structure of a paragraph in academic writing. For Sarah, a "paragraph has basically three parts." The paragraph begins with a main idea, called the topic sentence. Sarah further established this idea as fact by linking the notion of the role and location of the topic sentence to paragraphs in textbooks. Sarah suggested "that's why if you have to read six or seven chapters in a textbook the night before an exam you can skim them by reading the first sentence of every paragraph. . . . That way you won't get all the details and examples of what the writer is saying, but you will get the main ideas that the writer has because in the first sentence of each paragraph the topic of what that paragraph is going to be about." After the topic sentence, asserted Sarah, come the supporting details, the examples or data, and then the concluding sentence. Simply put, "so a paragraph has three parts." In summation Sarah stated the following:

> It [the paragraph] can't have one [sentence] because if it has one you're only going to have a topic sentence and you don't have any support for it. The minimum number is really three. You have to have one topic sentence, one sentence of support, and one concluding sentence. A good academic paragraph is going to have seven to fifteen sentences. But there's no such thing really as a one-sentence paragraph except in something like creative writing or journalistic writing, not in academic writing.

But One-Sentence Paragraphs Do Exist!

With this reassertion of her belief that academic writing does not permit the inclusion of one-sentence paragraphs, Sarah framed her two-class discussion of the paragraph in academic writing. The discussion began with the assertion regarding the allowable length of paragraphs and ended in the same manner. The whole discussion was thus framed with what might be considered a simplistic absolute that has, in reality, no validity. One-sentence paragraphs do exist and occur quite frequently in academic writing, both in published work as well as in unpublished manuscripts. In Raymond Williams's *Writing in Society* (1984, p. 152) I found the following one-sentence paragraph: "But these, I would argue, are in 1848 residual forms, in the sense that while they still command a majority readership among a given formed public, they are beginning to be written less." Out of context, the sentence lacks meaning; but in context, it serves as a transition from one topic, historical and costume novels, to a new one, the decline of such novels. I quote once again from Williams: "It is a tragic if temporary, even provisional, ending to the fiction of reform." This single sentence serves as the concluding paragraph to his chapter "The Fiction of Reform" (1984, p. 149). I found these two examples just by flipping through Williams's text. Now I may have just been lucky, so I moved on to another book, the edited volume *The Politics of Writing Instruction: Postsecondary*, which includes this one-sentence paragraph: "Obviously, at both practical and intellectual levels, this love/hate schema powerfully organizes discussion and action on a very complex, politically charged set of conflicts, concerns, and possibilities related to composition in the academy" (Phelps, 1991, p. 156).

And finally, I conducted the ultimate test in this minor experiment: could I find a one-sentence paragraph in an academic text written by someone from a more conservative perspective? I had to ask, because Williams is a well-known socialist literary critic and *The Politics of Writing Instruction* does lean to the left, so perhaps these pieces of writing were produced with a subtle intention of breaking established "truths" regarding academic form. Whom to turn to next? Right on the shelf above me sat *Cultural Literacy*, by E. D. Hirsch, Jr. (1987), a darling of the right, particularly in matters educational. I was nervous, but I proceeded with the same strategy applied in my experiment thus far: start from the back of the book, flip and scan. Eureka! On page 145 appears the following one-sentence paragraph, which once again is a concluding paragraph:

> I hope that in our future debates about the extensive curriculum, the participants will keep clearly in view the high stakes involved in their deliberations: breaking the cycle of illiteracy for deprived children; raising the living standard of families who have been illiterate; making our country more competitive in international markets; achieving greater social justice; enabling all citizens to participate in the political process; bringing us closer to the Cicero—main ideal of universal public discourse—in short, achieving fundamental goals of the Founders at the birth of the republic.

My purpose here has not been to ridicule Sarah but to highlight the arbitrariness of the rules that are often presented as absolutes in English and writing classes and in assigned rhetorics. One-sentence paragraphs do exist. Sentences may begin with "and," despite my high school English teacher's assertion to the contrary, and many accomplished writers use the personal pronoun "I" in academic work. Students, however, are penalized for engaging in the very behaviors that "come naturally to them" because these linguistic behaviors are deemed aberrant.

The Essay and Research Paper

At this point during her class, Sarah moved from a discussion of the paragraph to a discussion of the essay, stating that "An essay basically has the same three parts." By this she meant the same three parts as the paragraph. At this point Sarah was careful to make the distinction between the essay and the research paper, both of which will be required in the course. The essay was characterized as being based on personal experience and thus different from the research paper, which Sarah maintained calls upon other sources instead of just information from personal life experience in order to support the writer's thesis. It is not clear to me that Sarah really made a clear distinction between the essay and the research paper. This difference between personal writing and writing based upon source material was the main one offered, but in many other ways Sarah saw the essay as much like the research paper, only shorter. As Sarah maintained,

> However, in the research paper this general organization is exactly the same. We're just going to blow it up, make it bigger. Instead of having a one-paragraph introduction you might have a two- or three-paragraph introduction. Instead of having three or four or five or six paragraphs of support you might have seven pages of support. And instead of having a one-paragraph conclusion you might have a two- or three-paragraph conclusion. But the basic organization that we're working with is exactly the same. OK.

The language in which Sarah spoke is the language of absolute certainty, a language replete with assertions about the quantity of sentences, topic sentences, paragraphs, and parts of paragraphs found in her version of academic writing. Although she does not count words, she counts everything else. As Sarah commented in a moment of self-reflection, "I think I'm kind of numerically orientated." For Sarah, the world of writing was characterized by exactness. The essay, in Sarah's world of writing, was exactly the same as the research paper, but shorter. The world of academic writing Sarah presented to her students was not, however, an individual construct. Sarah had not extracted these rules solely of her own volition. Rather, the rules represented a compilation of "truths" regarding writing garnered from professors, mentors, textbooks on writing, and so forth, which she imparted to students with the best of intentions. She wanted her students to succeed in academia, to pass her course having acquired strategies that would serve them well both in upper-level courses and in taking the required writing proficiency exam at UMB. The rules Sarah imparted must be seen as part of a social construct representing "writing in the academy," which has been collapsed into easily codified rules, definitions, and strategies to be imparted to the students in her class.

Sarah continued her discussion of the essay by briefly clarifying, by genre, the differences between narrative, descriptive, expository, and argumentative essays. This information was conveyed in lecture format, as were all Sarah's classes. (She posed some questions to her students, but they were rarely answered.) Students were told that they would be responsible for writing an argumentative essay, and considerable time was spent defining the thesis statement. This discussion was organized around a handout Sarah provided to her students, which listed what she called four helpful hints. Sarah began by clarifying her use of the word "hints" in this instance: "I don't want to say rules." This was contradictory in that the main component of the course thus far had been the imposition of rules. The handout contained four helpful hints, in other words, rules, about writing a thesis statement. The "hints" were photocopied from a page of Dean Memering's *Research Writing*. The page began with a definition of the thesis statement. Once the thesis statement was explicitly defined, examples were given and students completed exercises in which they had to find the thesis statement in a sample paragraph. Then Sarah moved on to a presentation of the components and structure of the argumentative essay. She reduced writing an argumentative essay to a set of rules that, in this instance, were composed in part of strategies students were expected to follow. Sarah's explanation and justification for using the argumentative essay structure in her course is worth quoting at length, because it strongly reflects her ideological perspective regarding the teaching of writing and reveals, as well, many of the inherent contradictions within her practice.

Now, this is the first thing you need to do whenever you write an argumentative essay, because in an argumentative essay you're not just going to show your own side. In an argumentative essay you want to show the reader both sides of the issue, though you are going to favor one over the other. So the first thing you need to do is make yourself a list of what the two sides of the issue are and think about what the reasons behind each of those sides are, because as an intelligent human being who is writing an argumentative essay you need to have an understanding of both sides of the issue. You need to have in your mind what your side is, but you also need to have in your mind what the other side is, because argumentation is when you convince someone what is based on logic. There is a lot of writing and a lot of speaking that also tries to convince people, but they are based on emotions. All right. Politicians are great at it. OK, but argumentation is when you are trying to convince someone else and you base it on logic. Because of this argumentation always shows two sides or both sides of an issue but favors and develops one. So our organization of the argumentative essay keeps this in mind, and this organization that I am going to give you is also the organization that is used in an argumentative research paper. All right. There are a lot of different kinds of argumentative organizations, but I want you to um look at this one and use this one in your essays, because this is the one that you will be using in your research paper.

Historical Themes Revisited

First, Sarah did open the possibility that other forms of argumentation are available, but she did not explicitly relate any form to modes of academic discourse. Rather, her one reference was to the emotional language of politicians. Here she referred implicitly to the mind/body distinction prevalent in Western culture, which assumes a clear differentiation between logic and emotion. Logic is valued, while emotion is denigrated. Logic is male, emotion female. Sarah conveyed the negativity associated with emotion through her connection with politicians, as the word "politician" carries a very negative connotation. Her distinction also, interestingly enough, harks back to pre-nineteenth-century rhetoric: its goal persuasion, its presentation oral, and its status elite. Sarah, perhaps unknown to herself, had reiterated in highly encapsulated form the shifting focus rhetoric undertook as the academy moved from a classical orientation where rhetoric, taught as an oral mode, focused on persuasion. The academy then turned to the modernist focus on specialization of studies into disciplines and the elevation of the written word over the oral. As a result rhetoric was changed forever. Sarah's encapsulation captured the scorn the old rhetoric faced in the changing university and, at the same time, sought to establish a status not yet obtained for the rhetoric—however that might be defined—she was charged with teaching.

Second, Sarah revealed the ideological perspective that supports the notion that there are two, and only two, sides to an issue. This notion of opposing viewpoints allows no room for uncertainty: one is either for an issue or against it. Again I can hear my high school English teacher berating us with his authoritative-authoritarian scorn: "Remember, things are either black or white; gray is not an alternative." His notion, like Sarah's, highlights the tendency among people—Claud Lévi-Strauss considered it to be a universal, panhuman cultural characteristic—to make sense of the world despite the haze of its realized complexity and murkiness by viewing it through a socially imposed lens that splits reality, whatever that might be, into binary oppositions. This division of the world into dualities—good versus evil, black versus white, night versus day, heaven versus hell—allows for an assumed clarity of understanding that leaves masked and unrevealed the multiplicity of contradictory views that exist in all forms in the world of nature-the mind versus nurture-the environment. And here I have done it again: settled in the end on the conflict that afflicts and drives many disciplines, from linguistics to psychology to biology and on and on to this day. There is safety in duality; it assumes a rational order, not chaos, and that is reassuring. Writing in the academy, according to Sarah, is meant to reflect the logical, ordered, and rational state assumed to exist within disciplines and, by extension, in the world at large.

Third, Sarah stated that she was going to *give* the organization to the students. Her use of "give" suggested that she, perhaps as member (low as that might be) of the academy, possessed a form that she would now pass on to students in the class. There was also the underlying assumption here that students would "have" the form once its characteristics were described by Sarah. Once presented with the package, students need only fill it. The manner in which this conveyance is portrayed is interesting. Sarah so often spoke in the voice of the academic plural "we," but in this instance she was personally and directly involved in the giving, as reflected in her use of the personal, singular pronoun "I."

Fourth, while Sarah acknowledged that there are other forms of argumentation, she wanted (required) students to use the one she was discussing. The argument is tautological: students must use the argumentative form provided for the essay because the same form is required for the research paper. The argument, reformulated, is as follows: Since I want you (implicitly—you are required) to use this form in your research paper you need to use the same form in writing your essay. This way you will learn the form and be able to apply the same form to the research paper. The only difference is that the research paper will be bigger and will include points in support of thesis statements that are obtained through source material and are not just personal opinion.

Finally, Sarah's message was that issues are clearly formulated and can be separated into pros and cons and held within the mind prior to the writing of a paper. Thus the essay or research paper is seen as an external reflection of an internalized individual knowledge. This reflects an ideological perspective congruent with the cognitive approach to process writing, whose proponents regard language "as a system of rational signs that is compatible with the mind and the external world, enabling the 'translating' or 'transforming' of the non-verbal intellectual operation into the verbal" (Berlin, 1988, p. 483).

Once she had made the requirements clear to her students, Sarah went on to explicitly map out the format the essay should take. Sarah stated, "I want to have one paragraph that states the ideas for the other side but it doesn't go into them in great detail." She told the students that the rest of the essay would be the pros. In presenting the pros students were asked to give one point and support for that point in each paragraph. Students were asked to state their own side in the conclusion: obviously this would be from the section on the pros, because this is where the more detailed argument and supporting details were presented. Sarah did not emphasize that students are in a position to argue "for an issue," not against an issue. At this point in class, Sarah provided a model essay for students.

At the end of the class period, Sarah reiterated her main points for the day. She stated that in the research paper the students will be refuting the other side in detail, but in the argumentative essay there is not enough room to do all that. Kept alive is the metaphor of the container to be filled. The essay is a small container and as a result one is limited considerably in terms of what can be put into it; in contrast, the research paper is a large container and more can be packed into it. Sarah then handed out the assignment (the essay is due on Monday, giving students three days to prepare it), and she reminded students of the following:

> All right, this says that this paper is to be a three-to-eight-paragraph argumentative essay, and remember that a good, well-developed paragraph has seven to fifteen sentences. OK. It should be typed, and the final draft should not be more than three double-spaced typed pages. I don't want a five-to-seven-page paper. I want a two- or three-page essay, and it is due during class time on Monday, June 6. For a topic choose any controversial issue. I don't care what issue you use. It can be anything that people have two opinions about. If you don't know of a controversial issue you want to write about choose one from the list at the end of Memering [the assigned book for the course] or choose one from the list below [prepared by Sarah and on the handout].

This quote is striking as much for what it explicitly states as for what it does not. Sarah reiterated her concern for quantification. A paragraph is once again defined as containing seven to fifteen sentences. The number, as well as length, of paragraphs required is explicitly stated. This is presented in the language of what should be, thus form is imposed because it is expected. The notion of what is to be expected is subsumed by the statement that this relates to what Sarah wants. Thus imposition and desire connect directly to form. Content is irrelevant. As Sarah said, "I don't care what issue you use." What students might consider writing about was of little concern to her. Choice of topic will not be dictated; this is left up to the student. The only requirement was that the topic be controversial. Implicit here was the message that not only did Sarah not care what students write about, she also cared little, if at all, about their interests. She was concerned ultimately with form. Finally, Sarah suggested that students

> Choose a topic you know something about. This paper is to be from your own knowledge; no outside sources are to be used. I don't want you to go to the library and look for information about any of these things. We're going to do that soon enough next week. I just want you to use the information from your own minds because I'm more interested in you learning the organization of an argumentative essay because you need this organization in order to write an argumentative research paper.

Again Sarah reiterated the tautology upon which she based her presentation of the format of the essay. The essay must be structured as she required because she also required that the research paper be so organized. Further, she explicitly revealed once again that it was organization, that is, form, that she was most interested in having students learn. And though Sarah directed students, through the use of the imperative, to "choose a topic you know something about," this suggestion appears to stem more from her insistence that no outside sources be used than from an ideological perspective that links background knowledge or an emphasis on students' interests with successful reading or writing (Kintsch, 1977; Schank & Abelson, 1977).

In the third class Sarah offered the following as a review statement of her discussion of the essay:

> Yesterday we talked about essays . . . every essay begins with an introduction, and in the introduction you usually begin generally and then end with a specific thesis statement. The body of your essay is where you have the evidence or proof of what it is you're going to say. When you're doing an argumentative essay you always have as your topic some kind of an issue, and if you have done argumentative writing before you know that this issue is something that people discuss.

Sarah continued to lead students through the structure of the essay, mapping out each component piece by piece. As a result, students would perhaps view the essay, as well as the research paper, as entities that are clearly defined structurally. Each larger entity, the essay and the research paper, has the same clearly defined subcomponents or, if you will, slots to be filled with information, none of which Sarah was much concerned with.

The Rules Are Firmly Established

Thus after but four classes Sarah had established the rules that constitute writing in the academy. This world is self-contained and seeks itself as justification. Writing must conform to particular structures. Structures can be quantified. Sentences are counted, and the proper number constitutes a paragraph. Paragraphs are counted, and the proper number equals an essay. The essay enlarged becomes the research paper. In this world there are absolute restrictions about what is allowed and what is not allowed. In particular, one-sentence paragraphs are not allowed (in fact, they "don't exist"). Thus, a writing teacher who professed to adhere to a great extent to a process, rather than to a traditional, approach, has thus far not alluded in words or actions to the tenets of either the expressive or social/cultural process approaches and has alluded only superficially to the cognitive approach. What is most evident is a very close adherence to a traditional approach to teaching writing.

Choosing a Research Topic and Source Materials

During the first three classes, Sarah established the groundwork for formatting both the required essay and research paper in the course. She then began to deal with strategic rules for organizing the process of putting together the research paper. Once again these strategies were classified as rules because they allow for little if any flexibility in terms of process. One of the first rules stated was that a minimum of five sources is necessary for the writing of a research paper. These sources were to cover a range of materials, including books, magazines, and journals. Further, although for the essay Sarah stated that she did not care what topics students chose, she restricted the choice of topic for the research paper. While referring to a handout outlining the "Guidelines for Choosing a Topic," Sarah stated:

> The reason why I have the question here: "Is it too contemporary?" is that sometimes if you choose a topic that has just happened, for example, if you wanted to write your paper about the success of the Reagan-Gorbachev summit, you may not be able to find a variety of materials about that topic and this is because things that are contemporary are only written about in magazines and newspapers and it takes a while for journal articles or books to get published where people really think about what has happened. So you don't want to choose something that just happened in the last couple of months because you won't be able to find a lot of different kinds of sources and you can't write a research paper just from the newspaper and *Time* and *Newsweek* magazine. All right. Because you're writing on a controversial topic you're going to have to find sources where people have thought about this topic and they've expressed their opinions about the topic. So something that's too contemporary you won't be able to find a wide variety of materials about.

Revealing themes emerge in this strategic requirement, particularly in regard to the nature of truth, although reference is never explicitly made to that notion. Implicit throughout, however, is the conviction that the writing of a research paper is not possible unless a variety of sources are called upon. Presumably a variety of sources supporting one's argument adds validity to the argument itself. Never is the thorny issue raised that writers seek and select from the perhaps myriad perspectives available only those sources that support their perspective. Further, implied here also is the notion that contemporary topics are not appropriate for research because not enough time has passed to allow for a rational sorting-out of the issue, a process that once undergone would lead to some well-established views, that is, truths, relating to the subject. Sarah did not explicitly explain why a paper cannot be written solely from *Time* or *Newsweek*. Could it be that more weight is afforded information received in books or journals? If so, what does this say about the nature of academic writing? And are not books written that take entirely new, often revisionist, perspectives on issues long held sacred? What is one to do with these?

In a continuation of her discussion of sources, Sarah reiterated the need to use a variety of sources. She stated, "You can't just use all books; you can't use all magazines. Of your seven or eight sources you should have two or three books, two or three magazines, maybe a journal, maybe a newspaper article. All right.

Because you're not going to learn anything if you just use all books or all magazines. You're only going to learn how to find one type of information, so I'm going to require that you use a variety of different kinds of sources." In this statement Sarah revealed that she was interested in students learning how to find information and not in students learning from reading or from engaging in the process of sorting through information. What students would not learn if they were to rely solely on books or magazines is how to find journal articles, newspaper articles, and so forth. Quite clearly, the emphasis here is on how to track down information in the library rather than on how to sort out, comprehend, make sense of, and creatively reformulate what one has learned from reading about a topic.

Once students chose a topic, Sarah suggested they discuss the topic with friends. Brainstorming is supported within process writing, particularly within the cognitive approach, as a strategy helpful in sorting out the direction one's writing will take. Sarah had another agenda in mind when referring to talking with friends about the topic. Her agenda was totally pragmatic. As Sarah suggested,

> Discuss your topic with friends, teachers, and classmates. Revise the topic based on their opinions, suggestions, and your preliminary reading. Don't just sit in your own little cell and write your research paper. Tell people you're writing your research paper about whatever it is you're writing about. It's amazing how many people who might say to you, "Well, I read an article about that yesterday in the *Globe*." Well, there is one of your sources. Or "I have an uncle who works for such and such. You can interview him." There's another one of your sources. So it is very helpful that you talk to people about your topic.

What is interesting here is that Sarah began to work to break down the notion of the writer as solitary creator, but she did not go as far as Linda Brodkey does. Brodkey writes,

> Writing is a social act. People write to and for other people. Yet when we picture writing we see a solitary writer. We may see the writer alone in a cold garret, working into the small hours of the morning by thin candlelight. The shutters are closed. Or perhaps we see the writer alone in a well-appointed study, seated at a desk, fingers poised over the keys of a typewriter (or microcomputer) . . . Whether the scene of writing is poetic or prosaic, the writer above the madding crowd in a garret, only temporarily free from family and friends in a study, or removed from the world in a library, it is the same picture—the writer writes alone. (1987, p. 55)

Sarah did not wish to view her student writers writing alone, not because she particularly viewed writing as a social act, a communicative act, but, rather, because she recognized that people can provide sources for the researcher. What was important to Sarah here was the search for sources to support a premise already laid out in a very clear-cut manner. Nowhere evident in the pleas for students to get out of their own little cells as they work on their papers was the notion that discussion with another individual might have an impact on the direction the student's argument might take. There was no indication in Sarah's discourse that meaning or intent might be in any way muddled initially. One establishes a thesis and then finds evidence—or, in the case of the essay, provides support based on personal opinion—to substantiate the thesis. This is all quite straightforward and leaves no room for the doubting writer or for an illogical presentation of one's written work.

Two class periods later Sarah returned to this theme when discussing how to find information in *The Reader's Guide to Periodical Literature.* She had organized students' topics on a handout because, she maintained, she wanted everyone in the class to know what classmates were working on. This, she suggested, would be helpful for students because research is collaborative. Sarah discussed the collaborative nature of research:

> And what I've done is I've put all of your topics on this sheet for two reasons: one, so that we can do this exercise and two, because I think it's important that everybody in the class knows what everyone else is working on because then as people see articles or read articles in the newspaper about a certain topic you can come to me or you can go to the person and say that you've seen it. Because research is really collaborative. You don't want to research in a vacuum all by yourself.

Once again, collaboration means providing sources for, or seeking sources from, others and does not relate to a discussion of ideas or perspectives or meaning or, for that matter, to how information should be presented, as there are no options in this regard. In other words, collaboration is the getting or giving of information regarding where to find sources and not the mutual, dialogic construction of meaning or the opportunity to critically reflect on the substance of one's arguments.

The handout and Sarah's purpose in making it reveals further her notions of writing and the research process. The exercise was designed to elicit from students the time frame in which they would refer to *The Reader's Guide* for information on their topic. As Sarah stated, "So you need to look at your topic and decide when you're going to look. Are you going to look in 1988 or are you going to look in 1978?" This led to a class exercise in which students were asked what time frame their research covered.

More Numbers

Once the time frame discussion ended, Sarah moved on to the use of note cards. She assured students she did not care what color or size note cards students used, but she did, nonetheless, require that they be used. In response to a student question regarding how many were required, Sarah replied, "Well, you'll probably need anywhere from twenty-five to fifty note cards. All right. You may not use them all, but you want to research your issue so well that you have a lot of information at your disposal so that you know your topic well." Sarah continued with the following information, once more quantified: "A regular eight-to-ten-page paper usually has anywhere from fifteen to twenty-five references from sources, so you're gonna have to do more than that because when you're taking your notes you're not sure what you're gonna use and what you're not gonna use."

Summarizing and Paraphrasing

After Sarah covered how to find sources, where to record information, and how much information to record, she discussed how to include the information in the research paper. Sarah explained to students the differences between summarizing and paraphrasing. Students were then led through a summarizing exercise. Sarah initiated the process with the following: "All right, now we want to write a one-paragraph summary of this article, and because we're writing a one-paragraph summary of this article we want our paragraph to begin with a topic sentence because we are writing an academic paper. So our summary should begin like an academic paragraph with a topic sentence." Sarah continued by providing further explanation about what a summary consists of and how it is formed. This same process was discussed during the next class meeting when she presented the idea of the paraphrase. Sarah's explanation of paraphrasing is worth quoting at length:

> So what a paraphrase basically is, is it's taking something that a writer said and putting it in your own words, but you use all the information that the writer said. So a paraphrase includes all the same information as the original, so a paraphrase includes all the details, all the examples, and in the way it is different from a summary. Because of this we usually only paraphrase things that are two or three sentences in length. I am not going to paraphrase something that is a whole paragraph long, because if I have a whole paragraph then it's much better if I were to write a summary of the paragraph. All right so you use quotations, summaries, and paraphrases for different things.

At this point in the course students had been given all the necessary components needed in order to piece together a research paper. Overall format had been discussed, and the major components of the required papers, ways of condensing material from sources, and the glue to hold the parts together—transitions (these were provided in a handout)—had all been presented. Sarah then moved on to a discussion of outlining, how to document material, and how to develop a bibliography. Students were asked to use the Modern Language Association's format for referencing (MLA) because it is more difficult, and Sarah believed that if students later were required to use a simpler format, such as the American Psychological Association's format for referencing work (APA), they would have no trouble because they had already dealt with the most difficult referencing system in her class.

Clearly, Sarah imparted explicit statements regarding the form students should adhere to as they wrote their papers. Although she presented herself as primarily a process-oriented instructor, an examination of her practice reveals otherwise. The issues Sarah dealt with in class, the manner in which the class was structured, and the fact that she lectured most of the time all reflect a strong association with the traditional approach to teaching writing. The analysis presented thus far, however, is but part of the re-creation of Sarah's writing class. Apparent also within the structure of the class were some components of a process approach to teaching writing, most specifically of the cognitive approach. These components are highlighted in the section that follows.

Cognitive Approach Put to Practice

Sarah's course required students to write three drafts of their research paper. After each draft Sarah responded to students in writing and required that they meet with her for scheduled fifteen-minute conferences. Additionally, Sarah set aside a portion of the tenth class for what she referred to as a brainstorming exercise. Brainstorming, or the sorting-out of ideas for papers through discussion, is a major component of process writing pedagogy. Brainstorming in Sarah's class, however, took a different form. Sarah's students were given a piece of paper and asked to write their topic or thesis across the top of it and then to divide the paper in half and write the pros and cons for their thesis. After students finished listing the pros and cons they were to exchange papers with a neighbor in the class, who would then add pros and cons to the list. As Sarah stated, "In researching a topic you want to think of as many pros and cons as you possibly can and another person might be able to add some to your list." This reveals again Sarah's emphasis on quantification. More is better. Quantity is emphasized over quality. Further, the exercise again reflects the notion of collaboration as the giving and getting of sources or, in this case, of pros and cons for their lists. Once the written exercise was completed Sarah said, "All right. I'll give these back to you tomorrow. I just wanted to know what some of the ideas are that you're coming up with and I'll add to them if I can think of anything." Throughout the whole exercise there was no verbal communication among class members or between partners. Rather than brainstorming, a word that connotes energized, creative, verbally interactive turmoil with an effort to sort through ideas that might contribute to the development of a paper, students in effect took a quiz for one another and for Sarah.

Concluding Comments

An examination of Sarah's pedagogical practice reveals a close adherence to a traditional approach to teaching writing along with components of the cognitive process approach. In a way, Sarah's practice reflects, superficially, the revisionist perspective of the social/cultural approach, an approach that calls for the return to the explicit teaching of form while at the same time incorporating aspects of the various process approaches to the teaching of writing. And, while what was revealed in Sarah's practice in no way approximates assumptions and hypotheses proposed prior to the onset of the ethnography, there is no reason to assume that what is to be learned from the study and analysis will not be useful, if not important, in furthering the understanding of the acquisition of academic writing.

Before undertaking this study I anticipated that the instructor I would observe would exhibit entirely a process approach to teaching writing. I assumed so for two reasons: first, because Sarah professed to adhering to a process orientation; and second, because the director of the ESL program, Vivian Zamel, was a strong, well-known advocate of the approach. Since the director had been responsible for hiring Sarah, I assumed that she would not have been hired if her perspective or approach to teaching writing was too different from Zamel's These assumptions were wrong. Nonetheless, much can be gleaned about the relationship between ideology and practice, not to mention the tenuous validity of prestudy assumptions. I had actually thought that Sarah's practice would be much like my own: we were colleagues and fellow graduate students, and had experience prior to teaching at UMB working with ESL students in a variety of contexts, all of which suggest the strong possibility for commonality in approach to teaching. Thus I thought that whatever differences I would note would most likely reflect our personalities, and that we would not differ greatly in terms of ideological perspective and its relationship to practice. How wrong I was. Entering Sarah's writing class was much like entering an alien world, one where I saw a completely different method of teaching writing. And I left realizing how little we know of one another, even when inhabiting so many overlapping environments, including physical, social, and intellectual. And how rare it is that we have the opportunity to enter one another's space to the degree that I was allowed entry into Sarah's. For her permission, cooperation, openness, and critical reflection I am forever grateful.

7

PROFICIENT STUDENT WRITERS IN CONTEXT: ALAN'S AND ZOLA'S STORIES

> Anthropologists these days do not imagine themselves to be objective observers of empirical cultural facts, but understand themselves as actors whose research is a complex process involving the construction of meaning, power relations and the placement of oneself and the people one studies within a real continuing social and historical setting.—Robert A. Paul, "The Living Dead and the Puffer Fish"

In *Classroom Discourse: The Language of Teaching and Learning* Courtney Cazden (1988) comments on both the nature of educational research and the nature of the classroom experience such research attempts to capture. Cazden argues that most educational research examines the world of the teacher, a world Cazden characterizes as the "official world of the teacher's agenda." In so doing, much educational research implicitly assumes the perspective of the teacher. It was just such an agenda and perspective that the two previous chapters sought to capture.

However, the classroom, Cazden argues, also contains an unofficial world, the world of peer culture, the students' world—a world that should not be neglected. Cazden suggests that "Students, from their first year in school on, do not confine their actions and their talk to fulfilling the teacher's agenda, much as teachers might like that to be the case" (1988, p. 150). She argues further, now drawing from the work of another, that researchers who view students solely in relationship to their teachers and schoolwork are like "Colonial administrators who might be expected to write scientifically objective reports of the local populace . . . by ideologically formulating only those research problems that pertain to native behaviors coming under the regulation of colonial authority" (Speier, 1976, p. 99, quoted in Cazden, 1988, p. 150). Cazden maintains that teachers, unlike colonial administrators, perform valuable roles in society. These roles, she insists, should therefore be improved. In order to do so, researchers, Cazden argues, must "uncover and understand the voice of students" (Cazden, 1988, p. 150) as well as the voice and behavior of teachers. In chapters 7 and 8 I seek to do just that.

These two chapters each present case studies of two students. The case studies have been compiled through classroom observations, formal and informal interviews, and information gained from student completion of a written questionnaire. Three young men and one young woman participated in the case study component. Although I would have preferred a more balanced representation of women in the study, this was not possible because only one woman in the class I observed was a matriculated student at the university. The other women were from local colleges and had come to UMB because their institutions did not offer a summer course in writing. I chose not to interview any other women for the case studies because my focus was, in part, on students at UMB. This was so for two reasons: first, I was interested specifically in working with students who were under pressure as a result of the imposed writing proficiency exam at the university; and second, I was concerned that students who participated in the case study component be available, if necessary, for follow-up interviews.

Before entering fully into a characterization of the individual students it is important to qualify the extent to which I believe I will be able to capture who these four individuals are. And while my intent here is to give voice to each of the four students, I realize that the assumption that I am in a position to give voice to those who can in fact speak for themselves is presumptuous. By this I mean that despite my proclamations, it is I, the writer, who in this instance controls the storytelling, not the four individuals about whom I write. And although I quote each student to a great extent, I have controlled what portions of Alan, Zola, Tan, and Araya's interviews I have included in my discussion. So, too, did I in many ways control the original oral rendering of their histories as we met. As a faculty member, seated in my office as I asked questions of each student, I certainly had an impact on the sorts of stories the students related to me. Nonetheless, stories were told. In turn, I have developed a text, or four stories, if you will, in my own words as well as the words of each student. While the text—the two chapters—attempts to communicate to the reader who these four individuals are, obviously there are severe limitations in the extent to which I can capture and comprehend the people I write about here. What I can do is but relate a superficial rendering of complex lives. What role do I fill as I do so? Am I solely a researcher? Perhaps not. I would argue that I become, in many ways, a storyteller rather than merely a detached, objective researcher. By this I mean in my role as ethnographer/writer I select, I reformulate, I allow my perceptions to guide the unfolding text. I have the power to reshape another's reality—to make it, in part, my own. Thus, the four stories that follow are shaped as much by my perceptions of the four individuals as they are by each student's own rendering of his or her history. As I write the following two chapters, I break with the "once dominant model of the detached observer using neutral language to explain 'raw' data" and instead "engage an alternative project that attempts to understand human conduct as it unfolds through time and in relation to its meaning for the actors" (Rosaldo, 1989, p. 37).

To refer to what follows as case studies implies an objective, thorough, unimpeded rendering of an individual's history. The term "case study" implies scientific objectivity and discounts the notion of personal perception. To refer instead to what follows as stories depicts more honestly, perhaps, what a researcher does with the words of others. I can do no more than tell four stories with the understanding that they are told as much through my eyes as they are through the eyes of the four students, Alan, Zola, Tan, and Araya. Further, as I tell the stories, I do no more than fictionalize reality, in much the same way as do all tellers of stories (Scollon & Scollon, 1981). In the telling I thematicize each of the four individuals, and as I do so, real people become but characterizations of themselves. In what follows, Alan becomes "my student," Zola is "the resisting student," Tan is "the networker," and Araya is "the silent(ced) one." Most assuredly all four are far more complex than the limiting thematic characterizations I have bestowed upon them for the sake of conveying the results of my research. Therefore, I present but partial glimpses of four individuals. I suggest that, as ethnographers/writers, we can do no more. To suggest otherwise is in many ways a dishonest claim for all-encompassing scientific objectivity.

Alan: My Student

I know Alan not only because he participated in this study but also because he was my student in the first of the two introductory composition courses offered at UMB—101E ESL Freshman English I. I had had many opportunities to speak with Alan both in class and out during the course of the semester he was my student, and I found him to be engaging, intelligent, cooperative, and a strong developing writer. As a result, I was pleased he planned to take writing during the summer session in which I would conduct the classroom portion of my research; he was an excellent candidate to participate in the study as a proficient writer. In fact, as a result of reading the in-class writing samples, Sarah identified Alan immediately as a proficient writer and suggested that I choose him to participate in the case study component. Without hesitation I agreed, thus establishing a means by which I could come to know Alan even better than I did at that point in time.

Alan was born in Hong Kong on 9 September 1963, the last son, as he characterized himself, and ninth child in a family of ten children. His father, a retired custom tailor, and mother, an office assistant, left mainland China after World War II in order to escape Mao's Cultural Revolution. Neither received any formal education, and only his father is able to read the newspaper and write a short letter. Alan's mother cannot read but tries to pick up some words from the newspaper every day. Growing up, Alan felt no embarrassment because his parents had little proficiency in print literacy because most of his friends' parents were also uneducated and unable to read and write. All his brothers and sisters attended secondary school in Hong Kong, but only some had graduated. None has attended college.

Alan described himself as an average high school student, one who received Ds on essays and was more often interested in socializing with his friends than in studying. He describes his life as a high school student as being "just so easy." Never once in high school, for example, did he use the library to do research for a paper or even to borrow a book. When asked whether or not he had done much research Alan seemed amazed at his own lack of experience using the library. "The first time I use library is here. In my high school I never spend any time in library, but I don't know how I can get through. But that's the way. That's why my high school grade not very good. That's why. You know it's really amazing, you know I never spend an hour in my whole life in the library. I never borrow any book out of library. Yeah, it's my first experience."

Alan, nonetheless, did complete the sixth form in Hong Kong; completion of the seventh, however, is generally necessary if one wishes to go on to college. Although his parents would have supported him had he worked to get accepted into college, they did not urge him to do so. His parents felt that as long as he was able to obtain suitable employment after high school he would be fine. Since Alan had been but an average student, and because he performed poorly on the college entrance exams in Hong Kong, he had no choice but to seek employment upon completion of high school. Alan told me he did not "feel out of it" in doing so, though, because most students in Hong Kong work after high school rather than going to college. There are few colleges in Hong Kong, making competition fierce; thus entrance is limited to those whose families have the money and cultural capital to ensure admittance.

Upon graduating from high school at the age of seventeen, Alan obtained a job as an office assistant, a very low-level position, with a British tourist agency in Hong Kong. He quickly advanced through the ranks to become an accountant and administrative assistant to the manager of the company. No doubt he rapidly advanced due to the tremendous social skills he possessed. Alan may not have spent any time in the library, but he is more than adept at personal interaction. This skill served him well at work, led to many opportunities to speak with English and American tourists, and led to an apprenticeship with his American-born, English-speaking boss. These social skills, honed throughout school and mastered more fully in his professional life, served Alan well at UMB.

Throughout the seven years he was with the tourist agency, Alan took evening courses in English and accounting. As a result, he was able to raise his score on the college entrance exam within a few years from an E, the second-to-lowest possible score, to an A, the highest possible score. Alan's attitude toward education also changed considerably as he progressed in his career. Reflecting on his performance in high school, he comments, "You know, I feel bad. The more you are exposed to the real life then the more you want to get educated. And often we would say, 'when you are in high school you want to work; when you out at work, you want back to school.'" After a number of years of work, Alan realized that he had nowhere to advance to in the travel agency. The only promotions available would require a transfer to the United States, which was unlikely for a Chinese employee. Thus with this imposed constraint Alan began to consider options that would lead to his advancement both educationally and professionally. A move to the United States became a compelling possibility, made more so because of the impending political transition from British control of Hong Kong to control from mainland China.

Alan spoke Cantonese, Mandarin, and English and, as a result, was very important to his boss, who had been born in the United States and spoke only English. In addition to handling the company accounting, a great deal of the office operations including correspondence, and personnel matters, Alan also handled public relations. Alan's good looks—he is extremely handsome, compellingly so; he has an open and pleasing, charismatic personality; and he dresses in a stylishly classic, expensively appropriate manner—suited him well, I am sure, for such a position. Alan exudes an air of confidence and competence, but one that never touches on arrogance; this confidence was most likely present in his school days but then nurtured and enhanced during his tenure with the travel agency.

When his boss was tired or on vacation, Alan would often take over total responsibility for running the office. He always felt that his boss liked him very much and supported him fully. He was shocked and saddened to the point of tears, therefore, at his boss's response to his decision to pursue his education in the United States. When Alan told his boss that he wanted to leave the company, she responded by saying, "How could you! Your English is so bad. I mean how could you keep up with your university's work?" This response came from a woman who relied on Alan to write office memos and handle a great deal of correspondence for her, all of which she would correct solely for grammar. Though very hurt by this comment, Alan also realized that underneath his boss's expressed faith in his ability was a selfish dependence on his hard work and competence. As is often the case, Alan's boss had used him. Other professional contacts, including colleagues in the Jaycees, and friends were far more supportive of his decision to leave the company to seek a college degree.

Alan had another, more personal, reason for wanting to leave Hong Kong. As he recounted, "Last year was a big change. I had some personal change, which stimulate myself that I should get advanced by myself. I shouldn't just stay, I mean be satisfied with what I, I'm doing. Instead I should look forward, and look ahead, and I just want to learn whatever I can learn. I made a very strong to decide to learn and to what—go abroad and see new things." Alan had broken up with his woman friend of four years, a situation that caused him much anguish and led him to reassess his life. He felt that for the period of time he and his friend had been together he had spent too much time on her and not enough time on himself. This breakup and his experience at work with his boss led him to the following conclusion: "And I just think that I should spend more, more time on myself, rather than on some other people, I mean not working for other people, I should work for myself. Basically my job was working for her [his woman friend], and not for myself. That's why that's what stimulated me to get out that hell, no, that well. You know, life is like a well, I have to jump out and see the outside world."

When Alan left his position in Hong Kong he was earning a very comfortable salary, one that had allowed him to purchase his own apartment, pay for night courses, entertainment, and clothes, and to support his woman friend as they planned for their marriage. He was not leaving a mediocre position but one that many twenty-four-year-old college graduates would covet. Though he was economically successful, at least for his age, Alan did not consider earning money to be all that important. In fact he realized that his decision to come to the United States would more than likely impact negatively, at least in the short run, on his economic status. As he commented, "I'm prepared to earn less than before basically. You know the opportunity calls for me a great deal, but for me I think I'm still young. And money or income you can earn for the rest of your whole life, but if you miss the chance to come back to the university—I may never come back again."

Alan's parents, unfortunately, did not initially support his decision to travel to the United States to study because they felt his job as assistant to the manager at a tourist agency was too good to leave. Nonetheless, they had come to accept his decision to leave, and no major rift in the family had occurred as a result of the disagreement. Alan recognized that by the time he graduates from UMB he would most likely be far away from his parents "in terms of understanding and living style." He hoped, however, that this distance would not destroy the intimacy they have always shared. In fact, Alan went on to graduate magna cum laude, obtained a high-level administrative position at UMB (he has since moved on with an MBA in hand to a new professional context), married, and is now the father of two children. He regularly reports to the UMB alumni press with updates on his current personal and professional status; rare is the alum who does so. For Alan, UMB truly represented the fulfillment of dreams and desires obtained, appreciated, and never to be forgotten.

At the time of the study, Alan had been in the United States only one semester. He was living with a married sister in an urban area not more than thirty minutes from school. He owned his own car and had a good student job with the university. During his first semester at school he received all As and was elated and encouraged by his performance. In addition, he had become active in the university Asian Student Society and had a new woman friend. Thus, by the end of the first semester, Alan felt confident and somewhat comfortable in all domains of his life. However, this feeling of elation and confidence was soon deflated as he began his summer school courses.

As he began summer school Alan confronted many problems he had not anticipated. Alan had registered for two summer courses, one in accounting and the other the English course, with the anticipation that his twenty-hour-a-week job on campus would allow him the opportunity to study and do research in the library during the week after work. Summer library hours, however, were very restricted, and when Alan was out of work the library was closed. The only time available for him to do research was on the weekends. He had mixed feelings, too, when he was offered a second campus job, which he felt he could not turn down. Alan expressed the difficulty in the following: "I don't know, I have emotional problem now that really because the transition too much, too great. . . . You know it's unpredictable. I mean the change and, like I couldn't know the library would close and I couldn't know that I would be, get the other job."

Alan had a further problem.

> You know I was counting on your style, your way of teaching you know to make the decision. I'm not say something, I mean that is whose fault or something. It's nobody's fault. I mean I should expect something like this would happen, but it was my fault basically that I couldn't, I mean consider the situation. And I have to adjust myself, that's why I sign up for two course. I, maybe the other course, if I took it in the evening, maybe it would be better. I just have to spend my weekend keeping up the work which I couldn't do in the regular weekdays.

Alan was having a difficult time dealing with the change in teaching style he was confronted with in his English class. When asked why he found the transition from one writing class to the other so difficult Alan responded:

> Maybe because the transition is too short and too much. I mean your style and her style is completely different and the assignment is completely different. I mean we [in 101] have plenty of time and we have plenty of discussion about what we write, but here [in 102] nothing [said on a very high note]. And we briefly just through the instruction. And 'OK today's Thursday and I expect to have your paper on, due on Monday and that's it.' I mean nothing to talk about it. I mean everything is up to you to decide. I mean your format or whatever source of information you need to get is really up to you.

In 101E Alan had enjoyed exchanging ideas with others in the class and receiving feedback from his peers and from me. He felt that in 101E "We concentrate on the development of our paper rather than the development of the writing skill. We learn the writing skill throughout the course through the writing."

As Alan's former writing teacher, I was well aware of his love of discussion, the love he had of arguing and sorting through issues with others. To see him so frustrated now was disheartening. I was also conflicted in my expanding role. Originally his teacher and advisor, I now became not only a researcher but also Alan's confidante, and as such I found myself uncomfortably complicit (though implicitly so, because although I listened to his complaints and felt concern for Alan's situation, I never criticized Sarah or confirmed Alan's critique of her) in the negative evaluation Alan had of Sarah's performance as a teacher. I was not able to see myself solely as a detached observer in this situation but, rather, continued to view myself as Alan's teacher and advisor. Alan too continued to view me as his teacher and often sought my advice and evaluation of his work. It was only through great restraint on my part that I avoided responding to Alan's requests for feedback on his work as he went through the course. Nonetheless, I could not help myself from telling him that I thought he was doing very well and, early on in the course, that he should try to adjust himself to the new style of teaching.

Thus I was not able to release myself from my former role as Alan's teacher as I entered the new role of researcher. In many ways, Alan remained my possession, my client. As we continued in the advisor/advisee/confidante relationship, I played out my view of student as possession. My perspective, my way of viewing and relating to Alan, reflects what is to a great extent a cultural model prevalent in American education. It is not easy to relinquish our students, particularly our favorite students, to others. Throughout his course with Sarah, Alan remained my student and, thus, my responsibility.

Alan was confronted with a particularly distressing situation during the first writing class while working on his in-class writing sample. In front of the whole class, Sarah yelled at Alan for speaking quietly to a fellow classmate, a young man he knew from the previous semester. Alan sought to borrow his friend's dictionary to look up a word he did not know how to spell. He described what occurred:

> You know that time I was really mad at her. You know I couldn't, I just wanna look up a word and I couldn't finish it on time and then she was kind of pushing, you know. I feel very disappointed. Why shouldn't I? I mean it's not something which for me if I know that I write it correctly then I have, then I can continue to write. If I don't write, if I confuse or I have, no if I'm not very sure about it then I always keep on thinking that and it would distract my writing and I couldn't concentrate anymore.

At this point I asked Alan whether Sarah's yelling was disturbing. He was so upset as he responded that I couldn't understand him, and it is impossible to decipher from the tape what he said. When we were meeting I chose not to ask him to clarify his statement so as not to embarrass him. I chose instead to let him go on: "I'm upset because I'm upset with the way she teaches. That's why I'm kind of, kind of resenting, resenting it." As it was still the beginning of the course he remained optimistic, though depressed at the moment. He told me, "Yeah, I think I can adjust my life here [to the United States], why not to this!" He also recognized that first impressions may not be accurate. Describing Sarah's style of teaching, a style he finds distressing, Alan revealed that his first impression of me as a teacher was not very positive either.

> Yeah, I mean really her way of teaching is too pushing, really I mean. I don't know why she do it. I mean how she say OK, OK, this is very, I don't know, it's kind of peculiar. But I think that's the way, how she teach. No, to tell you the truth, the first, you at the beginning, when I have your class, I think sometimes

you're over, you're a little bit exaggerated. I mean your facial expressions or something like that. In fact, it does, it did help. It did help because it shows that you concerned about our thinking or our feeling. . . . But for her it just "OK." I mean it makes a difference if you allow people to feedback. I am not sure people will enjoy sitting there just like being fed—like fed ducks.

Alan had used this same feeding-ducks analogy to describe his high school experience in Hong Kong and, in fact, attributed his lack of academic motivation during high school in part to the feeding-ducks mode of teaching he experienced. "In our high school everything is just pushed in front of you. I mean no matter whether you like it or not, they just push everything. And then, remember I talk about feeding-duck system, feeding-duck system, no matter whether you, they, they've know that you're, you've, I mean you've had enough or not they still feed you to, I mean, to make you weigh more, heavier." Alan, though unaware of the analogy, might as well have been using Paulo Freire's notion of the banking model of teaching (1970). Freire describes banking as an educational model that seeks to fill students' heads with facts, as if their brains were vessels to be filled with knowledge the teacher has deemed important enough to be passed on and retained, then fed back through a process of examination (Shore & Freire, 1987). Alan was in many ways a keen observer of educational practice and one whose philosophy was clearly in tune with, though with no reference to or association with the field, the premises put forth in critical pedagogy.

Freire is careful not to equate lecturing, the mode in which Sarah teaches, with banking education, because as he notes, "The question is not banking lectures or not lectures, because traditional teachers will make reality opaque whether they lecture or lead discussions. A liberating teacher will illuminate reality even if he or she lectures. The question is the content and dynamism of the lecture, the approach to the object to be known. Does it critically reorient students to society? Does it animate their critical thinking or not?" (Shore & Freire, 1987, p. 40).

Alan linked the feeding-ducks approach to the reading assignments from *The Little, Brown Handbook,* one of the books assigned for the course, and he described how this approach made him feel. He also offered his own opinion about how one learns to write.

> If you are thrown a lot of stuff in front of you at one time I mean you just can't get it all. . . . You know I have been reading the *Handbook* for let's say fifty pages. You know, there's so much stuff to process, like from specific. I mean it's very difficult to digest it all at once. . . . It just make me so nervous. I mean did I follow what I am supposed to? Or, I just don't get used to it. . . . I mean people learn when they read other people's writing, but not some instruction which asks you to do it.

Thus far Alan had expressed a philosophy of teaching writing that includes a need for students to interact with the teacher and with one another as they sort through the myriad ideas that emerge when approaching a writing assignment. Alan found this verbal sparring, questioning, and reappraising of perspectives to be stimulating and helpful as he prepared drafts of papers. Further, he resented the lecture approach to teaching, not solely because he did not wish to be lectured to but also because the lectures that he had experienced in Hong Kong and now in Sarah's class served solely to impart bits of information at a rapid pace without time to analyze critically what one was being asked to absorb. Nor did the lecture format allow for interaction. I lectured in Alan's class, and I do to this day. So it was the opportunity for critique, analysis, and student input that Alan longed for, not free-for-all discussions. And finally, he believed that learning to write was somehow connected to reading the work of other writers, not to the absorption of rules for writing. Alan liked to have models before him to read, reflect upon, and emulate as he sought to acquire the forms required by the academy.

Alan elaborated on his philosophy of learning to write by drawing an analogy to learning to use the computer. "You know, if I learn computer of course I have to read the instructions, but I can have a lot of time to play around with the computer. Then I learn. Without playing around with the command key I can't do anything. Yeah, I mean it's just the same thing. You know, I think I learn by writing and by reading and not by, you know—it's just feeding goose like, like I mean, just like the experience I had in Hong Kong."

Alan's reaction to *The Little, Brown Handbook* was particularly strong. He continued:

> Basically, I mean, you know, if this is a book which I want to learn to read just like another story book I will read it on my own, but because it is too technical, I mean something which asks you, even influence you, I mean if you read something like that it seems to be a golden rule and then if you don't, if you see that you didn't follow all that, or you didn't see that from your writing then you're nervous or something like that. . . . I just don't want to think about it basically [in reference to the *Handbook* rules] even though I read it I don't, you know, I just don't, I think that I couldn't get that much out of it. It just waste of my time. Although I read it I couldn't memorize it for sure.

And further: "While I was reading the *Little Handbook* and I think what subject I have to, to, to, I mean to write about, only because we have to think of it on our own, I just, I mean my thinking was changing from step, I mean, I mean swung from one side to another. Yeah, that's right. I mean then I wasn't enjoying that much you know. I was too nervous, I was too nervous, I think I was too nervous." This nervousness has greatly affected his writing and how he felt about his work in the course. In fact, he asked me at one point during our first formal interview session what my opinion was of the first essay he wrote for Sarah. He expressed his concern about his writing: "One concern is really is coherent, does it jump all over the place, is it without unit, unitary?" What Alan expresses here is his uncertainty over the newly incorporated vocabulary of the *Handbook* and Sarah's imparted rules for writing.

Thus Alan, who finished the 101 course with both an A and great confidence that he had improved as a writer (and he had), was now in a situation that mirrored in many ways his high school experience in Hong Kong. Now, however, he appeared to have the resolve to continue with optimism and even admitted, "If I get a good grade [on the first essay] will maybe reinstate my, I mean my enthusiasm."

Always the pragmatist, Alan also said that if the situation changed a bit in Sarah's class he might reassess his opinion of the course. "Maybe once I start talking to her I will feel better, but it's up to her to take the first step. And I'm sure you know I talk a lot in the class." Alan did not start talking in Sarah's class; in fact none of the students did during the course. But whether a student talks a lot or not, or whether a student feels free to talk in class, may be a matter of individual perception rather than of reality (or, rather, the observer's perception of the situation). Tan, as I'll show in his case study, perceived Sarah to be a teacher who invited comments and questions in her class. The fact that students did not respond to Sarah's invitations to speak was not of significant concern; the invitation, in and of itself, was sufficient to communicate to Tan that Sarah was a teacher who was open to questions. Divergence in individual perceptions is quite normal, often caused by our past experiences; Alan had experienced a previous writing class where discussion and critique were central to the process of writing, but Tan had not had such an experience. Tan read Sarah's rhetorical questions and open requests for student response—though no one responded—as indicating the class was one in which student participation was encouraged and supported. The fact that student participation did not actually take place was irrelevant.

Alan did have his chance to communicate in this writing course; although this communication did not occur among his peers during class time, it did occur during formal writing conferences Sarah scheduled in lieu of class meetings. These conferences took place after students completed the first and second drafts of their research papers. An analysis of what occurred during these conferences is presented in chapter 9.

Zola: The Resisting Student

Zola, who was also chosen to participate in the study as a proficient writer, is a vibrantly attractive, dynamically outspoken, intelligent, heavy-smoking Moroccan woman in her late twenties who had been in the United States for three years and at UMB for one. Dressed most often in chic proletarian black, she moved with a kinetic grace, often punctuating her statements with cigarette in hand while displaying an intellectual intensity that demanded a presence, a critical space, for her in academia. Zola not only had opinions but also made them known, and she expected a response, recognition that she was engaging issues, important issues. Zola thought education should be as active as she herself was; thus her experience in Sarah's class was a disappointment.

Zola grew up in Morocco and lived there with her parents until 1980, when she graduated from high school and left to attend the University of Brussels. She described her early life in an in-class essay:

> My childhood was way back in the sixties. Along with my four brother and sisters, life could not be better for us and for our parents. Coming from a household of a working father and a housewife mother, I had all I wanted in and out home. Life was very different then, twenty years ago. . . . My life then seems to me now like a vacation, long relaxed days; peace was all around me and my family. I am wondering how thing changed without me noticing. My life change when I suddenly found myself a responsible young woman in Europe, just as my father said he found himself alone as he started his university studies.

What was this seemingly idyllic life Zola led prior to leaving her country to study abroad? What were the early influences in her life that made her the determined, hard-working, and academically motivated young woman she is today? Some of the answers to these questions lie in Zola's description of her early life with her family, a life in which learning was intermingled with daily living. The answers lie also with her deep respect and admiration for her father and mother, who were cousins and, thus, as Zola writes, "grew up almost in a similar situation, with the same mentality, succeeded in life and inherited the family success, the family's power, intellect, everything. We have to make it on our own nowadays."

Zola grew up in an affluent home. Maids tended to her family's needs, freeing her mother to spend considerable time with her children, time she often spent working with them on school assignments. In contrast, a stepmother who did not believe girls should be educated raised Zola's mother. As a result of her stepmother's restrictions, Zola's mother was unable to read or write when she was married at fifteen. However, once married, her husband supported her efforts and desire to learn. Through the years Zola's mother learned to read and to write and was able not only to assist her children with their schoolwork but also to learn with them as they progressed through the grades. Zola commented on her mother's education and early marriage:

> She learned how to read and write and study by herself with the help of my father. After she was married at the age of sixteen, fifteen, actually she was married at fifteen. That's how it used to be then: fifteen. If you got over fifteen, sixteen you're OLD to be married. And she learned and she had kids. She had five of us when she was not even twenty-two. But she learned how to practically do everything. She knows more than I do—general knowledge and even specific things like medicine, nutrition. Those were like her specialty.

Zola's mother spent long hours working on schoolwork with her children. This concentrated time spent learning together created a great bond between Zola's mother and her children. "My mother," commented Zola, "was definitely like a friend more than my father."

Perhaps as a result of the family focus on learning, Zola was very successful in school. She described her early experience with writing: "I was graded very nice, very well. And not only graded well, but also many times my papers were also read by the teacher to the students since I was about the age of eleven, twelve. I wouldn't give my writing to the professor before my father would have seen it and went through it. We used to take home writing. Usually we had a lot of take home writing." Early in her life Zola had learned the importance of revising her written work. She attributes this to her father's insistence that she always do the best possible work. Zola said of her father, "My father is a very tough grader. He would say 'What is this?' you know, 'Take it back and work on it.'" To this day Zola is often not satisfied with her work and, as she says, "I always change whether I like it or not." The need to change and work on her writing does not always work to her satisfaction. In fact, Zola seemed to wish she were not so compelled to revise. "I hate myself to change things all the time. Yeah, but if I keep my paper next to my eyes for one day I would always change it." To this day Zola shares her writing with others before she hands it in to her professors. With her friends she says, "We share ideas mostly. We don't talk about it as a writing."

This desire to improve her work she attributed to her father's influence. "Maybe yes, it was my father. Actually, yes it was my father. Definitely he was the type of person who was never satisfied or even when he was he would never say 'Oh, you're great!' because he would say these guys are gonna sleep and not do any efforts. It's true."

Zola's father was very concerned with his children's education. He was well educated with a master's in mathematics and languages, a degree he received from "the oldest university in the world." Zola described her father's professional position and his views toward education:

> My father is in education actually. . . . He is an, what do you call it? Advisor for the ministry in Morocco and also he did a lot of work like for planning. He was like a senator like here. He was pretty much involved in politics and that was his domain, education. And most all the family gave importance pretty much to learning and education more like than maybe business or some things like that. It was much relevant to them. Like I'm talking about grandfather and uncles and cousins.

Education is so important to the family that when one of Zola's brothers decided not to finish undergraduate school and instead to go into business in France, the family treated the decision as a disaster. Though the brother is not ostracized from the family, even the fact that his business is extremely successful has not changed the family's attitude. Zola told me, "Business has certainly no meaning; it is meaningless to them. You can always have a business but not your, at least you do not have a master's degree. It is like, you know, competition among family members and friends of the family."

After Zola completed two years of university-level work and obtained a degree from the University of Brussels she returned to Morocco to continue in school.

Her education was intermittent, however, because of the turmoil in the country. Zola wrote:

> My generation represents a whole new experience in my culture, in my country. By all means, we're "weird" in our parents' view. The country came upon a tremendous set of changes, which my parents did not have to deal with as young-sters. They lived in a more closed, traditional society. They lived an age where the short-run reform was unknown to the individual. The structure of the family and the people was meaningful to the individual. All that has changed and is changing fast now.

Zola described the situation in the early 1980s in Morocco: "We always had strikes. My generation was a generation of strikes. Because of the number of reforms." Zola participated in the strikes as did, she explained, all students. Zola described participating in the student strikes as extremely frightening. "It's a very frighten-ing thing when you go and the police and dogs behind you. It's very frightening. And like in Casablanca that very same year they shot two thousand people in less than four, five hours and there were children. They were shooting randomly."

The situation intensified to such an extent that continuing in school in Morocco became impossible and she decided once again to leave the country to continue her education. She went first to live with an aunt in Canada. After she arrived the aunt became ill, and Zola remained with her for a year, far longer than she had originally planned. From Canada Zola traveled to the Boston area and stayed with an Egyptian family in Dedham for a year before moving to Cam-bridge, where she continues to live on her own. She now receives financial sup-port from her brother in France so that she can attend school without having to take a job, unlike many students at UMB. For the two years Zola spent in the United States before beginning her studies, however, she worked to support her-self as a waitress.

When she first arrived in the United States, Zola spoke little English. She had only taken it in high school for three years in a course that met three times a week for one hour. However, she describes her command of Arabic, her native language, and French, her second language, as fluent. Of her command of English and her experience writing in English prior to coming to the States, she said, "Never English, I think maybe once classmates maybe, I think write to me a letter on New Year's—Happy New Year's—in English and I think I answered maybe once or twice, a few sentences, not more than four, five words in a sentence maybe." To improve her limited English upon arriving in the United States, Zola enrolled in a private English language institute, many of which are in the area, for an eleven-week intensive ESL program, a program she enjoyed very much. In addi-tion, she learned English through her two years of working as a waitress before she started at UMB.

Zola did not apply to UMB when she first arrived in the United States because she was not yet prepared to take the Test of English as a Foreign Language

(TOEFL) exam—required in lieu of the Scholastic Aptitude Test (SAT) for foreign students applying for college admission in the United States—or to deal with the amount of paperwork involved in putting together a college application. Her first real opportunity to write in English came when she took 101E Freshman English I at UMB. Zola enjoyed this course very much "because it gave me more confidence in writing in English for the first time." After discussing how much she had enjoyed her 101 course, Zola was quick to comment, "I'm not saying she [her 101 instructor, Vivian Zamel] was a better teacher than this one. I can't judge that." She suggested the following, however: "The course are very different actually. This [102E] is a more structured course. I guess. Maybe we will learn more from this course maybe on do research. I definitely learned from that course [101E] how to express and something that I have to say that I wanted to say."

Often in the 101E course Zola was not required to revise her work as were the other students. In 101E, Zamel corrected her grammar, and, interestingly, the one comment Zola remembers receiving from the teacher, other than statements of encouragement and praise, was that she "should not write a lot." As Zola commented: "Vivian had too much to read, more than what she required." In other words, Zola, because she loved to write, was writing longer papers than were required by the instructor. Zamel, obviously overburdened with student papers to read, asked Zola to cut back on the amount she wrote. Zola considered her 101E writing course easy "because it does not require learning much of new knowledge we lack. We learn how to write by reading and by practicing writing."

This philosophy of learning to write is much the same as that expressed by Alan, though Zola's analysis, and thus her implicit philosophy of writing instruction, is not as fully developed or as sophisticated as Alan's was. And although Zola is not as adamantly opposed to Sarah's approach to teaching writing as Alan, she is outspoken in one area. When asked about the first essay she wrote for Sarah, Zola responded, "I think I did all right. I did really good. I think I deserve an A. I got a B because, a B– actually. I think it was because I gave it late. You know my only problem actually with the whole system here in education is the timing. I mean I would rather have good quality, be late rather than I, I mean anything just on time." Actually, Zola's memory was a bit fuzzy here, even though she had just had the paper returned to her not long before she made these comments. What she received was a B– marked down to a C+ because the paper was late. Zola generalized her complaint about deadlines so that it was directed at the system as a whole rather than against Sarah as an individual. This is interesting in that, in my experience, not all instructors mark down for late papers. Sarah very rigidly marked down for lateness after spelling out at the outset of the course her requirements regarding on-time submission of papers so that students would know exactly what to expect. Zola, despite knowing what to expect, still seems somewhat outraged that she received a lowered grade, especially when she thought her work was of such high quality. In fact, Zola, who had done a number of papers for other courses since beginning school more than a year ago, had never been marked down despite the fact that she has turned in papers late. Zola expressed further her outrage at the "system" by commenting, "I really don't like the timing. I really don't give a damn about how fast the person is. If the person is not qualified or doesn't give me quality and I would be a teacher I, believe me . . . I don't think should be that important."

Ironically, Zola's final research paper for Sarah's course was also late, as was her second draft of the research paper. She was, however, not marked down in either instance because of the bizarre circumstances, entirely out of Zola's control, that caused her to turn in the papers past the due date. While visiting a friend at work as a night clerk in a prominent local hotel, Zola witnessed an armed robbery. During the robbery Zola had feared for her friend's life as well as her own. Not only was she shaken by the experience to such an extent that it affected her ability to complete her second draft on time, but also she was called to serve as a witness in court after the robber was captured. Zola was obligated to appear just as the final draft of the paper was due. Sarah was unaware that Zola had witnessed a robbery or of any of the pressures that Zola was under as the course drew to a close, and it was only after Sarah commented to me that she was surprised that Zola had not been in class, and that she had not turned in her second draft, that I informed her of Zola's predicament and obligations to the court. Shortly thereafter Zola contacted Sarah and arranged to submit her research paper to Sarah before final grades were due into the registrar's office. Sarah did not lower her grade, even though the paper was turned in late and was not typed. Zola received an A– on the paper.

While Zola may not have been able to control the circumstances that led to her final paper being handed in late, she could have controlled another resistant response she displayed, this time in reaction to Sarah's concern with being on time for class. In a handout she gave students during the first day of class, Sarah listed explicit rules for behavior in her course. Among these rules, in a section called "Class Policies," was the following: "No students will be admitted to class beyond 15 minutes past the hour." Zola consistently and blatantly disregarded this rule. She also often left the class, while Sarah was talking, to have a cigarette in the corridor outside the class. Sarah never commented on Zola's behavior or acknowledged her when she entered the class late. Further, Zola was able to circumvent two more of Sarah's dictates. Sarah stipulated also in the "Class Policies" section on the handout: "Attendance is required at all classes and conferences, and more than 2 absences may constitute grounds for failure in the course due to missed work." Zola exceeded the allowable two absences. And finally, Zola handed in her final research paper handwritten. Sarah required that the final version of the research paper be typed. Zola had earlier complained to me about typing because she had an aversion to it and had never wanted to learn. Secretaries typed, not Zola. Once again she used the armed robbery and her appearance in court as a witness as an excuse for her behavior. Confident, graciously outspoken, intellectually driven, and used to functioning in an adult world among peers, Zola did not take well to following rules, especially rules for which she could not find a rationale.

Zola, though a nonnative speaker of English and an immigrant, was navigating through a culture she knew well. Her position as a member of the upper class, her financial independence, and her seemingly "natural" association with academic culture through family ties and experience provided her with the appropriate cultural capital to succeed at UMB. She knew exactly how to manipulate the system to meet her needs. The fact that Sarah never made note of her tardiness to class, or to the fact that she often skipped out midclass for a cigarette, shows that Zola may, in fact, have had greater cultural capital than Sarah herself. In contrast, Sarah had not been at all hesitant about openly chastising Alan for speaking to a fellow student. Age did not play a role, because both Alan and Zola were in their twenties. Zola's actions were of such an extreme nature that to have called attention to them would have created the potential for a diversion from the task at hand; perhaps Sarah realized that the battle that would ensue was not worth it. I am sorry that I never directly asked Sarah to explain why she ignored Zola's resistant behavior, so I can only guess from my perspective as an observer privy to Zola's life experience. However, even though Sarah had not interviewed Zola, she had read Zola's essay from which I quote earlier in this chapter; Sarah was well aware of Zola's family's status in Morocco. Even if Sarah had not had access to the information through the essay, she probably would have been able to "read" Zola as a person from a wealthy family, with a strong sense of entitlement and resistance to authority from those she considered beneath her—a person who felt she was "above" the rules.

8

LESS-PROFICIENT STUDENT WRITERS IN CONTEXT: TAN'S AND ARAYA'S STORIES

Narrative is the art closest to the ordinary daily operation of the human mind. People find the meaning of their lives in the idea of sequence, in conflict, in metaphor and in moral. People think and make judgments from the confidence of narrative; anyone, at any age, is able to tell the story of his or her life with authority. The narrrative mode of thought comes universally to people as, for instance, mathematical or scientific reasoning do not. Everyone all the time is in the act of composition, our experience is an ongoing narrative within each of us.—E. L. Doctorow, "The Passion of Our Calling"

Tan: The Networker

Both Zola and Alan had received As in 101E English. Tan, on the other hand, had received a B–, a grade that is considered relatively low for an ESL writing course. At the outset of this study, however, I was not aware of Tan's previous performance in writing class. Therefore he was identified as a less-proficient writer solely on the basis of the in-class writing sample he completed during the first class of the summer session. Essentially, Tan was not evaluated in the same manner as Zola and Alan. I had already had Alan in one of my classes, and I was very familiar with his abilities and potential for growth as a writer. Also, I knew of Zola because I had observed her informally interacting with Vivian Zamel the previous semester when she was in 101E, and, in addition, I knew she was considered a very good writer. At the outset of the study, I knew nothing about Tan or Araya, the other less-

125

proficient writer chosen for the study; evaluative decisions about them were made entirely on the basis of the writing sample.

Who was Tan? What background experiences would be considered relevant to his present performance and development as a writer? Would he progress as a writer throughout the course of the semester, or would he still be characterized as less proficient when the course was over? Answers to these questions provide insight into the nature of the world of a student who is intent on survival in a new environment, in this case, the world of the academy. The answers reveal also that teacher perceptions may be far removed from the ongoing world of the student as it unfolds outside the walls of the classroom and of the institution.

In many ways, implicit rules of conduct of the academy become vague, and thus blurred, once one steps out of the confines of the anticipated scenario of the "student writing a research paper." What is this anticipated scenario? Generally, one envisions the student venturing into the library, once the topic has been chosen, to find sources for the paper. Once this is accomplished one further envisions the student taking notes and then writing and rewriting the paper, often into the early morning hours as subsequent drafts are produced and handed in to the instructor for feedback. This vision of the student writer is that of the writer in the garret writing alone. Of course it is expected that some student writers may discuss their papers with friends or family members or that they may, in fact, have others read their papers in order to receive feedback. Ultimately, however, the paper is expected to be *the student's own work.* The Social Darwinian ideology of the rugged individual struggling through a difficult project prevails in this instance. The extreme opposite scenario—that of the plagiarizing cheat—would be the student purchasing a paper written by someone else. When drafts are required this is, of course, difficult or even impossible (though perhaps there are individuals out there who will write draft after draft of a paper for money). Tan did not purchase a paper. However, the manner in which he wrote his research paper veers somewhat from the anticipated scenario outlined above, a scenario that I, and perhaps you the reader, can relate to as if it were second nature because we are so enculturated into the ways of the academy.

Tan is an extremely affable, endearingly fast-talking young man who sports a spiked haircut and projects the rumpled T-shirt, dirty sneaker look of the harried student. Tan was the archetypal opposite of Alan, the starched prepster whose appearance and manner were typical of the student in control. Tan seemed to leave a trail of bits of paper, notes displaced each time he opened his scruffy backpack or dug deep into his pockets in desperate search of a pen or pencil or a scrap of paper upon which to write yet another note. Alan was always poised, notebook on his lap, pen in hand, ready to proceed. Disheveled as he was, Tan was affable and extremely open, with eyes that were alert, deep pools longing to connect despite the fact that he felt he had difficulty expressing himself. As Tan commented, "You know for me I have problems to express. We, I think the Chinese all have a problem with express because they, they, when they have something they try to hide in the heart, but not to express. But when I doing my 101 English I try you know to express myself." Obviously Tan had had an instructor for 101 who focused on personal expression, no doubt process oriented and tied, overtly or not, to the expressive approach in process writing. Tan had learned, or had been coached, to express himself, because he did not seem to "try to hide in the heart" in his discussions with me. To the contrary, throughout the course of the summer session Tan shared many stories with me, leading me through a pastiche of emotional responses ranging from tears to outrageous laughter.

I learned that Tan had two goals. He wrote: "I want to be a part of US society and I want to be a electrical engineer. These are the purpose I go University of Massachusetts Boston." The goals he expressed and the circumstances he found himself in were far removed from the circumstances and goals of his early life. Born in war-torn Vietnam on 18 November 1962, Tan lived with his parents and siblings in the ethnic Chinese community in Saigon until 1978, when he left the country illegally by boat with his two older sisters and older brother. None of his immediate family members has a college degree. Tan told me his father is a tailor, although he identified him as a journalist on the written questionnaire he filled out at the outset of the study. His mother is a housewife. His father's occupation was but one of a number of contradictions that emerged as I came to know Tan.

Tan left Vietnam when he was sixteen and in his ninth year of school, at which point he had taken courses in physics, chemistry, and pre-calculus, among others, to prepare for a career in medicine. He was bilingual in Vietnamese and Chinese, but he did not begin to learn English until he lived in a refugee camp in Manila, where he received approximately one month of English instruction. By the time he was admitted to the United States in 1982, after two-and-a-half years in the refugee camp, Tan was able to carry on a simple conversation in English. Faced with an uncertain future at age nineteen, Tan decided to enroll in high school. At first he was refused admittance because of his age and his low score on the standardized test in English grammar he was given at the school. School officials suggested Tan enter an adult GED program, but Tan persisted and arranged to meet with the director of the bilingual program at the high school where he sought admittance. As Tan recalled,

> Then I went to Chelsea High School and, first of all, they reject me because, you know, because I was so poor in English. I mean when I try to get in. Then I think that I got improve in my mathematic, you know, exam so then the bilingual director, he give me a chance to stay in Chelsea. . . . I try to talk to the director because, you know, the people is, is not that great for me because I think they are older and it might embarrass me, you know, because I am in between high school and adult school.

Tan's argument worked; the director argued that he be allowed to enter high school. The thought of Tan sitting in a class of students older than he, students who might have had families of their own, must have swayed the director. I know I would have argued for Tan's admission to high school. Certainly he was in this awkward position, entering high school when he was nearing adulthood, through no fault of his own. The repercussions of the Vietnam War had created the context in which he found himself with no options but to flee as a boat person to life in a refugee camp—adolescence lost, family splintered, hopes frayed. We owed him high school.

Once in high school Tan was designated an eleventh-grader but placed in ninth-grade classes. Though embarrassed to be in classes with students so much younger than he was, Tan complained that the "program, you know, it wasn't that great. . . . They wouldn't let me, you know, to begin with high school like in ninth grade because my age. So they put me in eleventh grade and I have to catch up the material and uh classes." The following September Tan was placed in twelfth-grade classes because "I think I was doing good progress on the grammar and the simple, you know, conversation. So they let me into English 12 class." Tan recalls what it was like to take twelfth-grade English after being in a new country for only half a year: "It was hard to me because I had to read *The Great Gatsby* and *The Old Man and the Sea* from the novel, you know, from Hemingway. But I have a problem. I have, you know, to marry with the dictionary and this point I have write some writing, you know, about the novel."

His "marriage" to the dictionary did not preclude time for play. Through friends from Chinatown, Tan learned of a local high school with a large population of Vietnamese students that had what Tan characterized as an Asian League basketball team. Though Tan was not a student at this school he was recruited by his friends with the consent of the coach, who spoke only English, to play on the team. So Tan spent his weekdays in classes at one high school and then traveled far across the city for after-school basketball practice at another high school. Why did he join the team when he realized "It's really cheating" to do so? Tan offered this reason: "We have one purpose, you know, we want to play, you know, good basketball so, you know, we try, you know, to get a good team." The masquerade, however, did not last and the team, though the league winners, were not able to claim the championship. As Tan recalled, "By the end, you know, they figure out, you know, that I not in Brighton High. Then they reject, but we didn't care. We didn't care about that because we just want to play basketball."

Tan's English improved after he spent a year and a half in high school and, upon graduation, he decided to enroll in a local two-year technical school. He did so on the advice of a high school counselor who told Tan his English was not good enough for him to go on to college and that he should get a skill. This kind of advice, given no doubt with all good intent, may have swayed many nonnative English speakers from dreams of college and the possibilities that an advanced degree would perhaps provide. I know that the director of applied linguistics at UMB, who arrived in the United States from Cape Verde at sixteen not speaking English, was given similar advice from his well-intentioned guidance counselor at English High School in Boston. Choosing not to take his counselor's advice that he become a television repairman, Donaldo Macedo is now distinguished professor of liberal arts and director of the Applied Linguistics Program at UMB, author of numerous books and articles, and a firmly established scholar with an international reputation. At seventeen Macedo's English might not have been very good, though he did already speak two other languages (and now has command of five), but he did know that the technical field offered to him as his only option would not be the route he would follow. So Macedo found another advisor, and UMB, and a future filled with hope and possibility, not one constrained by the limits imposed by people who assume that a poor command of English equals a lack of intelligence. In contrast, Tan followed his advisor's recommendation and sought admission to a technical school to receive training to enter a trade. After a half year in the technical school, however, Tan was in a serious car accident and had to drop out of school. The accident put him in a position to reconsider his path in life, and he reasserted his desire to obtain a university education.

After he recovered from the accident, Tan registered for a summer course in 101E English at UMB, but, as a result of his score on the standardized text used by the ESL program to place new students, he was asked to leave 101 and take the entire ESL sequence of courses. The ESL sequence of courses does not provide credit toward graduation, but it does provide backdoor access to acceptance at the university. Students who successfully complete the courses do not have to go through regular application procedures. This means, for one thing, that they are not required to take the TOEFL exam. Once he completed the ESL courses Tan was accepted into the university and was then able to register for 101E English, the first required university writing course. So at the time of the study, Tan had not had much experience with higher education other than his short time at the technical school, the ESL program of courses at UMB, and, like Alan, one semester of credit-bearing course work. These experiences do not fully provide a foundation for success, because their requirements are far less stringent for the most part than what students will encounter in university-level courses.

Further distancing Tan from the realities and expectations of the academy was the fact that he had not had much experience writing in his native language because he had had little opportunity to do so in school in Vietnam. He said that what little writing he did at school in Vietnam was evaluated by his teachers to be average. However, Tan did begin to write after he escaped from Vietnam and offered the following explanation for his change in status from nonwriter to writer.

> But then, you know, I escaped from Vietnam to Manila to the refugee camp and then I start to write because, you know, I had, I was, I had, you know, emotion to, you know, try to express something because what I, what I experienced, you know, in my life because, you know, it was hard and some thing to me is very, you know, strongly because when I left home I have to, you know, leave my parent and I have to, you know, I have to, you know, I have to, you know, leave my sister because she was dead, you know, while we, you know, escaped. I mean she died, I mean, you know, because, you know, we, I remember when we, you know, in the boat, then we gots at one night, you know, I still

remember just the boat was, you know, checking out by the rock, you know, was close to the coast so the boat, you know, just hang, just, you know, I mean check out, can not go because, I mean the sea water's going so low at that time and then my sister tried to went down and tried to, you know, push the boat because there was a lot of people. There was I think, I believe a hundred refugees. So they have to, need some, you know, uh people, I mean to push the boat off the rock. Then my sister, when my sister went down to the sea, then he [*sic*] was disappeared.

Tan recalled further the circumstances of this traumatic event:

Yeah, I don't really know what happened. It was, it was, it was a dark, darkness night, you know—no moon out, no star or anything. I think, I think it was cloudy, cloudy and then the uh, midnight my brother, my older brother figured out, you know, my sister were missing. Yeah, it is so uh this too going, thinking of to me one experience is because after you leave my parent and my sister too, you know different experience, you know, one is my parent still alive after, you know, leave them. One another thing is my sister he [sic] died and I won't see anymore.

Tan began to write after his sister's death for two reasons: "One thing is to try to express myself and then the second thing is try to tell the situation to my parents." He describes his state of mind at the time as confused and worried about the future. He was in a state of emotional turmoil not only as a result of his sister's tragic death but also because his brother, his remaining sister, and he were denied admittance to the Philippines. They spent eight months living on a Taiwanese ship with two thousand other refugees before finally being allowed to enter the Philippines. This was a particularly grueling experience. While living on the ship and later in the refugee camp Tan learned, out of necessity, to ask others for help because, as he explained, "When you need something you have to ask because they don't usually provide enough, you know, water or food to the refugees. When we need something we have to write to the, our center or write some letters to the outside Chinese community for some help." In other words, in order to survive in the adverse circumstances Tan found himself in, he had to learn how to develop a network of support. He needed to write to his parents to inform them of their daughter's death, he found he needed to write in order to work through his sorrow, and he needed to write to seek support from as many outside sources as were available to him and his siblings. Tan was in survival mode, and he surged ahead amid horrendous odds. Rules you or I might understand did not exist in the new world Tan was thrust into, where one could not survive alone. Tan did everything in his power to ensure that he and his remaining siblings would survive, and they did.

This need to develop a network of support reemerged after Tan entered college. As Tan recalled:

I remember when I went to UMass Boston the first semester and I am learning. I was learning everything so independent, but it works out so slow because you know I have some question that have to, you know, to solve it by myself. Then the second year, the second semester, then I find out I should, you know, find a group of people to talk about, you know, the subject I want to learn because, you know, this is a quick way to learn it because people can tell you right away what the, he, you know, get from the topic. So I just gather, you know, the idea of the group of people and I, this is a quick way that I learn.

The skills Tan honed on the refugee ship and in the refugee camp served him well in academia. In order to survive his experience in Sarah's class, he created a network to support him through the process of researching and writing the required papers. First, he had the tutor assigned to the course assist him in finding sources for his paper, despite the fact that Sarah assigned specific grammar exercises for the tutor to go over with the students during the tutoring sessions she scheduled for each student. How was Tan able to circumvent the grammar exercises and enlist the tutor's help in finding sources for his paper? As Tan explained, "He [the tutor] know me and know shouldn't be any problem with grammar." Tan commented further that the tutor, "doesn't make the grammar to be the important part. What he concern is the research paper." In addition, the tutor, as an English major preparing to teach at the secondary level, had taken courses in literacy theory and was familiar with and supported the antigrammar perspective of process writing pedagogy. Thus the tutor was more interested in meeting Tan's needs than Sarah's requirements for tutoring sessions, because these requirements were at odds with his own theories of teaching. The collusion between Tan and the tutor can be viewed as a form of resistance that positively affected Tan's progress in the course. Had Tan and the tutor spent tutoring sessions going over the assigned grammar exercises, Tan might not have found the sources he needed to write his paper.

Tan also enlisted the support of his sister's boyfriend to help him through the course. As Tan explained, "I got, my sister got a friend, you know, who is American who live in Cambridge. So when I have a paper, you know, I will, you know, write down the paper first and then go to discuss with him so he will give me some suggestions. You know, what was my problem and so on and so on."

How did Tan find people to help him with his schoolwork? He explains the process he went through when attempting to enlist support: "I do some preparation about that. I try to figure out that person. You know, what he interest in, you know, like he interest in, in Chinese and then I say 'Well, I can teach you Chinese and can you read my English paper? We can get an exchange, you know, experience.'" In addition to his sister's friend, Tan also relied on a high school teacher he met through a mutual friend to assist him with his work in the course. The teacher, Joe, a forty-year-old Harvard graduate, had taught math for about eight years. Tan explained that Joe had become somewhat disillusioned with his American students and what he perceived to be their lack of interest in math and had, in turn, become involved with some of his Asian students who were interested in and quite good at math. Joe saw his Asian students as needing his assistance more with their English than with math, and he had thus begun working with some students informally after school hours.

With Joe, Tan maintained he did not go through the typical procedure used to elicit help because Joe was, in Tan's words, "really interested in helping people." Nonetheless, Tan and Joe were to travel together to China at the end of the summer session. Tan planned to travel first to Hong Kong where he would meet Joe, who was leaving on the trip a week before Tan. Tan planned to leave the United States as soon as the summer session ended. In fact, he completed his final research paper prior to the due date in order to maintain his departure schedule. While in Hong Kong, Tan and Joe planned to attend Tan's brother's wedding, after which time they would travel to mainland China together.

How did Joe help Tan with his writing throughout the summer session? He first helped Tan with his essay. Sarah gave the assignment—to write a three-to-five-page argumentative essay—to the students on a Thursday and required that they hand it in on the following Monday. Tan wrote an essay in which he argued that the United States should not establish a legal drinking age. Tan explained how Joe assisted him with this assignment:

> First of all I did something wrong on this essay, you know, the one due on Monday. I wrote something down and then I went to, you know, to my high school teacher, you know, my advisor home and we discuss, you know, the uh my topic. Then I figure out it was something wrong. Because I think that I'm not that participate good in the American society. So I got some wrong idea. So he points it out for me and argue what, what the point is my paper. Then we do a lot of argument and then I wrote my letter, I mean wrote my essay and then we discuss that, you know, on another time on the Sunday night. I live over there for two days. Yeah, you know, because we haven't seen for a long time.

Tan continued to explain how Joe helped him:

> He say, "This sentence, well your ideas is right, but, you know, you might, but your sentence structure have a problem." So he structure the sentence and sometime I have too much sentence. I have a problem sentencing. I have too much, too many sentences to say one thing. So he said I have a problem with vocabulary. So he said if you use the right word—this is a new word, you know. This is a word, you know, for the whole paragraph. So he just tell me how to learn from the vocabulary.

During weekends throughout the summer, Tan waited tables on Friday and Saturday evenings, so he generally worked on his writing during the day. For this particular essay, Tan and Joe discussed the topic until very late Saturday night and then, Tan reported, he wrote all day Sunday. Joe was surprised, Tan said, by how hard Tan worked. "He can not believe it, you know. I can sit down there and do my paper, you know, the whole day and then he ask me to go out and play basketball with the, my friend, you know, because my friend is live near there." Earlier in the summer, prior to being interviewed, Tan had responded on the written questionnaire to the question "Do you enjoy writing?" with the following: "In fact, I don't really enjoy writting, because I just can't sit down and write for hours." So in the end the question remains, did Tan sit all day long and work on his essay, or was Joe's intervention and assistance so great that the task of completing the essay was not overwhelming? Although Tan did not spend another weekend staying over at Joe's house, he continued to rely on him for support as he developed his research paper. This was done over the phone.

At this point I believe it is important to step out of Tan's story to provide my own commentary on his relationship with Joe. In our academic culture the relationship between Joe and Tan is implicitly suspect. Generally considered, it is the teacher's role to assist students during the school day or after school on school grounds. Rarely would one consider having a student spend the night at one's home in order to work on a paper. To do so raises the question of the possibility for sexual exploitation given the power differential between student and teacher. Since Joe was not in a position to evaluate Tan, however, the power differential rests more with the age difference and Tan's real need for assistance. Perhaps Joe truly was kindhearted and assumed the role of parent figure—a member of the family—with Tan. Tan did invite him to his brother's wedding, and he obviously planned to include him as a family member in the celebration. Nonetheless, a cynic (as I am) might suggest that there was more to the relationship than what Tan chose to reveal to me. And that was his right. He was making his way through yet another alien culture: the culture of academia. Whatever and wherever he could find support seems appropriate. Tan was apprentice to Joe, and that is a far cry from purchasing a research paper off the internet.

The relationship is further suspect because the help Tan received from Joe implies that Tan did not do all of his work himself. To not do all of one's own work is cheating. However, would the same implied accusation apply to the native-born middle- or upper-class student who worked on a paper with the help, for example, of his mother, an English professor? I believe not. We anticipate and encourage family support at all grade levels; we do not, however, accept support from outside the home unless it occurs in an institutional context, such as help received from paid tutors. And this practice is becoming more and more common. I have friends who have paid more than seventy-five dollars an hour to have a tutor come to their homes to help their children with their math homework. And one recently paid twenty-five hundred dollars to have a tutor prepare her son, once again in math and in her home, for his second try at the SATs. A one-hundred-point score increase was guaranteed. But of course our system is democratic, equitable, and merit alone counts, and these practices of the native-born members of the middle and upper classes are in no way suspect in our culture. In contrast, in order for Tan to survive the course and to develop as a writer, he needed to venture into areas of marginal acceptability within the academy. Had he remained within the limits implicitly and explicitly defined for the course, Tan may not have fared as well as he did. In Tan's case, behaviors considered unacceptable, indeed marginal, to academic culture served to ensure his success in the course.

Back now to the story of Tan's writing of his papers: The first major problem Tan had with his research paper was choice of topic. Initially he planned to write about the Vietnamese refugee situation and tie this to a discussion of the relationship between the U.S. and Vietnamese governments. Joe told Tan he thought the topic was feasible, but once he began researching, Tan found that he was having difficulty finding sources. While scanning the newspaper index, Tan discovered that there was a glut of sources on AIDS, so he approached Joe about the possibility of doing his paper on AIDS. Joe agreed he should change his topic, and he suggested Tan focus more narrowly on a discussion of condom advertising on TV. While his original topic was perhaps more interesting and relevant to Tan's own experience, it was beyond the scope of a ten-page paper. When Tan approached Sarah with the request to change his topic, she allowed him to do so. In addition, Tan continued to discuss his research paper with and seek correction and advice from his sister's friend when he visited their home.

Throughout the course Tan worked aggressively to complete his research paper successfully. He had a strong motivation to do so because he needed a grade of B or better in the course to be accepted into the Electrical Engineering Program, his chosen major. Tan commented on the pressure he was under to perform and offers his critique of the course grading system:

> Actually I got a comment right now on my 102 class because I really, you know, don't like the grading system because it seems to have a pressure to me because if I got a bad grade I won't get accepted, you know, from the engineering department. So if this course is like have no grade system I can do it more freedomly, more freedomly. I can do whatever I want so I don't have to worry about, you know, if I got a bad grade, I got a bad result. I mean so I'm nervous about that.

Despite the fact that he felt pressured because of the grading system, Tan liked the 102 class because he felt free to ask questions. "I believe is the mostly is very freedom, you know, in the class. I can ask questions, you know. Yeah, because especially, you know, if you ask question, you know, she won't thought you stupid. Classmates won't laugh at me." Tan was particularly sensitive to teacher response to questions because he had had a bad experience in a course the previous semester. He recalled, "I remember when I ask question in my electrical circuit class and my instructor, he, you know, think I'm stupid, you know, and how come it so simple question and seems so silly question. So he make me so my confidence not that strong."

Unfortunately Tan's experience in the electrical circuit course was not unique. Despite UMB's professed mission to serve the underserved, to reach out to a diverse, urban population in an effort to provide a college education to minorities, refugees, immigrants, and members of the working class generally stepping for the first time into the context of higher education, much prejudice existed. For example, instructors often made the false assumption that the inability to produce what is generically referred to as standard English in either oral or written form (or both) was a marker of lower intelligence. For students like Tan, whose first language was not English and who spoke with an accent and with marked grammatical errors (and wrote in similar fashion), courses outside of the ESL program, where grammar correction was not emphasized, often posed extreme hurdles, many of which were impossible to overcome.

By the end of the writing course with Sarah, however, Tan's confidence had grown. Further, he had completed his research paper, as well as the course, with a grade of B+, ensuring acceptance into the Electrical Engineering Program. He accomplished all this by establishing a strong network of support outside of the structure of the academy. Whether he stepped beyond the bounds of acceptable behavior in doing so is difficult to assess. In my opinion, he did not. Tan did not grow up in a community in which he received support in learning academic forms of language. Thus, after finding himself in a new community whose ways with words he did not know, Tan very reasonably concluded that the most efficient way to learn how to use the language of the community—in this instance, how to write a research paper—would be to call upon others for support. In doing so, he expanded the number of individuals available to help him through the socialization process necessary to begin, at least, to acquire the discourse of the academy. In my opinion, his approach to surviving in the academy was quite commendable, and certainly pragmatic.

Finally, at the outset of this section I commented on the notion of varied perceptions. The fact that Tan viewed Sarah as open to student participation while Alan viewed her as pushy and unreceptive to comment during class was as much dependent on the different background experiences of the two students as it was on the classroom environment itself. Is the reality, then, of the classroom as varied as are the participants and observers within its walls? And too, how did Sarah perceive Alan and Tan? Certainly she saw them as hardworking students struggling to write a research paper while meeting her deadlines and fulfilling her requirements. Other than seeing them four days a week sitting silently before her in class and meeting with them for approximately fifteen minutes on two occasions, Sarah had little contact with the two students. Clearly Sarah knew nothing of Alan's resentment toward her, because he kept his feelings hidden completely when in her presence. In fact Alan succeeded quite nicely in ingratiating himself to Sarah during his conference sessions with her. In like manner, neither was Sarah aware of the network of support Tan had created to assist him through the course. Sarah assumed that Tan was writing his paper alone and revising it based solely on her written and oral comments.

Araya: The Silent(ced) One

Araya, a slight, extremely pleasant, exceedingly shy, twenty-four-year-old Ethiopian, had been in the United States for three years and at the university for one when he entered Sarah's research writing course. Araya was not only one of the less-proficient writers in the course but also, I learned once I began speaking with him, the least orally proficient of the students participating in the case study component. This was the case despite the fact that he had studied English in school in Ethiopia for ten years as well as formally for one year of the three he had been in the United States. Why was his English still limited, despite his years of study in Ethiopia and the length of time he had been in this country? What was it about Araya's history and present social situation that might begin to explain his lack of proficiency in oral and written English? And how would he progress through 102 English?

Araya was born in Addis Ababa, the capital of Ethiopia, on 8 January 1963, one of twin sons of a textile exporter and a housewife. Though uneducated, Araya's father was an extremely successful businessman and the family was affluent. Maids and other household help tended to the family's needs, and, as a result, Araya and his siblings never worked until they were in their twenties. Araya's family valued education, and his father worked to provide support for his children to attend schools in the United States. And though Araya's father did not attend college, his brother graduated from the University of California at Berkeley and is an engineering professor at the University of Maryland. In fact Araya also planned to major in engineering. As he commented, "I want to study engineering, civil or electrical engineering, and if it is possible I would like to get my doctorate or something like that."

Despite the turmoil in Ethiopia due to its war with Eritrea and the famine in the area, Araya's family remained untouched by trauma. Their lives continued peacefully in the capital city through Araya's twelve years of schooling. After he and his twin brother graduated from high school, both began taking extension courses at the local university because they had not been accepted as full-time students. Araya explained that there is only one university in Ethiopia, and competition to get in is very intense. Since he and his brother had been average students in high school, they were not accepted. Two of Araya's older brothers and his older sister attended college in the United States because their opportunities for advanced degrees were limited in their own country. One older brother, a judge, remains in Ethiopia. One of the two older brothers in the United States is a surgeon practicing in Chicago. He is married to an Ethiopian woman, and they are the parents of two young children. The other brother is ABD in biology from Boston College and works at an inner-city parking garage as he considers the possibility of writing his dissertation while longing to return to Ethiopia. As Araya explained his older brother's status, "He works for his doctorate degree in Boston College, but he didn't got. He already passed the exam, but he has to write a paper." Araya's sister has her master's in economics and is married to an Ethiopian. She and her husband live in Atlanta. Araya's family was driven to succeed academically, and Araya's closeness to his family was evident was he told me about his family in detail.

Araya's life after high school continued peacefully until, solely by chance, he was conscripted into the Ethiopian army. With conscription came the risk of seeing active duty in Eritrea. Araya's father arranged for him to leave the country in order to avoid the service. As there was no possibility of obtaining a student visa once he had been drafted, Araya had no other choice but to walk out of the country. To do so is not that unusual for Ethiopians because many seek to escape the poverty and war-torn conditions in the countryside. The affluent also leave by foot, like Araya did, if they cannot obtain legal exit visas. In order to arrange the illegal expedition and ensure a guide and protection for his son, Araya's father had to pay one thousand dollars—a huge sum in Ethiopia. While these arrangements were being made the family was also able to secure a student visa for Araya's twin brother, who has been attending school part-time since he arrived in the United States three years ago and has yet to be accepted full-time.

Araya's journey across Ethiopia to Sudan, a journey he described as being "very scary," took fifteen days. Once he reached the border, Araya said, "the guerrilla fighter on the border, they help us giving food and help to get out." Once in Sudan he had enough money to secure a hotel room. Araya explains what happened next. "After that I was in Sudan and I make a phone call to here to my brother and my brother came over there and arranged the whole thing to come here." Araya stayed in the hotel in Sudan by himself for fifteen days while he waited for his older brother to arrange to come and get him. In all Araya spent thirty days in nearly complete isolation, first on foot with fear lurking at every step, and then in a strange country with no contacts, waiting for his brother to rescue him. With his brother's help, Araya was able to obtain refugee status and was thus able to enter the United States without any problems.

Once they were in the United States, Araya's brother helped him set himself up in an apartment in Cambridge, which he now shares with his twin brother. The family makes every effort to remain close despite the thousands of miles between them. Every fifteen days—there seems to be a magical quality to this number—Araya calls his brother in Chicago, and he visits him twice a year. He has also visited his sister in Atlanta a number of times since he arrived in the United States. And Araya's mother has visited twice and his father once, just six months before he began summer school. Araya and his twin brother live together and eat their meals out together every day—usually at Chinese restaurants, but occasionally at one of the few Ethiopian restaurants in the area—because they do not know how to cook. And they work at the same parking garage as the brother who is ABD, with whom they spend a lot of time. Rarely does Araya have occasion to interact with native speakers of English. Even in class he spoke but once when Sarah called on him to supply a short answer to a question on a homework assignment. In class he spoke to only one other student, a young Haitian woman who sat behind him. Araya and the Haitian woman were the only two students in the class who were Black. None of the other students sought them out. Alan, Zola, and Tan, on the other hand, asked a number of questions of Sarah throughout the summer session and spoke openly and often to classmates before and after class and sometimes discreetly during class.

Now that he lives in the United States, Araya is economically independent. Though his father has enough money to support Araya, he is not able to send money out of Ethiopia. Araya is able to pay his expenses by working in the parking garage sixteen hours each weekend. He was able to obtain the job through another student from Ethiopia. Weekend day jobs are coveted by Ethiopian students because the garages are not that busy during the day on Saturday or Sunday and students are able to study while at work. But here they toil completely isolated, in a glassed-in cell of sorts; the only opportunity for speaking English occurs when a driver approaches the window to pay. And anyone who has parked in a downtown garage knows that little conversation occurs between the ticket taker and the driver leaving the garage. Araya is completely isolated from English speakers. His main interaction is with his twin brother and visiting family members. His familial community is strong and supportive, but it leaves him no opportunity for entry into the larger English-speaking world of Boston. Even his choice of restaurants limits social intercourse in English, because Chinese waiters generally speak Mandarin or Cantonese, not English.

Prior to coming to UMB, where he took the sequence of ESL courses before being admitted as a full-time student, Araya had little experience writing in English. As he recalled, "I studied English because you need English to go to the university. But I didn't take any writing." Araya explained further that while he only wrote short answers or did multiple-choice exercises in English classes, he did write in his native language, Amharic. As he explained, "In high school in my language I use to write some kind of essay." How was he graded in these essays? Araya recalls, "In my language I got OK." The most experience he has had writing in English was in 101E at UMB.

When questioned about his experience in writing class Araya seemed somewhat confused about the language—the discourse of the writing class—I was using. When I asked whether he had ever written drafts for a paper he responded with the following: "No, it's not a draft, but you can write two times or three times. You can write at one time and she make a comment on it. And you can write it again." When asked later in the interview whether he saw any differences between the 102 class he was presently taking and his 101 course Araya responded, "I don't see difference. You have to write and you have to give a draft." This same confusion emerged on his written questionnaire. In response to the written question "Did you write drafts for your last English teacher, or for any other English teacher?" Araya wrote, "No, I have never gave drafts to my English teacher before." But his response to the next question—"How many drafts did your last English teacher require you to hand in before you submitted the final paper?"—contradicted what he had just written; Araya wrote "2 drafts." Araya was more familiar with the language of the traditional approach to writing, because he was able to tell me that he had had experience with narrative, descriptive, and argumentative writing and that he liked argumentative writing the best. The three other student writers in the study preferred personal narrative.

When asked on the written questionnaire to characterize what sort of writer he was in his native language—good, average, or bad—Araya wrote good and then scratched out his answer and failed to supply an alternative assessment. When

I asked him how he had been graded as a writer here in the United States he told me he had received a C, an extremely low grade, in 101. He continued with the following assessment of his writing: "It's very difficult to write an essay for me and most of the time I got C+ or C. I never get an A. And I'm working on it I think."

Araya did appear to work hard at his writing, and he reported that he spent seven or eight hours writing his first essay for Sarah's class. How did he go about writing the essay in which he argued against legalization of drugs? Araya explained, "Write it one times. Take two hours and then go back again and write it again." And further, "She told us about organization. . . . So first I make an introduction and then the support for legalize the drug idea on the second paragraph and on the third paragraph the reasons why's not good legalization of drugs and then the conclusion. I arrange it like that."

Araya followed the model Sarah provided very closely as he went through the process of writing his paper, and he was very conscious of how many sentences he had in each paragraph, trying to make sure he had more than seven in each. When asked if he constantly counted his sentences, Araya responded that he did and that he "tried to get more sentences in each paragraph." Once the paper was written he stayed up until 2:00 in the morning typing it. Araya explained why it took him so long to do so: "My typewriter is simple typewriter. When you make a mistake you throw out paper. I don't have much experience so I make many mistakes." No one proofread his paper, which was replete with spelling and grammatical errors when he handed it in to Sarah. Araya attributed his problem with spelling to his difficulty with pronunciation in English. What Araya needed was a computer with spellcheck, though such a purchase was impossible for him because he was on his own financially. He also needed a network of support, a helpful friend who could speak and write well in English.

Despite his problems with writing, Araya attested to liking to write and to realizing that writing is important. Araya asserted, "It's very essential to writing courses. I always felt eager to know how to write correctly for my future when I have to write good papers and otherwise. Yes, it's very important. I have to keep study writing English. I have to take more course in the future."

Though he was one of the least successful and least improved writers in the course, Araya was the only student in Sarah's course to evaluate her on the official teacher evaluation form as excellent. (Sarah gave me permission to read the official evaluation forms. This was necessary because department policy prohibits access to evaluations to anyone other than the instructor evaluated and to select members of the personnel committee charged with ranking instructors for merit raises.) Araya also evaluated the course as excellent. Certainly the manner in which Araya evaluated Sarah and the course points to the problematic nature of student evaluations. Was Araya's evaluation based on his perception of how much he learned in the course or on how comfortable he was with Sarah's teaching methods? Araya was unaware of the extent to which others in the course were receiving assistance from Sarah (as discussed in chapter 9), and never once did Araya even hint to me that he was displeased with anything having to do with the course or Sarah. Overall, the others in the course evaluated Sarah and the course as good. Alan evaluated Sarah as good and the course as poor; Tan evaluated her as very good; and Zola—surprise, surprise—was absent the day official evaluations were completed. Araya wrote on the final evaluation form that "By taking an account of my instructor comment I improved my writing. Those comments helps me to overcome most of my writing problem." With these words Araya ends his story of 102 English. It is a short story and one without a happy ending.

To obtain information about Araya I relied more heavily than in any of the other case studies on his responses to the questionnaire that I asked all the students to complete for me. Araya was difficult to speak with. His shyness was overwhelming, and his desire to please quite sad. He wanted so much to do what was right, yet he was clueless about how to engage in his new cultural context. Araya had no sense that within the communicative context of professor/researcher and student he, as the initiate to the community, was expected to perform. All the others—Alan, Araya, and Tan—understood and acted in the appropriate, expected manner in response to each question I posed, and what followed was a free-flowing conversation in which the students took full opportunity to tell me as much as possible about themselves. In so doing, they were able to further insinuate themselves into the culture of the academy by learning from me, engaging with me, moving in rhythm with me as our conversation flowed. Araya, in contrast, treated each encounter as an exercise. I posed a question and he responded with a short answer. Our meetings were filled with silence, and I was left feeling that if I were to probe further I would seem intrusive, loud, and inappropriate. No sense of hostility existed when we were together, just the discomfort—on my part—from too much silence. I wanted to transport Araya to a community of friends so he could socialize with someone other than his twin brother and become socialized into the communicative patterns necessary for success at the university. But who was I to even consider such a thing? They were twins, and they no doubt enjoyed each other's company immensely. And Araya's siblings were academically successful, so perhaps, once he entered the mathematical world of engineering, he would not need the communicative behaviors that I so wished he would acquire. Araya was the one student of the four who did exactly as Sarah said, yet he gained nothing of note from the course other than a low passing grade and college credit. And I had failed him as well.

9

THE DIALOGICAL CONSTRUCTION OF SUCCESS: ALAN IN CONFERENCE

> The experience of a perfectly tuned conversation is like an artistic experience. The satisfaction of shared rhythm, shared appreciation of nuance, mutual understanding that surpasses the meaning of words exchanged . . . goes beyond the pleasure of having one's message understood. It is a ratification of one's way of being human and proof of connection to other people. It gives a sense of coherence in the world.—Deborah Tannen, *Conversational Style: Analyzing Talk among Friends*

In Sync

In this chapter and the three chapters that follow, I present both an overview of what transpired between Sarah and her students during their conferences and a more detailed analysis of selected portions of the discourse of each of the conferences. These analyses will be carried out at both the macro and micro levels. In my analysis of the interactions between Sarah and Zola, Tan, and Araya, I will return to the analysis of the interactions between Alan and Sarah as a basis for comparison. As has been the case throughout the book, I privilege Alan over the other students. In this instance Alan's interaction with Sarah, which I have deemed successful, becomes the point of reference for analyzing the interaction of each of the other students involved in the study with Sarah. In all ways, Alan is the model student.

The words from Deborah Tannen's *Conversational Style* that appear in the epigraph at the beginning of this chapter capture the aura and essence of the interactions that occurred between Alan and Sarah during the two occasions when they met to discuss the first and second drafts of his research paper. When in conference, Alan and Sarah were completely in sync with one another as demonstrated through not only their words but also their behaviors. Sarah relaxed with Alan; she leaned forward when he spoke, and he did the same when spoken to. Their interactions displayed the components of a well-choreographed dance; there were no false steps, because these participants were well practiced in their roles. Both conferences between Alan and Sarah—and here I privilege Alan by mentioning him first because he was the one in control—were marked by a sense of harmony and mutuality of intent and an understanding of goals. Further, throughout the conferences Alan was the one who acted; he was in control of the direction of the discourse. This control, however, never extended beyond the confines of the barriers established by Sarah's comments on his paper, and so Alan implicitly abdicated an acknowledged power to his instructor while at the same time he made sure that he gained as much as possible from the time spent together. And finally, the prominent linguistic pattern displayed throughout is one that I refer to as the fill-in-the-blank pattern. The two were so in sync that they often completed the other's utterances with the called-for word or phrase. This was unique to the exchanges between Alan and Sarah. In what follows I describe in more detail and provide examples that confirm the generalizations I have made here.

On Time

On the day of his conference with Sarah to discuss the first draft of his paper, Alan arrived approximately twenty-five minutes before his scheduled conference time. Sarah had suggested students arrive approximately ten minutes early so they would be able to review her written comments before meeting with her. Sarah noted that Alan was early, because she was able to see him in the hall outside her office, and asked him if he would like to start his conference with her before his scheduled time. Sarah decided to ask Alan to take an earlier time slot because her previous appointment with Araya had ended quite early and the student with the next scheduled appointment, Tan, had not shown up yet. Alan said he needed time to look over his comments and would prefer to finish reviewing them before he met with Sarah. Alan had asserted his control of the situation. Ever the good student, he had arrived for his appointment well ahead of the scheduled time. In doing so, Alan situated himself within a cultural framework of being organized and on time (in fact ahead of schedule), which is music to the academic's (and potential employers') ears. In declining Sarah's offer to meet earlier than scheduled Alan did not rebuff his instructor but, rather, further insinuated himself into the appropriate cultural framework as the student who intends to be well prepared for the meeting to ensue. Once again his actions display characteristics valued and rewarded in the workplace, a context with which Alan is most familiar and where he has met with much success.

Maintaining Face

When Tan had still not arrived about ten minutes later—behavior not condoned either at school or at work—Sarah once again asked Alan if he would like to begin his conference earlier than scheduled. At that point Alan agreed because he had now had enough time to review Sarah's comments. Thus in these early moments, even prior to the scheduled conference, Alan was able to assert his needs and not abdicate to Sarah's agenda. At the same time, however, he was able to communicate to Sarah the serious manner in which he regarded both her comments on his paper and his responsibility to review them prior to meeting with her.

While in conference with students, Sarah sat in her desk chair. The chair, however, was moved away from the center of her desk, which was up against a wall, so that she sat at one corner of the desk and the student sat at the side of this corner. Thus there were no extreme barriers between Sarah and the student with whom she was meeting, as would be the case if she had chosen to sit at a desk facing outward, with the student on the opposite side, placing the whole desk between student and instructor. Sarah's arrangement allowed her to use the corner of her desk to lean on if she chose or for the student to place papers if necessary.

During the conference with Alan, Sarah and Alan sat facing one another, often leaning toward one another as they spoke. Alan sat with pen in hand, taking notes and making corrections on his paper as Sarah responded to his questions and comments. And though he looked exceptionally tired during his first conference, Alan was, nonetheless, dressed crisply, despite the hot weather, in white pants, matching white Reeboks, and a pink polo shirt. The pink pen with which he so copiously copied Sarah's suggestions matched his shirt exactly. Alan displayed a nearly perfect package: here was the appropriately dressed student who exhibited all the overt behaviors expected within the context of the writing conference. An instructor could ask for no more.

At the outset Alan seemed somewhat dismayed by the grade of B– he had received on his first draft. This dismay was conveyed through a slightly distraught look but was never verbalized. Nor did he allude to the grade he had received on the first draft at any time throughout the conference. Once again a very appropriate choice on his part: instructors wish to believe that their students do the work they require purely for the intellectual benefits, not for the grade. In fact, discussion of grades is taken to be crass and most inappropriate, and when students do bring up the topic most instructors cringe and then file away on permanent record the fact that this particular student is not to be taken seriously. Faculty so dislike discussing grades that the most progressive often choose to give all As, inflating their unsuspecting students' egos, while at the same time enhancing their own chances for both avoiding uncomfortable confrontations and encouraging positive student evaluations. Sarah did not take this approach. She was a hard grader, yet she was fair, because she gave students guidelines and percentages clearly outlining the basis upon which a grade was given. This action on her part distanced her personal involvement in the "giving of the grade" and presented to the students the notion that the process—which is so very subjective—was based on objective criteria.

The Conference Begins

Sarah had greeted Alan in the hall outside her office, so once they were both seated—a process that proceeded without a hitch—she began the conference by asking, "Do you have questions?" Alan responded in the affirmative and proceeded to read directly from the comment sheet Sarah prepared for each student. This sheet was attached to Alan's draft of the research paper, which also contained written comments directly on the text. Alan began by referring to the comment sheet and then continued in a systematic manner to lead Sarah, page by page, through nearly all the twenty-eight comments she had made on his paper. As he did so he asked for further clarification and elicited suggestions for revision from her. The exchange between Sarah and Alan was harmonious and marked, overall, by a mutual understanding of purpose and clarity of intent.

Furthermore Alan was very much in tune with what Sarah expected of him in terms of revision, so much so that throughout the conference he was often able to complete statements Sarah had begun. This was generally done by overlapping her words or by picking up the stream of talk as Sarah paused. This was accomplished without causing aggravation as it might have if Alan had overlapped to change the topic of conversation or to set his own agenda, for example, communicating that he did not agree with a particular suggestion or comment Sarah had made on his paper. Rather, Alan's overlapping served to confirm the direction Sarah's turn-at-talk was taking and to communicate to her that he was completely in sync with the flow of discourse. By the end of the conference Alan and Sarah were so much in agreement that, at times, portions of their interaction took on a singsong quality. By this I mean that their intonation patterns were mirror images of one another. The final exchange in the following sequence, which occurred near the end of the conference, illustrates this.

T1   I think the problem here is with your use of this colon.

A2   A dash will do.

T3   Yeah, a dash will do, a little dash will do. (uttered with a lilt, as a joke.)

A4   You mean this one. (does not respond to the joke.)

T5   Well, no, I mean again this is an integration problem.

A6   You mean I have to say why I use things.

T7   Right.

A8   And what word this for.

T9   Yep.

A10   (pause as Alan makes notes on his paper) Just use a comma, but will be a too long sentence. It will be too long sentence. If you, comma.

T11   No. (high tone)

A12   No. (low tone)

T13   No. (high tone)

A14   Yeah, this should be a comma instead of

T15   Right, yeah, it should be. That's fine.

A16   Yeah?

T17   Yeah.

A18   And here, stopping here.

T19   Yep. (rising intonation)

A20   That's it. (rising intonation)

T21   That's it. (rising intonation)

In addition to the synchrony displayed through intonation, this sequence is also illustrative of other patterns that emerged elsewhere throughout the conference between Alan and Sarah. When, in T5, Sarah told Alan he has an integration problem, Alan was not content to accept a single-word analysis, but rather responded in A6, A8, and A10 with his interpretation of what Sarah meant in this instance. Alan went so far as to reword Sarah's comment in A6, "You mean I have to say why I use things," and in A8, "And what word this for." What Sarah called "an integration problem" was reconstructed into language that Alan could understand. By doing so, Alan was assured that he understood what Sarah intended. Sarah confirmed Alan's rewording of her comment in T7, with the single-word response: "Right," and again in line T9 with the single-word response: "Yep." There is no ambiguity here. Communication is clear.

Spelling, Punctuation, and Grammar

The extent to which punctuation was being considered in this exchange between Sarah and Alan is striking. Although the professed purpose of the first conference was to discuss bigger-picture research and writing issues, as discussed in chapter 6, Sarah spent considerable time discussing punctuation with Alan during this conference. What is important to consider here is not that Sarah has failed to read Alan's text for meaning but, rather, the degree to which meaning is ultimately related to issues—punctuation and grammar—considered by process-oriented theorists and teachers to exist apart from meaning and intent. The theoretical distinctions made between meaning and grammar or between content—that which the writer wishes to communicate—and what are characterized as superficial aspects of language creates a false dichotomy between features of written language and a false hierarchy as well.

Spelling, punctuation, and grammar do affect meaning, and they really cannot be treated separately from the overall communicative intent of a written text.

I know that my argument will raise the hackles of those who adhere to a process approach, because it represents a devaluing of a fundamental premise of the approach: deal only with meaning at the start, and deal with more superficial features of language only when the text has reached its near-final stage. That approach works for academics and novelists, for example, because, for the most part, the features that need attending to at the copyediting and proofreading stages of the production of an article, academic book, or novel will be superficial in character. In most cases, the writing will already be good enough that the meaning is quite clear; these writers of articles, academic books, or novels accepted for publication have been at their trade for a while, they have apprenticed, and they are now members of an elite club. Students are not.

I can remember quite clearly that when I was an initiate into process pedagogy—before I was even aware of the theoretical distinctions made within the field—I was willing to give up correcting grammar, spelling, and punctuation at the early stages of students' work on papers. This was the case until, after handing back a first draft to a class of 101 students, I was approached by a Haitian student after class who told me, "Professor, while you may have gone to Harvard, I did not. And I won't have a prayer of getting there unless I learn to write like a Harvard student. Now, you have not taken any time to correct what I imagine are many mistakes in my paper, and I need you to do so. Unless I know exactly what I have done wrong, I can't hope to learn what I need to do to be right."

I paraphrase this young man's speech. His false assumptions about my association with Harvard and his tempered plea that I assist him in acquiring the language forms that would allow him to become an apprentice to the dominant culture I clearly represented struck me as so to the point that I was left questioning my own intentions in adhering so uncritically to a specific methodology. I did what he asked, while at the same time attempting to clearly articulate in class the need to focus as well on overall text structure, audience, clarity of purpose, and so forth in addition to points of grammar, spelling, and punctuation. I wish I knew for sure that this well-spoken man did get into Harvard. I am pretty confident in assuming that he has succeeded in academia, whether at Harvard or elsewhere. This student sure taught me a lesson, and it is not the only one I have learned from my students, who have led me to rethink my practices so that I might better serve their needs.

Confusion

Although by the end of Sarah and Alan's conference they have achieved clear and direct communication, the beginning of the conference did not go as well. At the very beginning of the conference after Sarah asked if Alan had any questions, Alan told her he did. The fact that Alan was able to respond immediately in the affirmative and then to move directly to Sarah's comment sheet helped to set the tone for the conference: Alan was serious about this meeting. Alan then proceeded to read from the comment sheet attached to his paper a portion of what Sarah had written about his draft: "After giving the information from." His tone here indicates confusion, which had arisen because he had not seen a small arrow directing the reader to continue to the back of the comment sheet. Once Sarah directed Alan to the back of the paper he continued reading her comment and then proceeded to paraphrase what she had written. Sarah had written, "After giving information from a source, tell the reader how to interpret it, emphasizing what is important about it." Alan paraphrases in the following manner: "Oh, uh huh, OK you mean first we indicate where it come from and then quote it and then afterward express in our own word, that's it?" Sarah then clarifies for Alan: "Yeah, you don't necessarily have to express it all in your own words." Alan interjects with "the main point," which leads Sarah to continue: "Right, the main point. Why did you include it? What do you want the reader to see from it? What conclusion can be drawn from this piece of evidence?" Once Alan understood that Sarah's comment was continued on the back of the comment sheet, he was able to read it and restate it for Sarah. In this instance, the misunderstanding stemmed not from an inability on Alan's part to interpret Sarah's words but, rather, from his oversight. He had not noted the arrow directing him to the back of the paper. Alan never commented to Sarah on this confusion, for to do so would have diverged from the intent of the meeting between the two. There was no point in Alan commenting on the fact that he had failed to see an arrow or even the need to apologize. There was no time for such digressions; the purpose of the conference was to understand what Sarah expected him to do to improve his draft.

The next exchange between Alan and Sarah was also marked by confusion. This confusion emerged over Sarah's first comment on his paper. She marked the sentence "Nowadays, there are about one half of the college students are Part-time students." in Alan's introduction with the comment: "sentence structure." Alan looked at Sarah's comment and said, "um, is it the idea's incomplete?" In class Sarah had defined a sentence as a complete thought. Alan had logically deduced that if she has indicated he has a problem with a sentence it might very likely be that he has not presented a complete thought. This is not what Sarah was referring to in this case, however. Sarah attempted to clarify the intent of her comment with "No, no, it just means that you have here, I write sentence structure when I don't know what to call it. All right, it's not a fragment and it's not a run-on, OK, but you have 'nowadays there are about one half of the college students are part time students.' You have two ideas." After Sarah finished reading his sentence, Alan attempted to interject with "what." However, Sarah continued with her comment: "you have two ideas." At this point Alan responded incredulously with "Two ideas!" Sarah then says, "What were you going to say first?" Alan, who was now quite flustered, answered, "No, I just want to indicate I mean, I mean, nowadays I mean, I mean recent, there are about one half of students they are part time students." This should not be interpreted as two ideas; Sarah responded with, "But you've said it in two clauses. One clause you've said 'there are about one half of the college students.' In your second clause you've said 'they're part time students' and you don't have any link. This 'college students' here is doing double duty."

Alan began to read again the problem sentence: "There are but one half of the stu . . . OK, I try again." Sarah interjected with "OK, yeah you just need to restructure it a little bit. OK." Thus ended a very problematic exchange between Sarah and Alan, an exchange that could have been avoided had Sarah just indicated that the problem was grammatical and all Alan needed to do was drop the first "there are." Alan, sensing their exchange was leading nowhere, had the good sense to end this portion of the conference by indicating he would try again. Just two questions into the conference, Sarah and Alan have met only with confusion.

Back on Track

Had the tone that had been maintained to this point continued throughout the conference, the final outcome would not have been so positive. But at this point the tone and the direction of the conference changed. Alan was quite deft at redirecting the focus of the conference so that the interaction reflected positively on the work he had put into his paper thus far. He was able not only to redirect the focus of the conference to the amount of work he had done but also to indicate to Sarah that his knowledge of reference materials in the library was quite sophisticated. Further, Alan was able to communicate to her that he was more than a mere initiate into the community of writers and researchers, despite the fact that he had but limited experience doing library research. The following exchange, which began immediately after Sarah suggested Alan need only restructure the problematic sentence under discussion, illustrates how this was accomplished:

A1   You know here
T2   Uh-huh.

Alan was referring here to the following paragraph in his paper, next to which Sarah had written "Can you find a source to support this?"

> There are several arguments against students having part-time jobs. First of all, part-time jobs distract students' study. Once students engaged in part-time jobs, their purchasing power becomes much stronger. They can afford more consumable goods which non-working students can not obtain. The more they can earn, the more they tend to work. Monetary power in this capitalistic society distracts students' interest from study to work. Student may decide to drop-out of school as they think the opportunity cost—their earning power and the huge tuition bill accumulated till their graduation—would be outrageous. The virtue of liberal art education will be overridden by the material world.

The exchange between Sarah and Alan in reference to this passage continued:

A3   You know this is only based on, I mean my own interpretation.
T4   Uh-huh.

A5　I mean I couldn't find anything. Now maybe there's two information, two sources which I, I think is very useful.

T6　Uh-huh.

A7　There's maybe, as you can see my list of sources, I have too much already.

T8　I know. I know. I know. Well, I think maybe what you can do, I mean, I don't think you need to get more information, but here you said that part-time jobs distract students' study. That's the argument, all right?

A9　Yeah. Well, mental because they got more money and then they interest on getting more money rather than on getting to study.

T10　RIGHT. All right, if you can maybe, have you looked at those sources? (referring to his reference list)

A11　Yeah. Most of them.

T12　Most of them. OK. Well, it would just be good if you could find something that would substantiate this. (light laughter here from Sarah)

A13　If not, then do you mean that I have to develop another argument and then take it out?

T14　No, no, no, you can still use it. You can still use it, but in a research paper it is always good if you make a claim

A15　(overlaps with "make a claim") support it.

T16　Right, so maybe just kind of, um, go through those sources or, um, I'm trying to think where you might find this kinda information.

A17　You know, it's kind of economic aspect.

T18　Yeah, it's an economic aspect, but it's also a psychological aspect.

A19　Yeah. Yeah, I tried to find some book that's psychological effect on this issue but there's nothing.

T20　There's nothing!

A21　I mean, I used ERIC. I used educational index.

T22　Yeah, right, right.

A23　And I used, I mean the computer source from the public library for all the journal article and nothing about, I mean, this.

T24　Yeah.

A25　Nothing about psychological effect.

T26　OK.

A27　Or maybe I, I can use the reference from all these articles they have reference.

T28　Yeah! That's a good place to look! I know that's really a long search. The other thing you might do is tell the librarian specifically what you're looking for.

A29　Uh-huh.

T30　Say I'm looking for a source that would tell me the psychological aspects, the psychological effects that part-time jobs have on students.

A31　Uh-huh.

T32　And the librarian might know more where to look. I mean you might try psychological abstracts. I mean that's an index of psychological journals, but a lot of them are very, very involved.

A33   They involved more than that. I mean it's very, it's very abstract.

T34   Right, right! It is, it is. You're right, you're right, you're right! (light laughter) But I would ask a librarian before you go into psychological abstracts.

What did Alan accomplish in this exchange? How did he turn the conference around so that it continued to reflect positively on his achievements? In this exchange, Sarah remained rather neutral in her response to Alan until he, in section A7, commented on the number of sources he had for the paper, thus directing Sarah to a positive aspect of his work. Then, in T8, Sarah responded in the affirmative. In fact, she emphatically agreed that Alan has a good number of sources. This is revealed in the three-time repetition of "I know." Sarah then stated directly that Alan need not get more information, and she turned instead to an examination of his argument that part-time jobs distract students from their schoolwork. Alan then categorized his argument, in A9, as relating to student psychological considerations by referring to "mental." Sarah, in T10 and T12, emphatically agreed with Alan's assessment and suggested he review the sources he already had to see if he could substantiate the argument. At that point, in A13, Alan wondered aloud whether he could leave the argument in his paper if he was not able to find a source to substantiate it. Sarah, in T14, assured him that he could leave it in, despite the fact that the argument was based entirely on supposition. Sarah either shared Alan's opinion on this matter or had been convinced by his argument, and she was willing to accept it whether the argument was backed up with a reference or not.

Alan Insinuates Himself into the Discourse of the Academy

In Alan's next response a pattern of interaction was established that was repeated throughout the conference. Sarah stated in T14, "but in a research paper it is always good if you make a claim." In A15, Alan completed her statement with the correct answer as he overlapped "make a claim" with "support it." This fill-in-the-blank pattern, if you will, occurred over and over as the conference continued. Another pattern that continued throughout the conference emerged here also. Sarah often repeated verbatim what Alan had just said, and by doing so she both affirmed and confirmed his words. This is seen in A17, when Alan said "you know it's kind of economic aspect," and Sarah responded in T18 with "yeah, it's an economic aspect, but it's also a psychological aspect." Of course Alan had already in A9 commented on the mental aspect of this issue. By T18, Sarah not only repeated Alan's words but also mimicked his intonation. This occured in the repeated "there's nothing," uttered with the same rising intonation Alan used. The sequence ended with Alan displaying his knowledge of ERIC in A21, of the psychological abstracts in A33, and of his understanding that when Sarah mentioned, in T32, that psychological journals are very involved, she was in fact referring to the abstract issues with which they deal. By this point in the conference, Sarah and Alan were engaged in a conversation that could occur between peers who are commiserating over the density of particular source materials and the difficulty of finding sources for their work. This was not a conversation in which Sarah was at all times the all-knowing teacher who provides her student with answers to his questions but, rather an exchange in which colleagues share inside jokes about the difficulties of doing research. Thus, in a very short period of time, Alan had been able to begin to insinuate himself into the discourse of the academy. In other words, he had begun the process of proving to Sarah that he belongs.

In the second, and again in the final, draft of his paper Alan made only grammatical and structural changes in the paragraph in which he argued that part-time jobs distract students from studying because they become enticed by the ability to purchase material goods. Nor did he revise another paragraph in which he presented an unsubstantiated argument. Later in the conference Sarah suggested Alan interview a student who worked part-time in order to substantiate his argument. He never followed through on this suggestion, nor did Sarah ever follow up on whether or not Alan had revised as she had suggested. Alan did follow through on Sarah's comment that he evaluate information from a source or, as Sarah refers to the process, "integrate." He does integrate where Sarah has directed him to do so throughout his second and final drafts of his paper.

How to Get an Extension

At the end of the sequence discussed above, Alan sought a due date extension for his second draft.

A1   OK, before I ask any more questions can I know when the second draft is due? (Alan knows very well when it is due.)

T2   Sure, Tuesday.

A3   Oh, I hardly have any time.

T4   I know, that's the problem with taking a course in the summertime.

A5   (overlaps Sarah beginning with "taking") Yeah, because you know I have to work on Friday the whole day and then the afternoon is closed, everything is closed, and then Monday is closed because

T6   Oh right.

A7   holiday and the weekend I, I, I'm going to New York, going down

T8   Right.

A9   I mean,

T10   Yeah, that's the problem with taking a course in the summertime.

A11   Yeah, you know even if I don't go down to New York I have no, no time to look up these sources.

T12   Yeah, well I'll tell you what, if you sign up for a conference next Thursday instead of Wednesday, you could give me your paper Wednesday.

A13   OK.

T14   But, I mean I really have to have it then

A15   Yeah, sure.

T16   because the following Wednesday is the last day

A17   Uh-huh.

T18   and the final draft is due.

A19   Yeah. I mean once I sign up I have to do I mean if that's the, I mean

T20   I mean that's as much as I can give you in a six-week course. (Both laugh)

Alan never asked Sarah directly for an extension but, rather, maneuvered her to the subject indirectly by expressing how hard it was for him to work on the paper. Alan argued he would have difficulty meeting the Tuesday deadline because he works, because he was planning to travel to New York for the weekend, and because the school library would be closed when he returns due to the Fourth of July holiday. Sarah initially resisted his attempts to get an extension, as seen in T4 and T10, but she finally agreed as Alan continued to add reason upon reason for his inability to do the research in the next week. Sarah ended by offering Alan an extension even though he never directly requested one. Though Zola, Tan, and Araya were just as pressured as Alan, none received an extension for their second draft. From this point on the conference between Alan and Sarah continued harmoniously.

Fill-in-the-Blank

In what follows I present another example that illustrates the fill-in-the-blank structure that occurred frequently during the exchange between Sarah and Alan. This recurring pattern is striking not only because of the manner in which it illustrates how much Sarah and Alan were aware of one another's intent but also because the pattern does not occur in the interactions between Sarah and Zola, Tan, or Araya. Clearly, Alan was the most in tune with the instructor. This is apparent in the following exchange between Sarah and Alan in which they discussed Alan's use of brackets around the word "work." Alan had written the following: "In Mary Roark's opinion, [work] promotes developmental growth in college students in ways that are not available through academic and social experience alone . . . ."

A1   (mutters as he looks through paper) What's this indicate?

T2   Yeah, yeah, and this you can only use brackets

A3   inside.

T4   Right.

A5   Uh-huh.

T6   So if you just, is this your own word that you just put in there? (referring to "work")

A7   Yeah, because it in fact it in this source it said "it" instead of "work."

T8   Oh does that change the meaning?

A9   No.

T10   All right, well then you could you could

A11   leave this out. (overlaps with second "could")

T12   Right, right, because you're not quoting it.

A13   Yeah.

T14   So you'd just begin your quotation marks over

A15   uh-huh because the word, I mean the, the, the word "it" represent "work" but I can't quote I mean

T16   Oh, I see. OK, all right, OK.

A17   So I should just leave this bracket out and this should do it.

T18   Right, yeah, yeah, that would be fine then.

In this exchange the issue of concern was Alan's use of brackets around the word "work." Brackets should not have been used because "work" is outside the quotation marks. "It" was used in place of "work" in the original source, but Alan decided to use "work" because the quote, out of context, would have made little sense if it contained a pronoun without a referent. Here, a great deal of effort went into negotiating the issue of punctuation despite the fact that, as mentioned earlier, punctuation was not the professed focus of the first conference. In this exchange Alan was very clearly in tune with what Sarah was concerned about regarding the brackets. Before Sarah was able to complete her explanation in T3 of where brackets can be used, Alan supplied for her the appropriate answer. Once Alan indicated that brackets should only be used inside quotation marks, the implication was that they should not be used in this instance. Then in T6 through T8, Sarah tried to clarify whether Alan has chosen the word "work" himself or whether "work" did, in fact, come from the quote. Once Sarah was sure that the quote did not include "work" and that "it," as used in the quote, did in fact refer to "work," she once again set out to tell Alan how he should handle this technical issue by giving him explicit directions. And finally, in this section of the exchange between Alan and Sarah, Alan completed statements begun by Sarah in A3, A11, and A15. These three examples illustrate clearly the fill-in-the-blank pattern seen throughout the conference. In turn, the pattern establishes the extent to which Alan was able to anticipate the direction of Sarah's talk.

Prior to turning to a brief analysis of what transpired in the second conference between Alan and Sarah, I present one more example of an exchange that illustrates the fill-in-the-blank pattern described above. This exchange occurred near the end of the conference.

A1   You know here

T2   Uh-huh.

Here Alan refers to a paragraph near the end of his paper in which he discusses a work program at Berry College in Mount Berry, Georgia.

A3   It's, I have already told, I mean, indicated on the paper that it's from this college.

T4   Uh-huh, but where's this from? This seems to be from like

A5   Yeah, it's from the page. I mean it's a quotation from.

T6   Right, but it seems here you've said a student work program has been a vital part of Berry's founding in 1902. OK here this is, it seems to be

A7   I need to, some kind of introduction to indicate it.

T8   You're right, this is an introduction to this long quotation, but you don't need to quote this because it is very, it's fact the college provides valuable learning experiences and helps students.

A9   But I need, it's a, it's a writer's word or theirs.

T10   Right. So I would paraphrase it

A11   Paraphrase it and then

T12   and not, and not um, endnote because it just says a student work program has been a vital part of Berry since its founding in 1902. That's just a fact. OK. I mean it's not anybody's idea. It's just saying it's the state of the way things are.

A13   Uh-huh, and then this can serve as the introduction for this quotation

T14   Uh-huh. Right. (overlaps this quotation)

A15   and then integrate at the end.

T16   Yep.

A17   I mean why I need to say this.

T18   Yeah, because you have shown an example of a college who has this. What do you want the reader to get from that example?

A19   Yeah. This whole thing.

In A1 Alan oriented Sarah to the point in his paper he wishes to discuss, and then, in A3, he attempted to clarify his intent in the section under discussion. In T4, Sarah asked "Where is this from?" She was referring to a quote Alan had used in his paper. This first quote was followed by a longer, indented quote that discusses the philosophy of Berry College. The first quote was: "The college provide valuable learning experiences and helps student meet educational expenses. A student work program has been a vital part of Berry since its founding in 1902." Alan had not indicated in the text the source of the quotation. This was a common issue of concern throughout his paper. In T4, Sarah continued with "This seems to be from like. . ." and in A5, before Sarah could finish, Alan completed her statement and continued with "I mean it's a quotation from. . . ." Then, before he could finish Sarah broke in, in T6, indicating that she seemed concerned about where the student work program was from and not where the quotation was from. By A7 Alan sorted out what he believed Sarah wanted him to do in this instance. He thought Sarah wanted him to explain where the quote came from by providing an introduction to it. In T8 Sarah indicated that she agreed with Alan, but her agreement was with something other than what Alan had said. Sarah saw the quote as an introduction to the next quotation in his paper. Though the two were in agreement, they were, in fact, agreeing to two different things. Alan believed Sarah wanted him to introduce the first quotation, while Sarah wanted him to use the information contained in the first quotation to introduce the second quote. Now that the two had come to a tenuous agreement, they continued to sort out what Alan should do to revise in this instance. This sorting out continued through T7 and A8. In both utterances Sarah and Alan countered one another's words with *but,* showing contrasting views of what Alan has done and then should do to revise. Finally, in T10 the issues of concern were sorted out. Sarah agreed with Alan and suggested how he should correct the problem. Sarah suggested that, rather than quote the section that explains when Berry College was founded, Alan should paraphrase it. Then the two worked harmoniously to map out the steps Alan should take. In A11, in response to Sarah's suggestion that he paraphrase, Alan said, "Paraphrase it and then. . . ." In T12, Sarah continued what Alan had begun and supplied more direction and a rationale for paraphrasing. In A13, Alan once again built on what Sarah began and indicated that he now understands what she meant by "introduction." This was done implicitly, because nowhere in the exchange did either indicate that a misunderstanding might have occurred. Finally, in A15, Alan completed the sequence by explaining that at the end he will integrate, as Sarah had suggested he do by writing "integrate" on his paper. By indicating that he will integrate Alan meant that he would explain to the reader why he wrote what he did. Throughout this exchange Sarah and Alan worked through a misunderstanding concerning the use of "introduction," and by the end of the exchange they were able to play off of one another's comments. Never, in either conference, did Alan openly express frustration or disagreement with anything Sarah said although, as is the case above, they were initially engaged in instances of miscommunication.

The Second Conference

Before turning to a discussion and analysis of what transpired in conference between Zola and Sarah, I discuss briefly the pattern of exchange between Alan and Sarah, which occurred in the second conference. The purpose of the second conference was to deal with problems related to grammar, punctuation, and spelling as well as issues of organization, content, and research. Throughout Alan's second draft, Sarah marked errors in verb tense, formation of plurals, spelling, sentence structure, spacing, and so forth. Two of her comments dealt with the content of the paper.

The second conference began, as had the first, with Sarah asking whether Alan had any questions. He immediately responded in the affirmative and focused directly on the text, referring Sarah to the first comment she had made on his paper. The problems Sarah focused on now in Alan's paper could be dealt with quickly and without extended negotiation. The following exchange, which occurred at the very outset of the conference, illustrates the pace at which Sarah's comments were dealt with. Sarah had just asked Alan whether he had any questions.

A1   Yeah, I mean is that you just want me have a single one space maybe like this?
T2   Yeah, it should be like the whole rest of the paper.
A3   Oh, really.
T4   Uh-huh.
A5   Oh, OK. Yeah, is it the wrong word you say?
T6   Yeah, the wrong word.
A7   How about it has gone down?
T8   Let's see. (spoken as Sarah reads Alan's paper.)
A10   Or it went down or it has gone down.
T11   Yeah, you can either say it went down or it has gone down. Either one is fine.
A12   OK.

Here Alan elicited from Sarah first the correct manner in which she wants him to reformat his paper and then a verb tense correction. Alan did not ask Sarah directly for the right answer but, rather, offered his suggestion for change and waited for confirmation that what he had said was correct. After these two corrections Alan dealt with two more that concerned misunderstandings on his part about how to use particular phrases in English. In each case Sarah explained the problem and then confirmed or elaborated on Alan's suggested correction.

After dealing with these four problems Alan sought confirmation from Sarah that the conference could continue in the manner in which it had thus far.

A1   I spend some time just to see what corrections I can make and see if it makes sense to you.
T2   Yeah sure.

Alan asked a question, although he used a declarative statement. His statement/question reflects the manner in which the conference had proceeded thus far. His statement was direct, explicitly stating the manner in which he hoped to proceed in this conference, if Sarah approves. Alan took time to correct his mistakes throughout the paper and then seek confirmation from Sarah about the appropriateness of his changes. The conference continued in this manner, with Alan and Sarah often joking about changes and errors as they went along. This is apparent in the following exchange.

A1   Uh-huh. OK. (reads) Now I think I shouldn't use semicolon.
T2   Right, you can only use a semicolon if you have two complete sentences on either side of it.

A3   Yeah, I don't know how it is it was there.

T4   Oh, it just popped up from outer space, right?

Sarah's willingness to joke with Alan, to deal with every correction he chose to make on his paper, to grant him an extension, and to interact with him as a near equal all indicate the extent to which she viewed Alan as a student writer in control of the development of his paper. Never once, for example, did Sarah become frustrated with Alan or lapse into lecturing as a form of conveying information to him. Rather than dealing with generalities when discussing his work, Sarah and Alan focused on very specific aspects of his paper that needed correction more than revision.

10

STUDENT AND INSTRUCTOR SPAR FOR CONTROL: ZOLA IN CONFERENCE

> Unsuccessful conversation is maddening.—Deborah Tannen, *Conversational Style: Analyzing Talk among Friends*

Who Is in Control Anyway?

Zola's conferences with Sarah, although amiable for the most part, differed overall in tone and focus from Alan's. Whereas Alan's conferences with Sarah were harmonious, Zola's interactions with her were often marked by tension and conflict, in particular over the direction and goals of the conferences. It was at these points, when communication broke down, that each or both of the participants, Sarah and Zola, surely felt this maddening state that Tannen describes in the epigraph to this chapter. While Zola took control in her conferences, she did so in a manner far different than Alan had. Zola was not at all constrained by Sarah's comments. Sarah and Zola often overlapped one another, and, in so doing, each sought to establish the direction of the talk through a process of verbal dueling. And finally, whereas Alan had, when appropriate, made indirect requests of Sarah, Zola was overly direct in circumstances deemed inappropriate within academic culture, contributing to the tension between her and Sarah.

Zola was kept waiting past the time at which her conference was to begin while Sarah continued to discuss Alan's paper with him. By making Zola wait, Sarah implicitly conveyed the message that she, Sarah, was in control of the conference. Zola was put in her place. Though she attempted to get Sarah to begin

159

her conference on time by calling into the office from the hall when it was time for her appointment, her efforts failed. This was coupled with the fact that Zola, who was used to receiving As on her written work, had received on her first draft of this paper her second low grade from Sarah; she received a C+ on her previous essay and has received a C on the first draft of her research paper.

Do Not Speak of Grades

When the conference between Zola and Sarah finally began, the grade was the focus of Zola's concern.

T1   OK. Come on in, Zola.

Z2   I'm going to have surgery on that. (referring to her draft, which she holds)

T3   Your paper is going to have surgery?

Z4   (moans)

T5   You have questions

Z7   Oh, my god, you don't know how much I got. (laughs)

T8   I mean that's fine for a first

Z9   Nooo. Oh, I got a C, really!

T10   Really it's not. The final draft is worth 30 percent of your grade and the first draft is only worth 10 percent, so don't worry about it. All right now, your question.

Zola entered Sarah's office attempting, in Z2, to make a joke of the state of her first draft. This is in sharp contrast to Alan's first remarks during his first conference. Alan never alluded to his grade but, rather, went right to the business at hand—trying to understand Sarah's comments and figure out specific strategies for revising his paper. In T3, Sarah responded to Zola by asking a question to clarify whether Zola was referring to her first draft when she mentioned surgery. By T5, Sarah directed Zola to ask questions about her paper. Zola, though, was not yet ready to settle down to the task at hand by asking a specific question and, while sitting slumped back despondently in her chair, once again derogatorily joked, in Z7, about her draft. In T8, Sarah attempted to reassure Zola, but before she could complete her comment Zola interrupted, in Z9, to contradict Sarah. In T10, Sarah explained her grading policy in a further attempt to allay Zola's fears and to end the discussion so that they might begin the conference.

In this exchange, Zola repeatedly stepped out of the confines of expected conference behavior by discussing issues of concern only to her (her low grade) and not to Sarah. Academics do not wish to discuss grades. Students should be motivated not by the desire to achieve good grades but by their deep and singular interest in the subject matter in which we wish to engage them. In other words, Zola was expected to ask questions in reference to Sarah's comments and not to veer from this implicitly established pattern for interaction in the writing conference. Both in T5 and T10, Sarah focused Zola to this pattern.

How to Not Get an Extension

Though at the beginning of the conference Zola behaved quite differently than Alan, at the very end of the conference she began an exchange about due dates with Sarah in much the same way Alan did when he asked Sarah when the second draft of his paper was due. (No student in Sarah's course should have been confused about when assignments were due because she had provided them with a calendar showing each day of the course. This calendar, as well as the syllabus, gave due dates for papers, descriptions of assignments, and dates for quizzes and the exam.) In Zola's case, however, the outcome of the exchange about the due date of the second draft was very different than Alan's had been.

Here is the final exchange between Sarah and Zola during Zola's first conference, an exchange in which Zola asks when the second draft is due and, by doing so, indirectly requests a due date extension.

Z1   OK. I think I understand this thing now. (mumbles) All right.

T2   OK.

Z3   When do we have to. . . . Oh, I have those things. (in reference to handouts Sarah gives her anticipating the exchange to follow.)

T4   Tuesday.

Z5   Second draft?

T6   Yep.

Z7   Ooohhh.

T8   This course is a killer in the summertime.

Z9   I have two courses.

T10 You do?

Z11 Yeah.

T11 What's your other course?

Z12 Psychology. (Zola goes on to explain that she has two papers in psychology that are like exams and has already had one other exam in the course)

T13 My word, you're pretty busy these six weeks. (both laugh)

Z14 I had just a week between semesters.

T15 [Zola], we have the open book exam in class.

And thus ended the conference between Sarah and Zola. Zola had unsuccessfully attempted to get an extension for her second draft; although Sarah acknowledged that Zola was extremely busy she did not demonstrate any sympathy, nor did she volunteer to give her an extra day as she did with Alan. This may be the case because Alan used a very different ploy in indirectly asking for an extension. Even though he too had a second course, he did not mention it in his discussion with Sarah. He focused solely on her course and his concern that he would not be able to do the work she required because he would not be able to get to the library (because he worked and because the library would be closed over the holiday weekend). Alan also mentioned that he was traveling to New York over the weekend.

Zola also had to contend with the holiday weekend, but she chose to focus on the fact that she had two courses, diminishing her focus on and interest in Sarah's course. And even though going out of town on a holiday weekend does not seem to be a very fitting excuse for an extension, Alan got one and Zola did not. I believe this is because Alan made Sarah's course and the work he had to do for it the central focus of his concern, whereas Zola focused on the fact that she was very busy with her second course. Sarah strongly believed that English should be regarded as just as demanding a course as any other course in the university. Anyone who has had the experience of teaching knows that central to academic culture is the notion we all share that "our course" is the one that students should focus on. To suggest otherwise is to denigrate not only our perceived status but also the status of our course. Sarah had gone to great lengths to establish credibility and status for 102, and she had expressed a concern that some students did not take the writing class as seriously as they did their other courses. In privileging the demands of her psychology course over those of her writing course, Zola has broken an implicit cultural assumption that Sarah holds dear. In addition, Alan may have succeeded in getting an extension because he brought up the subject at a high point in his interaction with Sarah, whereas Zola waited until the end of what was, at times, a frustrating conference to deal with the issue of when the next draft was due.

Minor Editing: Who Gets Help and Who Does Not

Another exchange, this from the second conference between Zola and Sarah, illustrates the difference in the quality of the help Zola received from Sarah compared to Alan. In this exchange Zola attempted to elicit from Sarah the correct spelling for two words Sarah had marked in her text as being misspelled.

Z1   OK. Now. (pauses as she looks through paper for next comment from Sarah) How do you spell *interfere*?

T2   Ooohh, do you have a dictionary?

Z3   I do have a dictionary, but I don't know why, with an *re*, right?

T4   Yeah, that's what you need.

Z5   Oh, this has the same thing (refers to text as goes through it) Now I can see what I did. What is the spelling this word?

T6   OK. [Zola], I know you're tired, but I have another appointment at 1:30 and there's somebody else who missed his appointment this morning that I have to see.

Z7   Oh.

T8   OK.

Compare this sequence between Zola and Sarah with the following, which occurred during Alan's second conference with Sarah.

A1   And here, you think there should be a y there?

T2   Yeah.

A3   OK. Check out.

T4   Spelling.

T5   Yeah.

A6   I mean I used this as an adjective not verb.

T7   Right, but when you use it as an adjective

A8   it should be f

T9   (pause) and just a comma here describing the whole thing.

T10   Right.

A11   Should be a colon.

T12   Yeah, you could use a comma, colon there. Yeah that would be fine.

A13   I thought this, all this is, is parallel.

T14   Yeah.

A15   No, "the actual feeling" (and mumbles "parallel").

T16   Let me see. (reads silently) Yes, that's fine. I must have read it wrong, sorry.

A17   I bet because you have so much to read. (both laugh)

In Z1, Zola asked very directly for the correct spelling of *interfere,* which she had misspelled in her paper. In T2, Sarah countered with another question: "Oh, do you have a dictionary?" This was an indirect request that Zola look up the word and not ask Sarah how to spell it. Sarah was very much opposed to giving answers to students when she felt they should be able to get the answer themselves. In fact, she had told students in class that she was not going to tell them how to spell words. In class she told the following anecdote about librarians.

While I'm talking about librarians let me say one thing. All right? Librarians: A librarian's job is to help people find information. Don't ever be afraid to talk to a librarian, and don't feel that a librarian is going to think you're stupid. All right? That's why we have courses in research writing. Tomorrow when I take you on your tour—I'm not a librarian, but since the library doesn't do tours anymore I have to do them—you might ask me a question and I will say I don't know, and after the tour together we will go ask the librarian. I was once in a public library and I was at the information desk. And the telephone rang and a woman called and asked the librarian how to spell a word. Now, if I were the librarian I would've probably gotten pretty upset. I would have said, "Don't you have a dictionary? Can't you look it up?" Instead the librarian got her dictionary out, looked it up, and told the person on the other end of the phone how to spell the word. All right. So you can ask the librarian anything. And a lot of people think, "Oh well, I'm going to ask this question and the librarian's going to think I'm so stupid." All right? Never, ever think that way. That's their job. All right?

Looking up words in a dictionary may have been part of a librarian's job, but it was not part of Sarah's. Her students were to be self-sufficient in the literate environment of the university.

In Z3, thinking perhaps that Sarah meant she should have looked up the word before putting it in her paper, and not that she should now go look up the word, Zola tried a new tactic for obtaining the correct spelling from Sarah: She supplied an alternative spelling herself. Sarah responded by verifying Zola's spelling change. Then in Z5, Zola tried again to get Sarah to respond directly to her request for the spelling of another misspelled word in her paper. Sarah, now very frustrated, explicitly acknowledged that Zola was tired and as a result was, perhaps, not quite of sound mind. (Sarah was aware that Zola had stayed up all night the night before the conference to study for a psychology exam, leaving her too tired to attend to the writing conference in an appropriate manner.) Sarah dismissed Zola's questions by not responding or commenting directly on Zola's request to have the word spelled. Instead Sarah told Zola that she had an appointment at 1:30 and another one thereafter. Sarah indirectly communicated to Zola that her time with Sarah was limited and should be spent on matters more important than spelling. In other words, Sarah would not and could not, as she had other obligations, attend only to Zola's needs.

In contrast, the exchange between Sarah and Alan proceeded in an entirely different manner, despite the fact that both students were dealing with issues related to very minor editing. In Zola's case, the exchange ended in frustration. But in Alan's case, the exchange ended on a very positive note, with Alan expressing his understanding of how hard Sarah must work in order to read all her students' papers. Why did the exchange between Alan and Sarah end successfully, while the one between Zola and Sarah met with failure?

Both sequences start with the students attempting to elicit from Sarah the correct spelling of a misspelled word in their text. However, while Zola asked Sarah directly how to spell the word, in A1 Alan asked Sarah whether a "y" should be placed where he indicated in his paper. Sarah answered without hesitation in the affirmative in T2. Alan then, in A3, began to announce he will check it out, and before he could complete his intent, Sarah, as was often the case, completed his statement with "spelling." Then in A6 Alan, now discussing a different misspelled word, commented about the part of speech of the word. In T7 Sarah responded in the affirmative, confirming that Alan had correctly identified the part of speech of the word. Alan had correctly identified the part of speech, but he used this as a way to elicit the correct spelling changes. In T7 Sarah began to explain that when the word in question is used as an adjective it is spelled a particular way but, before she could finish, Alan, in the fill-in-the-blank pattern that characterized his conferences with Sarah (see chapter 9), provided the correct answer in A8: "it should be *f*." Alan had thus been able to get confirmation of the spelling of two words in his paper while Zola had only been able to get the correct spelling for one word. Thus, in two very topically similar exchanges between Sarah and two of her students, very different outcomes emerged, based primarily on a subtle difference in linguistic style. Zola, who was very direct in her request for the correct answer (as she had been for an extension as well), failed to achieve an entirely positive response from Sarah. Alan, who requested the correct answer (and an extension) indirectly, achieved positive results in each instance.

Zola Speaks to the Issues

Overall, Zola's conference with Sarah was quite different from the conferences between Sarah and Alan. Alan and Sarah never discussed issues dealing with the arguments he presented both for and against students working, other than to indicate how one example could be related to his topic.. In contrast, Zola wanted to talk about issues. Zola was not led through the conference solely by Sarah's written comments on her paper; Zola was willing to step out of the text or, rather, away from Sarah's comments on Zola's text, in an effort to sort through issues in which she (Zola) was interested. The following exchange took place at the beginning of the first conference. Zola had been trying to work out how to introduce quoted and paraphrased material in the body of her text. One issue Zola attempted to clarify was how to cite information that comes from an article for which the author is not listed. Further, she was attempting to explain that much of the information about her research topic was people's opinions and that the foundation for either side of the argument was not fact.

Z1   I think so. It was Hayakawa.

T2   OK.

Z3   And don't need it here. (referring to adding "U.S." to her text. She now begins a new topic in the next utterance.) When I, I find like something with a line in an article and doesn't say who said it I just put according to the article published in *New York Times.*

T4   Yup, right, right. (Sarah overlaps with Zola's "*New York Times*") And here, I mean in the body of your paper

Z5   so

T6   you don't even have to tell when it was published because all the information is going to be on your endnote page.

Z7   Yeah. OK.

T8   OK, but there are a lot of magazine and newspaper articles where the author isn't listed.

Z9   Yeah, this is the thing is not a single person or somebody did the research something like a lot of these just say, it's more political actually.

T10   Right, right. (overlaps "political actually")

Z11   than something scientific or you know.

T12   Right.

Z13   Like they throw things at you.

T14   Right.

Z15   Everybody has his argument.

T16   Uh-huh.

Z17   And I don't know if you saw the show on Monday at 10:00 p.m.

T18   No.

Z19   about language. My professor must be seeing this I'm sure.

T20   Noooo.

Z21   (unclear overlap section with drawn out "no") so they had Jerry Williams on Channel 25.

T22   Oh.

Z23   This debates between the pro and the entire ELA (English Language Amendment).

T24   Oh.

Z25   I recorded it. If you want to see it I have a copy.

T26   Oh, that's great.

Z27   I have it on a tape and uh it was two against the amendment and two pro.

T28   Well, you can use things from that.

Z29   I didn't want to use it until I asked you

T30   Oh yeah.

Z31   put it and everything. They were just throwing things, they have no, I mean nothing is like evidence,

T32   Yeah, right, right.

Z33   especially the English Only movement members.

T34   Uh-huh.

Z35   You know, I think was odd, you know like they even told the lady like uh he the one who was from the US English movement even said that accusing, that the non, the anti-ELA are against this amendment just because they want to make sure that there will be enough jobs for bilingual teachers.

T36   Oh yeah. (mutual laughter)

Z37   Discussions usually end with even in the newspapers articles something like that.

T38   Um, well, you're not going to find any evidence that it has to be this way or it has to be that way, you're, you're only dealing with people's opinions.

Z39   Yeah.

Z40   So I just have to report the people's opinions.

T41   Right.

Z42   So I try to. OK. (at this point Zola turns to a comment on her paper and proceeds to give a long explanation of what she had been attempting to say.)

What is interesting about this exchange between Zola and Sarah is, first of all, the amount of talking Zola did compared to Sarah; and second, the fact that Zola, not Sarah, initiated the topic. Zola was not content to deal with a succinct discussion surrounding the issue of how to introduce paraphrased and quoted material but, instead, needed to explain that, due to the nature of her topic, she could not find sources that reported factual information based on scientific research. Zola illustrated the political nature of her topic by recounting a television program that featured individuals arguing for and against the English Language Amendment. Clearly Zola wanted to talk about her topic and, in so doing, attempted to sort out the various arguments that surface surrounding the issue. In class, Sarah talked and students listened; while in conference with Zola, Sarah did a lot of listening and Zola did a lot of talking. In class Sarah introduced topics for discussion; in their conferences, it was Zola who often introduced the topic for discussion. By doing so, however, Zola spent time away from direct response to Sarah's comments on the paper. And though she did consider most of Sarah's comments on her paper, Zola also considered issues relevant to her interests and concerns.

Structural Confusion

Zola also, unlike Alan, did not deal with the comments Sarah made on the evaluation sheet attached to her paper. One comment in particular was not dealt with at all during the first conference. Sarah had written the following: "What side of the issue are you on? Your paper shows you are for the amendment, but your conclusion seems to say differently." In indicating that Zola's paper shows she is for the amendment, Sarah meant that Zola had organized her paper so that the arguments against the ELA were presented first and the arguments in favor followed. Zola's conclusion took a stand against the amendment. In fact, in class Sarah had provided the required format for the argumentative paper: the paper should begin with an introduction, a section with the arguments against the issue the writer supports (the cons) should follow, next should be a longer section with the arguments for the issue the writer supports (the pros), and then the paper should conclude with a summary statement of the writer's side. Zola reversed the order of presentation of the pros and cons, but this issue was not dealt with directly at any time during the first conference.

The fact, however, that Zola did not support the ELA was conveyed implicitly throughout the first conference, such as in Z35, when Zola commented that during the television show one woman supporting the ELA suggested that people opposed it "just because they want to make sure that there will be enough jobs for bilingual teachers." The fact that Sarah and Zola were able to laugh together about this argument implied an understanding that they both ridicule the pro-ELA position. Despite Sarah's written comment on the first draft regarding format, however, Zola used the same structure for her second draft. On the comment sheet attached to the second draft Sarah wrote, "Good organization and good evaluation of the arguments. A few points need clarification—see my questions. Your conclusion gives the reader the impression that you agree with the other side. Do you?"

Here, and in the comments on the first draft, Sarah did not specifically explain to Zola that she needed to change the order in which she had presented the arguments for and against the ELA. It was not until the final paper was handed in that Sarah dealt directly in writing with the issue. At the very end of Zola's final paper Sarah wrote the final comment: "Good—but from your conclusion you really should have switched the order in which you presented the sides." Sarah persisted throughout in reading through form—the structure of the paper—Zola's perceived position vis-à-vis the ELA, yet Zola's conclusion, as Sarah did note, indicated she was against the ELA, and Zola's comments throughout the two conferences implicitly, and at times explicitly, conveyed her opposition to the amendment. Here is an example of the power form plays in conveying meaning. Sarah had explicitly taught the form she expected students to follow in the presentation of the opposing positions in their research papers. And despite face-to-face encounters with Zola, who had reversed the required format, Sarah failed to read beyond form.

This inability to read beyond form was compounded by the fact that students are generally prohibited from introducing directly their own perspectives on an issue in the papers. "I" cannot be used; the opinions of others can be presented in support of a position, but only if these opinions can be documented. Students are asked to take "sides," but they are not allowed to insert their own voices into the papers directly. They must do so through form—how the arguments are presented, and in what order—and in the amount of attention spent on one side versus the other. The arguments against an issue are given less space; the pros—the side of the argument the student has chosen to support—have more paragraphs than do the cons. Zola had devoted more words and paragraphs to her position regarding the ELA. However, she privileged her position by placing it first in the research paper, which was "against the rules" and obfuscated Sarah's ability to truly read for the meaning and intent of the author, Zola.

Which Side Are You on Anyway?

During the conferences, and in the comments that were written on Zola's paper, Sarah never commented explicitly about whether Zola was for or against the English Language Amendment but, rather, referred to the anti-ELA position simply as "the other side" in her query regarding Zola's position. Zola would have been helped far more had Sarah commented more specifically, as in the following.

Are you opposed to the English Language Amendment? If so your paper should present the arguments for the ELA first, and then you should follow with the arguments against the ELA. Since you are opposed to the ELA (your conclusion seems to indicate that this is your position), your paper should include more arguments against the amendment than for it. If I am correct about where you stand on the issue (and I believe I am) your paper should follow the format I have just presented. This format will allow your conclusion to flow more naturally from the arguments you present against the amendment. In addition, I made it clear in class that I require that your paper be formatted in the manner I have just described.

Zola received an A– on the paper. The paper was well written and well researched—Zola had already had a class (101E) that took the English Language Amendment as its central focus for reading, discussion, and writing, so she was well informed about the topic. She also had numerous sources for the research paper already in hand because she was able to use the course packet from 101E as a resource for her research paper. Zola's final paper had only two minor errors in the text. Thus, not until it was too late to change the organization of the paper did Sarah deal explicitly in writing with the issue of the structure of Zola's paper.

The issue of organization was dealt with verbally in the second conference, but in an exchange filled with misunderstandings and confusion. The discussion of which side of the issue Zola supported proceeded as follows.

Z1   Um (mumbles, turns to the last page of her draft). Oh, I support the other side. (This comment is in response to Sarah's written comment after Zola's conclusion, "your conclusion sounds as though you are on the other side!")

Because Zola has structured her paper in the manner she has, Sarah assumed erroneously that Zola supported the ELA. Zola's conclusion, however, indicated otherwise. In her conclusion Zola had written,

> By its own account, the "official English" movement seeks to stimulate debate on the sensitive issue of language. However, the movement makes language the rallying point for simmering intolerance, frustration, fear and distrust. State declaration of an official language invites legal, political, and cultural challenges to bilingual services and to other programs. Thus, we may soon have to determine how far these declarations can go to mandating the needs of non-English speakers. The equal protection clause of the Fourteenth Amendment prohibits state action limiting the rights of language minorities. These declarations will only stand as hollow symbols of our generation's xenophobia.

The exchange between Sarah and Zola in reference to the conclusion continued.

T2   Well (laughs), then maybe you should change around your sides or change your conclusion because you wanna conclude, I mean you want, you've presented in your paper the side, that side that you're presenting, if it's not your own side in your conclusion you should at least should sound like it is your side or

Z3   Uh, I'm on the side of the, uh, anti-ELA.

T4   So you think that we should have the ELA.

Z5   No, we should not. We should not have the English Language Amendment.

T6   Then you should switch the sides of your paper because the cause

Z7   That's what I've done before, but it didn't work that way. I know whatever the cause because, I don't know.

T8   If your thesis is that we should not have the ELA

Z9   It's just a question actually.

T10   All right.

Z11   Should we have it, all right?

T12   Should we have it? (overlaps with Z11 at "should" midword)

Z13   Do we need an ELA and what would be its implications?

T14   But if you're, all right, but if you're going to conclude that we should not have it then you should mention the other side first which is that we should (pause)

Z15   Yeah, OK, so I should ask the question just in other words.

T16   Because right now you're gonna

Z17   That's why I asked you about it a long time ago, remember, in the library I said I have to switch my, uh, that (unclear) to cause you know whether to have

T18   Well, to have (overlaps from unclear word in Z17) Well, now it sounds like

Z19   I still have a problem with that I don't know

T20   'cause (overlaps "know")

Z21   In order to speak about the ELA I have to speak about the common language (pause) see like instead of talking about the healthy person have to switch something to say sickness you know and I don't know how to try.

T22   Well, you don't really have to do that if your conclusion is going to be that we should not have the ELA, then the other side is gonna be the reasons why we should have it because right now your conclusion does not naturally flow out of the rest of your paper. Your conclusion seems to be something very different from the argument that you have been building in the last part of your paper.

Z23   Yeah it goes mostly with the first part.

T24   Yeah so it should

Z25   What's wrong with that? (overlaps with "so it should")

T26   Well it's not as convincing as it could be if your conclusion flowed naturally out of the arguments in the second half of your paper.

Z27   OK. I'll see what I can do about that.

What is the basis for the confusion that persists throughout? How do Sarah's assumptions about what issue is at hand differ from Zola's? A line-by-line analysis of the exchange sheds some light on the nature of and basis for the miscommunication. In Z1, Zola, after reading Sarah's final comment on her second draft, stated that she supports the "other side." By "other side" Sarah meant the anti-ELA position. In T2 Sarah laughingly suggested that Zola should change sides or change the position she takes in her conclusion. By suggesting that Zola change the position she has taken—from against to for the ELA—Sarah discounts the possibility that Zola might have strong convictions regarding the English Language Amendment. Rather, Sarah suggests that the taking of sides is merely part of the exercise of writing an argumentative paper. In other words, personal conviction plays little or no role in the choosing of sides. Zola does, however, oppose the ELA passionately. She has alluded to her opinion in conference with Sarah and has stated it in the conclusion to her paper. Then in Z3 Zola explicitly stated her position: "um, I'm on the side of the, uh, anti-ELA." Sarah still misunderstands Zola, even though she has very directly stated she is against the ELA, and she responds by asserting that Zola supports the ELA.

Form and Interpretation of the Writer's Intent

This misunderstanding between Zola and Sarah highlights the importance of textual form in the interpretation of texts. Since Sarah assumed that the beginning of the argumentative research paper presents the side that the writer opposes—the cons—she had difficulty reading beyond form and attending to the message Zola had presented both in writing and in speech. In an effort to make her true intent known after Sarah's misinterpretations of her statement in Z3, Zola explicitly stated her position again in Z5, this time choosing different wording in an effort to more clearly communicate her position. "Anti" became "should not have" and "ELA" became "English Language Amendment." In T6 Sarah suggested Zola switch the sides of her paper, meaning the order in which Zola presents the arguments for and against the ELA. Zola insisted she had tried to switch the sides but it did not work. (This could very well mean that Zola had intellectually toyed with the prospect of supporting the ELA through a serious consideration of the arguments ELA supporters present, because she perceived herself to be an intellectual, or it could mean she actually tried rearranging the sections of her paper and didn't think the new structure worked. Implicit throughout this exchange between Sarah and Zola is Sarah's belief that the technical problem concerning the issue of the ordering of the arguments in Zola's paper would be solved if Zola switched her position. Zola, in Z15, referred back to her thesis question and assumed that Sarah's comment meant she needed to rewrite her thesis question, but she never did so.

The Final Draft

The thesis question in Zola's final paper read exactly as it did in the second draft. In T16, Sarah attempted to respond to Zola's question about rephrasing her thesis question, but Zola interrupted and referred to a discussion the two had had previously in the library regarding her thesis statement. In Z17 and T18 neither completed a statement. By Z19, Zola acknowledged that she still had a problem with her thesis when, in fact, Sarah was concerned not with the thesis but with the manner in which Zola had organized her paper. In T22, Sarah referred again to her concern that Zola's conclusion does not flow out of the rest of her paper. In Z23, Zola acknowledged that the conclusion is different from the arguments that precede it. In response, Sarah, in T24, attempted to explain to Zola what she should do about this. Before Sarah could complete her statement, however, Zola interrupted to ask what was wrong with the order in which her arguments had been presented. In T26, Sarah said that Zola's argument was not as convincing as it would be if her conclusion "flowed naturally" out of the argument presented in the second half of the paper. Sarah's assertion that the order she suggests to Zola is natural is striking in this context, because the organization Sarah suggests is not natural but, rather, is contrived and most certainly a social construct. The structure for the argumentative research paper Sarah requires students to adopt is a mere construction of writers of research writing textbooks; it is in no way a natural phenomenon. In the end, Zola resisted Sarah's suggestion to reorder her paper.

Back on Track

The examples given thus far of Zola and Sarah interacting in conference have emphasized the fact that portions of the conferences were marked by miscommunication, frustration, and interruption. When Alan and Sarah interacted they often completed one another's utterances. In contrast, when Zola and Sarah interacted they often interrupted one another, changing the topic under discussion or contradicting what the other had previously said. Though this pattern was prevalent throughout the two conferences between Zola and Sarah, there were, nonetheless, times during the two meetings when they worked collaboratively to improve Zola's paper.

During the second conference, Sarah and Zola discussed the following portion of Zola's text: "Still, most of the language used now-a-days in the political process, is misunderstood even by Americans whose English is a native language and it certainly places non-English speaking citizens in a great deal of difficulty to deal with and fully understand these issues." Sarah had commented in writing at the end of this section, "What point are you making by comparing these two groups?" The following exchange is an example of the positive interaction that Sarah and Zola were occasionally able to achieve.

Z1   Yeah, when I here wanted to show that, here I talked about the for this, and who are not, whose for whom English is not a native language.

T2   Uh-huh.

Z3   OK. But here I added this to show that English for Americans over here when English is was always their native language

T4   Right

Z6   they had also this problem.

T7   OK. All right

Z8   This is what I wanted to add.

T9   Right, and you did, but then what does that show the reader? What does that contrast show the reader? I mean, why did you put in

Z10 Basically I put it here because I wanted to show other things in the end. (overlaps with Sarah's "put in" and spoken with great frustration.)

T11 OK, but the question is why did you put it here?

Z12 To show how hard it is.

T13 Right! And that's exactly what

Z14 Yeah, but that's obvious (overlaps at "exactly"). (both laugh)

T15 But it's not obvious, I mean you may think it's obvious 'cause it's up here in your head.

Z16 Eeh.

T17 OK.

Z18 OK. (laughs lightly) Right, so how would I put that?

T19 I mean, I don't know, but I think you need a couple of sentences or at least one sentence that

Z20 Uh-huh.

T21 that emphasizes the point that you're making.

Z22 OK. (weak)

Zola revised the paragraph as follows: "Still, most of the language used now-a-days in the political process, is misunderstood even by Americans for whom English is a native language." All Zola had done was change "whose" to "for whom" and deleted the second half of the sentence. Next to this portion of her text in the final draft Sarah wrote "Good." Essentially all Zola had done was correct the grammar. What she had done, however, in conference was prove to Sarah that she had a command of her subject matter and was able to understand what she was driving at as Sarah pushed Zola to make explicit her reasons for including the information in her paper.

Even though Sarah and Zola were at odds with one another during the two writing conferences, in striking contrast to the harmonious nature of the conferences between Sarah and Alan, in the end, Zola's strengths as a writer carried her through the course and led to a strong final grade. Zola entered Sarah's course with the cultural capital and a written discursive advantage that positioned her for success. Despite the fact that Zola resisted most of Sarah's imposed rules and expectations regarding due dates, attendance, typing, and structural form, she nonetheless did well in the course. The communicative breakdowns apparent during the two conferences and Zola's failure to revise according to Sarah's requirements were not offensive enough to affect the overall evaluation of her final product or the final grade for the course. One can only wonder what Zola's potential for growth as a writer might have been had she and Sarah been able to negotiate a more positive exchange pattern throughout the conferences.

ORAL COMPETENCE SUPERSEDES WRITTEN COMPETENCE: TAN IN CONFERENCE

Flattery will get you everywhere.—Candace Mitchell, maxim surmised as an observant youth and used to great advantage from then on

Privileging the Instructor's Position

While both Alan and Zola acted in setting the direction of their conferences with Sarah, Tan displayed a lack of assurance and hesitancy in his interactions with her. He deferred to Sarah throughout, speaking less than Zola and Alan had in their conferences. He was, however, able to move the direction of the conference to the personal without meeting resistance from Sarah, and he did this through a subtle privileging of her position.

Tan missed his first scheduled conference with Sarah but then contacted her to reschedule. Once he finally made it to the conference, no mention of his having missed the first meeting was made. Sarah began her conference with Tan in the same way she began the conferences with the three other students, by asking whether he had any questions for her. Tan's immediate response was, "uh, no." He followed, however, with "I think its, well, its ideas are so, I mean, I did it so quickly, so I made a lot of mistakes." At this point Sarah broke in with "Oh, well. Uh, do you know what you need to do to revise?" Tan responded in the affirmative and pointed to the first paragraph of his paper, where Sarah had commented "found where?" The exchange between Sarah and Tan (designated in these exchanges as S, for "student," to avoid confusion with T for "teacher") continues as follows.

175

S1   For example this one.

T2   Uh-huh.

S3   According to the statistics. This supposed to be one quote for two sentences.

T4   Oh, OK.

S5   Yeah, what should I do about that?

In S5 Tan finally asked Sarah a direct question and thus moved into the required discourse of the writing conference. By this I mean he directed Sarah's attention to a comment on his paper and asked her opinion about how he should correct or revise in that instance. Sarah responded, "Well, what you need to, instead of saying according to the statistics, it's OK to have two sentences with the same endnote"—Sarah understood that in S3 Tan meant "endnote" when he said "quote"—"but you need to tell the reader where you found the statistics, or who compiled the statistics."

The interactional pattern displayed in this first exchange between Sarah and Tan was repeated over and over during their two conferences. What is striking about the exchange and every exchange between the two is that Tan listened attentively to Sarah as she spoke and never interrupted her. Tan waited to speak until he was absolutely sure Sarah had completed each statement. Sarah, in contrast, did overlap Tan on occasion. Unlike Alan, Tan often seemed unsure of the direction Sarah was going in as she discussed issues of concern in his paper. And unlike Zola, Tan at times failed to display mastery of his topic, fumbling in confusion in his attempts to answer Sarah's questions regarding his paper.

Power in Powerlessness

The insecurity Tan displayed in his first exchange with Sarah continued. In fact, it took Tan a bit of time before he was quite sure of how the conference should proceed. After dealing with the second comment brought up by Tan, the next exchange occurred.

S1   And uh, sorry. I have to get all, read it, and do one by one. Can I do that?

T2   Oh yeah, that's fine, sure, sure.

S3   I'm not sure do that here.

T4   Yeah, that's fine, that's fine, that's why we have the conference.

S5   OK. (laughs)

Though Sarah provided no specific guidelines for the conference in terms of how it is to proceed, we learn from the successful interchanges between Sarah and Alan that she did have an implicit framework for the conference: the student was to review her comments one by one on the paper and use these comments as both the structural framework for the conference and the foundation for questions. The only cue she gave students to this implicit notion of conference structure was the question she posed at the start of each conference: Do you have any questions? Now, of course this could mean "Do you have any questions in general?" or it could mean the more specific question "Do you have any questions regarding the comments I have written on your paper and that I have assumed you have reviewed in the time you have set aside to do so right before our conference began?" Only Alan understood Sarah's opening question to mean the latter, and this is the case because he had had practice the previous semester in this discourse pattern and had, perhaps, experienced this discursive pattern while interacting with his boss at the tourist agency.

Tan struggled with how to proceed, though he soon took the initiative and asked Sarah directly whether she wishes him to follow her comments one by one as they unfold before him on the written text. Once sure of how to proceed, Tan dealt with each comment or question Sarah marked on his paper, taking detailed notes as she spoke. Often, he expressed gratitude for her suggestions. Overall, the first conference was carried out without much confusion or instances of miscommunication.

Eliciting Compliments

Near the end of the conference, after having dealt with minor details concerning endnote style, Tan flipped through his paper and commented, "It's good enough." Sarah responded, "It's very good, yeah, you're coming along well." Thus began a section of discourse in which Tan continued to elicit compliments from Sarah and, without asking directly, was able to negotiate a change in schedule for handing in his final draft of the research paper. Tan needed to finish Sarah's class three days early because of his planned trip to Hong Kong to attend his brother's wedding. The first conference ended with the following exchange between Sarah and Tan.

T1   So who's getting married in Hong Kong?

S2   My brother.

T3   Uh, is he older or younger?

S4   Older.

T5   Oh.

S6   Oldest.

T7   Oh, the oldest. Is he the first one to get married?

S8   Yeah.

T9   Uhh! This will be a big celebration, huh?

S10   Yeah, that's why my parents getting so excited you know.

T11   Yeah.

S12   You have to be making a party.

T13   That's right. (mutual laughter) Well, I think we can work it out.

S14   OK. Thank you for your help.

T15   Sure, sure.

S16   OK. See you later. See you next week.

T17   All right. OK.

It was only Tan, the most adept of the four students at creating networks of support, who was also able to elicit interest from Sarah in his personal affairs and to engage her in dialogue on personal matters.

The Second Conference: Getting Personal

The second conference between Tan and Sarah began quite differently from her conferences with the three other students. Just as Tan's first conference had ended on a personal note, so too did the second conference begin. At the beginning of the second conference the two spent considerable time discussing the problems Tan had just encountered as he attempted to get his passport from City Hall, which had been closed as a result of an electrical failure. Sarah was extremely interested in the situation at City Hall because she had to go there herself within the next day or two. Sarah listened attentively to Tan as he described the problems he encountered, and she expressed considerable sympathy throughout the story. Her final words of sympathy were "Oh my, oh dear. Well, I hope it works out." to which Tan responded, "Sure." At that point Sarah initiated the formal beginning of the conference with "All right, well do you have any questions about your paper?" With this question she explicitly marked the end of the personal exchange and the beginning of the writing conference, even specifying that she is looking for questions *about his paper,* which she had not done with the other students. A change in discourse mode is implied. Tan, who was now aware of the expected procedure of the writing conference responded, "uh yes," without hesitation. But, rather than waiting to hear his question, Sarah broke from the direction the conferences had generally taken and took the opportunity to compliment Tan on the progress of his paper by stating, "OK, it's coming along very nicely." In so doing, she continued the personal involvement that had begun during their discussion of Tan's problems obtaining a passport, and she linked back directly to the manner in which the first conference had ended. Tan took advantage of the opening and replied, "It's pretty good 'cause I was so tired and running, you know, back and forth, New York and Boston." Again expressing sympathy, Sarah responded with yet another "Oh my." The pattern here is that Sarah compliments and then Tan denigrates his work. To Sarah the paper was "coming along very nicely" while to Tan the paper was only "pretty good" and "not very good." The exchange continued as Tan expressed how tired he was from traveling, and how he felt that he "didn't do good on the second draft, maybe." With these words he was able to elicit more reassurance from Sarah, who told him, "Yes, you did."

Getting Explicit and Helpful Feedback

Finally Sarah focused the conference on Tan's paper and not on issues peripheral to the text. The two then proceeded to go through Tan's text comment by comment with Sarah giving explicit directions about how he should revise. Tan asked, "What is that mean 'restate why this is so'?" in reference to a comment Sarah had written after the following sentence in his text: "Clearly, the strategy of condom ads is more useful and legitimate than the sponge advertising for the public." This sentence appeared at the end of a paragraph in which Tan discussed the fact that contraceptive sponges have been advertised on television. He used this information as support for the argument that condom advertising should be allowed on TV. The gist of his argument was that if contraceptive sponge ads can be aired then condom ads should be too, particularly because condoms serve not only as contraceptive devices but also as a means to prevent the spread of AIDS. In his discussion of the issue, however, Tan had not stated directly the fact that condoms help to prevent the spread of AIDS.

Sarah and Tan's exchange continues when Sarah told him,

> Restate why this is so. OK. You're building your argument comparing the sponge to the condom, the sponge commercials to the condom commercials. OK, down here you said, "Clearly the strategy of condom ads is more useful and legitimate than the sponge advertising for the public." All right. Restate why they are more useful and legitimate. OK, because before you've just said what they do. You said in one sentence what they do and what they show, which is prevent AIDS. In the next sentence you've said that they're more legitimate than the sponge ads. You need to link it. You need to take it one more step further and say they are more legitimate because they prevent AIDS.

Sarah not only explained what she meant by her comment but also provided Tan with specific directions for revising the text in question. As Sarah spoke, Tan took notes and then revised the section in the following manner in the final version of his paper: "Clearly, the strategy of condom ads is more useful and legitimate than the sponge advertising for the public because condoms can stop AIDS as well as prevent pregnancy, so condom ads are an important piece of information to educate public against AIDS."

Joking

During her conference with Tan, Sarah also allowed moments in which the two joke together. In the following exchange, Tan had come upon a comment on his paper that he was unable to decipher. Rather than telling Sarah he was having trouble reading her writing, Tan instead used a different approach.

S1   Oh, what does that mean, the nar . . .

T2   Transition. (overlaps "nar")

S3   Oh.

T4   Oh man, my writing is really bad.

S5   (Tan laughs along with Sarah)

T6   Oh, I can read it perfectly.

S7   You should be a doctor, you know.

T8   I know. (laughter) I know, I know, yeah you need some kind of transition there for those two paragraphs. OK.

S9   OK.

The fact that Sarah allowed for a moment of levity in conference with Tan signifies that she had made a personal connection with him, in much the same way that she allowed, once again through joking behaviors, Alan recognition as a person as well as a student. The expressed humor allowed Tan and Alan to enter a space, an opening, if you will, to access further the discourse of the academy. The offered opportunity for access is a privilege, one not allowed to Zola or Araya. I do not suggest that Sarah explicitly acknowledged the differences in discourse style or that she was even aware of the subtle differences in style that allowed for the differential access enjoyed by both Alan and Tan. The humorous exchanges were but seconds in length, and they certainly did not represent the primary mode of discourse observed between Alan and Sarah and between Tan and Sarah. Yet just seconds within the narrow confines of the writing conference, restricted both in length and in numbers of allowed meetings, could leave a lasting impact on the perceptions both student and teacher retained after the event.

Terrible Confusion, Great Frustration

The conference proceeded without a hitch until Tan came to the second-to-last paragraph of his paper, where the first sentence read, "Subsequently, with the powerful sex drive among youths in the United States, and the fearful expansion of the acquired immune deficiency syndrome disease, AIDS, we need more than just high moral teaching to curb the teenage pregnancy and AIDS epidemic we need a strong nationwide program to address these epidemics." Next to this sentence Sarah had marked: "R–O," which meant that the sentence was a run-on sentence. Tan asked Sarah, "Why do you say this sentence is a run-on sentence?" Here are Sarah's response and the exchange that followed.

T1   Because it has two ideas in it with no connection between them. (Sarah reads from Tan's paper) "Subsequently, with the powerful sex drive among youth in the United States and the fearful expansion of the acquired immune deficiency syndrome disease, AIDS, we need more than just high moral teaching to curb the teenage pregnancy and AIDS epidemic we need a strong nationwide program to address these epidemics." All right, where is the end of your first idea there?

S2   Oh yeah, the true idea is the power sex drive and the uh fearful expansion.

T3   OK. With the powerful sex drive and the fearful expansion, what do we need?

S4   Um. Let me put (mumbles to himself and pauses) this

T5   What did you write that we need because we have a powerful sex drive and a fearful expansion of AIDS? What did you say we need?

S6   We needed a, I mean do something um (pause) Yeah, it isn't clear over here.

T7   Well, it is clear. No, what you're saying is perfectly clear. The only problem is that you have too many ideas, too many things that we need to do in one sentence and you don't have any connection between them.

S8   So I would break it down. You know, by maybe two sentence.

T9   Yeah, you could fix it that way or you could put a connection between them. What's the first thing you say we need to do?

S10   Power sex drive among the, well, we have to, you know, educate the, I mean young people.

T11   OK.

S12   First of all.

T13   OK. All right, so you say we need more than just moral teaching to curb teenage pregnancy and AIDS. All right. What is the second thing you say we need?

S14   The fear for expansion and we have to stop it. We have to, you know, introduce the condom.

T15   Yeah, but what do you say in this sentence we need?

S16   Yeah, I have to make another sentence to support this. What you mean is

T17   No, no, what I'm saying is that in this sentence, your sentence here begins with "subsequently" and ends with "epidemic," OK? In that sentence you have two ideas and they're not connected. You're saying that we need two things. Well, first you're saying that we don't need high moral teaching. Then what are you saying we need?

S18   What you mean we need the

T19   Just read me what you wrote.

S20   I'm confused, you know. (laughs lightly)

T21   All right. OK. All right. Let's look at this sentence again. Do you know what a run-on is? (exasperated)

S22   Uh well, actually it's too many ideas in one sentence.

T23   Right, right.

S24   Right.

T25   Did you do the run-on stuff with [Sam, the writing tutor]?

S26   No, not yet.

T27   All right. Well, that's why you're having problems with this. There's a section to do with Sam for run-ons, OK. And what a run-on means is that you have too many ideas in this sentence and they're not linked together. OK, so instead of me just telling you what it is, OK

S28   Sure.

T29   go look at the run-on section.

S30   Yeah.

T31   OK, 'cause you have to do that by next week anyway.

S32   Sure.

T33   And if you still can't get it come back and talk to me about it.

S34   Sure.

T35   Or just show me after class.

S36   OK.

T37   OK. (pause)

In T1, Sarah focused Tan on the problematic run-on sentence by reading it from his paper. Sarah did not have a copy of Tan's paper, so she used his. After reading the sentence she asked Tan to explain where his first idea ends. This was an odd question, because the two had not yet reached an agreement about what his first idea is. Tan interpreted her question to mean that she wanted him to identify the fundamental, or initial, subject of the sentence she had just read. He responded in S2 by saying the "true idea is the power sex drive and fearful expansion," Tan was correct, in fact, in his response to Sarah's question. However, Sarah had another first idea in mind. In T3, Sarah attempted to elicit from Tan what he had asserted "we" need because of the "powerful sex drive and fearful expansion." Tan was then unable to respond and was left mumbling to himself as he attempted to sort out what Sarah meant. Then, in T5, Sarah explicitly asked Tan what he wrote that we need as a result of the "powerful sex drive and fearful expansion." Tan read his text and then assumed, in S6, that the problem was that he had not made it clear what was needed. In T7, however, Sarah asserts that what he has written is in fact clear and that the only problem is that there are too many ideas in the sentence. She tells him that these ideas have been presented without a connection between them. In S8, Tan offered a legitimate solution to the problem—he suggested separating the sentence into two sentences. While Sarah acknowledged that this was a possible solution, she suggested that he could also use a connection between the ideas. In T9 Sarah then asked Tan what he wrote was the first thing needed. In S10 Tan said that what is needed is education. In fact, he had written this not in the sentence under discussion at the moment but in the sentence that followed. But in the sentence under scrutiny, which begins with the word "subsequently," he had said that what is needed is more than high moral teaching. To say that more than high moral teaching is needed leaves open the question of what, in fact, is needed. What did Tan assert is needed? He very directly stated that what is needed is "a strong nationwide program to address these epidemics." He implied that "high moral teaching" is not needed. In the sentence under discussion Tan had really only asserted that one thing is needed, not two. Yet Sarah had asked him to repeat the two things she believed him to be arguing are needed. Sarah then, in T13, agreed that more is needed than high moral teaching in order to curb teenage pregnancy and AIDS. She then attempted to elicit from Tan what the second thing needed is. Sarah continued to read Tan's run-on sentence as presenting two things that are needed. She accepted that "high moral teaching" is needed, and that "a strong nationwide program to address these epidemics" is needed. It is not the case that Tan is arguing that these are the two things are needed, as Sarah continues to assert.

At this point Tan responded by saying that we need to introduce the condom. Tan was presenting his own answer to Sarah's question rather than referring to what he had written in the sentence under discussion. He presented two of the main themes of his paper, condoms and education, as answers to the question with which Sarah was trying to elicit an answer that showed that Tan understood why the sentence is a run-on sentence. In response, in T15 Sarah tried again to get Tan to refer to the particular sentence they were discussing.

At this point Tan was thoroughly confused, and he thought Sarah wanted him to add another sentence of support to what he had already written. He made this suggestion in S16. Sarah had suggested throughout the conference that what Tan needed to do in order to clarify issues and evaluate what he had written was provide more supporting evidence. After trying to focus Tan specifically on the sentence under discussion, providing for him the first and last words of the sentence to which she was referring, Sarah then reiterated the problem as she perceived it: The sentence has two ideas and these ideas are not connected. She then explicitly outlined one of the ideas for Tan and attempted to elicit from him the second idea. (Sarah had used the same strategy with Alan, but also to little avail.)

In T19, Sarah, in great frustration, asked Tan to "just read me what you wrote." Tan finally explicitly stated to Sarah, in S20, the obvious: he was confused. Then in T21 Sarah once again directed Tan to look at the sentence and then asked him whether he knew what a run-on is. Tan, in S22, very succinctly and correctly defines a run-on. Sarah confirmed the correctness of Tan's answer, but then she asked whether he had completed the run-on exercises with Sam, the writing tutor. Tan responded that he had not. Sarah then attributed the entire misunderstanding to the fact that Tan had not yet gone over the exercises on run-on sentences in *The Little, Brown Handbook*. She then reiterated the definition of a run-on sentence, and insisted that instead of her "just telling" Tan what to do he should work with Sam on run-ons. Tan agreed and Sarah then once again explicitly directed Tan to the section in *Little Brown*. She further justified her suggestion by stating the run-on exercises were assigned for the next tutoring session anyway. Therefore, she was not asking him to do more work than was required for the course. Despite the fact that Tan had been able to define a run-on sentence, Sarah could see in his paper the fact that he still produced them.

A Teachable Moment Lost

Once Tan told Sarah that he did understand what a run-on was, it might have been helpful for Sarah to intervene directly at this point. She could have provided copyediting instructions directly to Tan. Had she taken the opportunity to engage him in this "teachable moment," the confusion and misunderstanding surrounding his intended meaning might have been avoided. In other instances, such as in Alan's conferences, Sarah had directly intervened and provided copyediting suggestions. Although Alan's errors were more superficial and therefore less complicated, once Alan communicated to Sarah that he was aware of the nature of his specific error and that he was able to converse with her specifically about tense and its effect on spelling, for example, Sarah provided him with the specific copyediting suggestions. In contrast, Sarah's misunderstanding or, more accurately, misreading of this portion of Tan's research paper led him further and further into a web of confusion.

In his final paper Tan revised the run-on sentence in the manner he had suggested in S8, during the early part of the exchange. He broke the sentence into two: "Subsequently, with the powerful sex drive among youth in the United States, and the fearful expansion of the acquired immune deficiency syndrome disease, AIDS, we need more than just high moral teaching to curb teenage pregnancy and AIDS epidemic. We need a strong nationwide program to address these epidemics." Tan had done nothing more than place a period after "epidemic" and capitalize "We." This confused interchange could have been avoided if Sarah had simply asked Tan how he would restructure the run-on. This would have allowed Tan to show her his solution without making it necessary for her to provide specific copyediting advice, which she had been avoiding. Instead both student and instructor were at odds, ultimately perhaps leaving Sarah with a negative impression of Tan's ability to revise.

Decontextualizing a Sentence

What did Sarah do as she attempted over and over again in this exchange to get Tan to focus solely on the sentence she considers to be problematic? Essentially what she did was decontextualize the sentence from the rest of Tan's writing. By this I mean she isolated his sentence from the context in which it occurred, and from its intended meaning within the paper. In other words, Sarah treated the sentence as if it were an exercise in a grammar book. This decontextualization contributed to her misreading of Tan's intended meaning. Further, she insisted that the reason Tan could not provide her with the answer she sought was because he had not yet done the exercises on run-ons in the *Little, Brown* book. The fact that she attributed the confusion to this illustrates the extent to which Sarah connected writing with sentence-level work. She did not view writing as a means by which ideas are developed and expanded upon as papers are created. For example, we can see the logical development of a single idea in the run-on sentence and the sentence that follows in Tan's paper. For Tan to write that "more is needed than high moral teaching" implies that high moral teaching is already provided and has proved to be insufficient in dealing with the problem of curbing the AIDS epidemic. Rather than high moral teaching, what is needed, asserted Tan, is a "strong nationwide program to address these epidemics." And how will this be done? Tan suggested a "message should be proposed to educate the public." In the run-on sentence under discussion Tan had presented only one example of what is needed to curb the spread of AIDS, not two ideas as Sarah insisted was the case.

Final Grade

In the end how did Tan fare on his final paper? Not badly at all. He received an A– and the following comment from Sarah: "Good, well research [*sic*] paper." It is interesting to note that Tan was originally chosen to participate in this study as a less-proficient writer in the class as a result of an in-class essay that read in its entirety as follows.

> There are some differents in between I and my parents' live style. The major different which is my parents have an Chinese traditional philosophy to people and to the matters, and I have my own, mixture which compined Chinese and American philosophy to my live. For example, last fall, when my parents needed a washing-machine, they rather paid it by cash than the monthly instant payment. Then I asked why? My father said: "If you don't have enough money, don't buy it! I just don't like to spend the future-money, and the concern might come along with me until the payment is off."
>
> In the contrast, If I was my father, I would charged for it, because I might have the money to do other things; then, my money wouldn't get tied up.

By the end of the course, however, Tan began a ten-page, typed research paper in the following manner.

> One of the most controversial issues of today is the issue of condom advertisement on television. Since the epidemic of AIDS and teenage pregnancy have been present in our society, expecially in the United States, the subject of condoms, which was a neglected issue, has become a "heated issue" (1) for every one. According to the statistics of the Atlanta based U.S. Centers for Disease Control, there are at least one and a half million Americans who are already infected with the AIDS virus, and each one who gets it has a very high risk of dying. Every year, the number of victims multiplies by a factor of two. (2) The rate of teenage pregnancy, in much the same way, has alarmed our society. Each year based on several sources, there are at least five million American teenage girls who get pregnant, and about four hundred and seventy thousand of them deliver babies. (3)

One is struck by the written proficiency displayed in the opening paragraph to Tan's final paper compared to the lack of proficiency apparent in his in-class essay, written at the outset of the course. In the best of all possible worlds one might hope that this student had advanced considerably over the course of the summer semester. In fact, Sarah, who had no knowledge of Tan's network of support, gave him a grade reflective of the accomplishment displayed in the final research paper. Perhaps she assumed his high motivation—his desire to be accepted into the engineering program and his need to complete the course early to attend his brother's wedding—drove him to focus and produce a well-written paper. She also would have been disinclined to consider he had sought help as she had seen his various drafts and had noted the improvement as he revised. Sarah had also come to like Tan—he was likable—and this personal connection might have swayed her from considering the possibility that he was not working alone. Further, Sarah had too many papers to read and comment on and too many students to meet in conference. Tan's early work was far from her concerns at the time final grading was done.

12

DISCOURSE WITHOUT DIALOGUE: ARAYA IN CONFERENCE

Having a conversation should be as easy and as instinctual as singing along to your favorite song. Like singing, it is something we have been doing since we were infants. But having a good conversation, like singing well, is surprisingly difficult. Except for the rare prodigy, learning to sing well requires a good understanding of the dynamics of singing—and a lot of practice.—Steven Morgan Friedman, "Random Thoughts," cited in Lawrence Cohen, "Getting Along"

Stranger in a Strange Land

Negotiating his way through the writing of a research paper and the discourse of the writing conference in an alien tongue proved to be exceedingly difficult for Araya. As Steven Friedman notes in the epigraph at the beginning of this chapter, communicating well—having a good conversation, in this case a productive writing conference—is "surprisingly difficult" and takes "a lot of practice." The discourse of the writing conference—and the components of the "good conversation" embedded therein—were beyond Araya's scope of experience; and even once placed in the cultural context of the conference, he had no foundation upon which to practice the techniques that would lead him to membership in a community of apprentice writers. Araya was no prodigy, but neither was Alan, Zola, or Tan. And the latter three fared far better in conference than did Araya, because they each had previously acquired aspects of academic culture that provided the foundation and strategies through which to obtain a further, widening space for themselves within this alien, academic world. Araya, despite his best efforts, remained a fringe dweller, an outcast of sorts, stuck at the narrowly opened door of the academy.

Least Proficient, Least Feedback

Of the four students, it was Araya, the least-proficient writer, who received the least feedback from Sarah during their two conferences. This was the case because Araya appeared to be totally unaware of what was expected of him during the conferences. Tan was also unsure of how to interact in conference initially (see chapter 11), but he was able quite early on in the first conference to negotiate with Sarah about how the conference should proceed. He did so by directly asking Sarah whether he should ask questions based on her written comments. Tan had assumed a possible structure for the conference and then set out to confirm whether his assumption was correct. Had he made a false assumption, but nonetheless questioned Sarah directly whether this approach was what she expected, Tan would have provided Sarah (or whomever was conducting the conference) with the foundation upon which she could explicitly state to him her expectations. Of course, this is only assumption. If Tan had asked, "Should I ask you general questions about how I am doing so far?" Sarah (or any teacher) might have responded with "Yes, that will be fine." Such a framework could have led to a free-for-all and left Tan with no specific direction for dealing with the concerns Sarah had marked on his paper.

Even though Sarah had an implicit understanding of the discourse of the writing conference, she never stated directly what that structure was. Since Tan "guessed correctly" and posed his question in an appropriate form for Sarah to understand, the conference for the most part proceeded according to her expectations. (This, however, did not necessarily guarantee successful communication that would translate into appropriate revisions and improved writing [see chapter 11].) Once Tan was confident of the structure he was to follow in the conference setting, he dealt specifically with each question and comment Sarah had made on his paper. In contrast, Araya never reached a point in either conference with Sarah where the two dealt with specific questions having to do with the development of his paper. Rather, Araya remained in a discourse pattern with Sarah that mirrored the pattern of Sarah's classroom. By this I mean that, for the most part, during the conferences with Araya Sarah lectured on general issues, in much the same way she did in class, and Araya engaged in only limited dialogue with Sarah. He spoke primarily in response to Sarah's direct questioning and his responses were, for the most part, short. When Araya did speak, Sarah often overlapped his utterances before he was able to complete his statement.

Speaking outside the Text

Throughout the two conferences with Sarah, Araya asked only one direct question: "How about my grammar?" The question, however, was not directed to any specific point in his paper. In fact, the question was asked midway through the first conference, when the purpose of the meeting was supposed to be to discuss the overall development of the first draft of the research paper. Sarah did not mark for grammar on the first drafts, and she considered questions relating to grammar at this stage in the development of a student's paper to be inappropriate. However, as has been noted in the previous chapters analyzing the discourse of the writing conference, on more than one occasion the issue of grammar was raised and discussed during a first conference.

Only on two other occasions during the two conferences did Araya request help from Sarah, indicating on both occasions that he was having difficulty finding sources. During the first conference Araya told Sarah he was having problems getting sources for the general topic, welfare; and during the second conference he indicated that his difficulty was in finding sources that "talks about opposing welfare." Sarah responded to Araya's concerns by giving him explicit instructions about how to find more sources for his paper. The types of suggestions she gave him are discussed later in this chapter.

Sarah's Implicit Assumptions

Clearly Araya, the least-proficient writer of the four students, was also the least proficient in other forms of academic discourse. He was totally unprepared to interact in a writing conference. And although conferences were established by Sarah to provide all students in the course with equal access to her assistance as they set about revising their papers, Araya, who most needed assistance, received virtually none. This was the case because he knew none of the discourse strategies necessary to elicit from Sarah the kind of assistance he needed in order to develop and improve his paper. In other words, the writing conference and the expected behaviors and strategies employed in the conference setting were completely alien to Araya. This subculture of the discourse of the academy and, more specifically, of process writing theory and pedagogy, was a new culture for Araya. Araya had never before participated in a writing conference with an instructor or with a peer writer in class. (During their 101 classes, both Alan and Zola had met with their instructors, as well as with fellow students, to discuss papers as they prepared to revise their work. Tan, too, had met in the past with his 101 instructor to discuss his work, although he had not had as much experience in conference as had Alan and Zola.) Further, Sarah never made explicit to students what was expected of them in conference. Sarah was explicit in conveying information regarding some aspects of the conference—for example, she did tell students when to arrive, to look over their papers and read her comments before meeting with her, and that the conferences would last for fifteen minutes—but she never indicated explicitly that students should hold their papers as they met with her or that they should go through their text from beginning to end using each of Sarah's comments as a point of reference for asking her for assistance or clarification. Nor did Sarah indicate that as students went through their texts they should lean close to Sarah so that she, too, could read her comments and what the student had written. This was a necessary behavioral component of the conference because Sarah did not have copies of the students' papers with her comments. So with each question she needed to be reminded of how the question or comment she had marked on each paper related to the concerns raised by the students as they made their way through their commented-upon draft.

I would never suggest that Sarah should have been responsible for making copies of student papers after she made her comments and suggestions so that she would have a copy to refer to throughout the conference. This would have created a major burden for Sarah, who was already overburdened. However, she could have explicitly stated to each student as they entered her office to begin the conference that she would need to refer to her comments because she no longer had them in hand and could not remember specifically each issue she had raised when reading the papers. She also could have made it clear that she was sitting at the side of her desk so that the student could sit catercorner to her and place the draft on the corner of her desk so that they would each have access to it. Never did she model the forms of questioning the students should engage in as they sought her assistance; that is, she never explicitly told students that a commonly employed question in the writing conference is "What do you mean by [insert teacher's written comment]?" Nor did she tell them that once the teacher explained a comment, it was appropriate for students to suggest what they might do to revise the text in question and, by so doing, indirectly elicit more specific direction from the instructor. Sarah also did not indicate explicitly that students should take notes on their papers as she spoke or that if they came across a misspelled word or verb tense error she would indicate the correct form to them if they first suggested a correction. Finally, Sarah did not indicate that the conference was not only a meeting held for them to discuss and work on revisions but also a time when students had the opportunity to display their knowledge of and interest in the topic they were researching, as well as to comment on the amount of work they had thus far put into the project. All of these features—body placement and stance, questioning behaviors (direct and indirect), where the conference should begin and end, as directed by Sarah's comments on the students' papers, and the fact that the conference provided each student a space to perform, to demonstrate the effort they had put into the task at hand and the degree to which they had mastered the material they were researching—were culturally and socially generated. The cultural model of the writing conference was owned by Sarah, and, as a member of the dominant culture, she was in a position to judge each student's progress (superficially, their writing) based on conformance to, or inability to engage in, the behaviors she expected them to demonstrate. Sarah's position is not unique. I never explicitly stated to students in writing courses my expectations regarding the manner in which a writing conference should proceed, nor am I aware that explicit instructions of this sort exist. I did, however, provide model questions for students when they peer-conferenced in class.

All of these behaviors could have been made explicit through direct instruction and modeling. A student who had never engaged in the type of academic discourse and behaviors required in the writing conference was at a loss when attempting to participate in a conference. And although Araya was on time for his conference and was also appropriately thankful for Sarah's help, he engaged not at all in the other behaviors expected of a student during the writing conference. Nor did he engage in any of the more subtle sorts of behaviors students display when in conference with instructors, behaviors that might ingratiate him with the instructor. For example, he did not, as did Alan and Tan, indicate sympathy for how hard Sarah must have worked in order to read and comment on all the student papers, nor did he communicate to Sarah how hard he had worked putting together either of his drafts. He also never indicated, as had Alan, Zola, and Tan, how tired he was, which is perhaps the most common indirect way in which students communicate to their instructors that they have forgone everything, even sleep, to do the work required in the course. By doing so, students communicate to the instructor that her course has been put above all else in their lives, and is that not what we, members of the academy, wish to hear? Our course and the work we require should take precedence over all other aspects of the student's life; we are in control and expect total focus from those enrolled in our course.

The first conference between Sarah and Araya was begun by Sarah in the same manner as her conferences with the other students. Sarah asked, "OK, first of all, let me ask you, do you have any questions?" To this Araya responded in the affirmative and then proceeded to explain to Sarah that he did, in fact, have a problem (rather than a specific question). Araya answered, "Yeah, uh, I've got problem to uh get the contact some books. I got about six books." In suggesting that this was his problem Araya was responding to Sarah's first notation on the comment sheet attached to his paper.

Thus Araya's conference began with a concern that lay outside of his text. Never during the conference did Araya ask questions related to comments Sarah had written on his paper, nor did Sarah direct Araya to specific issues related to his writing. Throughout the first conference Araya also remained physically distant from his paper. When he finally sat down in Sarah's office—of the four students, Araya was the only one who was directed by Sarah to take a seat after he entered her office because it was clear that he did not know where he should place himself or in what manner—he placed his paper on her desk and never touched it again or referred to it directly. During the first conference Sarah did pick up Araya's paper to flip through it to see what comments she had made on it. Never, however, did she refer to a specific portion of his text or suggest to Araya that he could, and should, do so. Throughout the conference Araya remained not only distant from his text but also physically distant from Sarah. He never leaned forward as Sarah spoke to him but, instead, sat straight upright in his chair facing her. His body stance was the same as the stance he exhibited while sitting in Sarah's class at a desk facing her as she lectured. Sarah, like Araya, remained seated upright throughout the conference, with her back against the desk chair. Neither appeared comfortable in the other's presence. Just as Araya appeared unaware of how to proceed in the conference, Sarah seemed at a loss about how to deal with Araya. This was the case, perhaps, because he displayed none of the expected behaviors of the student in conference. In a sense, the conference set up a situation during which the student was to take the lead by following the teacher's written comments. Araya did not take the lead but, rather, sat back, just as he did and was expected to do during Sarah's class, and waited for her to tell him what to do. When confronted with this unexpected behavior, Sarah fell back into her classroom style of interacting with students: she lectured.

Lecturing in Conference

In order to get a sense of the nature of the communicative patterns displayed between Sarah and Araya it is useful to return to the beginning of their first conference, because it contains discourse features that were displayed throughout the two conferences. The initial exchange in the conference follows.

T1   Araya, come on in.

A2   Mmm, all right.

T3   How are you?

A4   Mm, good.

T5   Have a seat. OK, first of all let me ask you, do you have any questions?

A6   Mm yeah, uh, I've got problem to, uh, get the contact some books. I got about six books.

T7   Ooh, OK. (overlaps Araya's "six books")

A8   about the welfare system.

T9   Oh, OK. (overlaps "welfare system")

A10   But I don't got anything else. Is difficult.

T11   Have you, have you looked in the *Reader's Guide?*

A12   *Reader's Guide?*

T13   Yeah, the *Reader's Guide to Periodical Literature,* the green books.

A14   Green books, yeah, um, for magazines.

T15   Uh-huh.

A16   I got only one magazines, New York ones.

T17   Oh, OK.

A18   Yeah.

T19   Were there any other magazines there? I mean

A20   About welfare? Yeah, most of them, it's, they talks about the economics things.

T21   Oh, uh-huh.

A22   It's difficult to, uh, got research.

T23   Yeah. (overlaps "got research") OK, all right. What about newspapers? Did you try the *New York Times Index?*

A24 No, I didn't try.

T25 OK. (overlaps "try")

A26 But I got one newspapers.

T27 Yeah, (excited) I saw you have the *Boston Globe*.

A28 Yeah. (overlaps "saw")

T29 That's good, that's good. All right. Why don't you try the *New York Times Index*. (pause) It's up on the fifth floor of the library. (pause) OK, and then there's some, do you know what editorials are in the newspaper? (pause) OK, a newspaper has a page usually that's called the editorial page.

A30 Uh-huh. (pause)

T31 All right, and people write to the editor of the newspaper expressing their views about different things. OK, how they feel about current events and things that are happening.

A32 Uh-huh.

T33 OK. The, um, so the editorial page is a page in the newspaper that's only people's opinions.

A34 Uh-huh.

T35 OK.

A36 OK.

T37 There is an index of editorials. OK, I don't know exactly what it's called. OK, I'll, I'll just write down the editorial index, OK but if you ask, um, the librarian for the editorial index all right.

A38 Um.

T39 Tell the librarian what kind of information you're trying to find, OK.

A40 OK.

T41 That you're doing a paper on welfare and you need to find some sources about people who are opposed to the welfare system. OK, there are a lot of people in the United States who are, but a lot of time this is an opinion, so I think you'll find information in the editorial index.

A42 OK, OK.

T43 All right.

A44 All right.

T45 So ask the librarian for that. OK. All right. Do you have any other questions?

A46 Um no. Um how bout my grammar and

By A6, Araya had informed Sarah that he had found six books about the welfare system. Sarah would have known this already, because he had included the required bibliography with his first draft. In A6, Araya also indicated that he did have questions by responding to Sarah's question in T5 in the affirmative. However, he did not ask her a question but, rather, appeared to be indirectly requesting help in finding sources for his paper. By A6, Araya had established that this portion of the conference will deal with concerns peripheral to his existing written text. He had introduced the difficulty he was having finding sources for his paper as the initial topic for discussion in the conference. In T11, Sarah asked whether Araya had attempted to find sources in the *Reader's Guide*. In A12, Araya repeated the words "*Reader's Guide*" with rising intonation to indicate he was not quite sure what Sarah meant. In A14, he again repeated Sarah's last words, this time, however, with falling intonation. Araya often repeated the final words of Sarah's previous utterances. By A16, Araya indicated that he had found a magazine through the *Reader's Guide*—a "New York ones." "New York ones" is, obviously, not a magazine title, but perhaps "New York" is part of the title of the magazine Araya had found. This lack of specificity was also characteristic of Araya's discourse. In T23, Sarah directed Araya to another source, this time the *New York Times Index,* and in T29 she used the same tone of voice she used when lecturing to describe where to find this reference source in the university library. Sarah used this same lecturing tone throughout the conference, including in T39 and T41, when she explained to him how to approach a librarian.

Later in the first conference Sarah suggested Araya interview an individual "who had strong opinions about welfare" and use the individual as a source for his paper. Sarah made this suggestion because she had had a student in the past who had done a paper on the same topic as Araya, and this other student had interviewed people as part of his research. Sarah later admitted to me that this was perhaps not an appropriate suggestion for a student like Araya, who seemed to have no network at all and who was by all appearances extremely shy and reticent. Araya never interviewed anyone. Sarah had made the same suggestion to Alan, and although he was not at all shy, he also failed to follow her suggestion. During their first conference, Sarah gave Araya five suggestions about where to find more information for his paper. She suggested he consult the *Reader's Guide,* the *New York Times Index,* and the *Editorial Index,* that he interview people, and that he ask the librarian for help. All these suggestions were useful, but Araya could have found all of these ideas, except for asking the librarian for help, by reading the research writing text for the course. Students had also been provided with this information when Sarah took them on a library tour. All the suggestions were of a very general nature and did not deal with specific issues of concern related to what Araya had written in his paper.

The only other suggestion Sarah gave Araya during the first conference was that he needed to evaluate both sides of his argument. Once again, her suggestion was not specifically related to Araya's text but given in the most general terms. Sarah made this suggestion to Araya just as she finished discussing the issue of his need to find more sources for his paper. What she said, as well as his response to her, is included in the following exchange.

T1   OK, the other thing is you need to evaluate both sides. Do you understand what that is?

A2   Yeah, (drawn out) I write with the first part, but the second part I didn't write.

T3   OK, we got the pages in the right order now. OK. (said in reference to the fact that she found the pages of Araya's draft to be out of order.)

A4   (repeats what he said in A2, mumbled)

T5   OK. (overlaps Araya) All right. OK. All right. OK. All right. OK. So you need to do that. OK?

A6   Uh-huh.

T7   But I think the most important thing is to find more sources. OK and if you want to look around today and you're still having trouble come back tomorrow.

Sarah's Efforts to Get to the Text

Sarah explicitly told Araya in T1 that he needed to evaluate both sides of his argument. She had written this comment on his cover evaluation sheet also, and she was referring to her written comments at this point in the exchange. She then asked Araya whether he understood what she meant. Araya responded in the affirmative and then indicated to Sarah that he had evaluated the first part but not the second. By this he meant that he had provided an evaluation of the arguments against welfare but not an evaluation of the arguments in favor of welfare. In T3 Sarah ignored completely what Araya had said in A2 and referred instead to the fact that she had discovered that the pages of his paper were out of order. When responding to Araya, Sarah used the inclusive "we"—"we have the pages together." Araya was not at all involved in reordering the paper, thus it is odd that Sarah chose to include him in the process of reordering the pages. Or was she incorporating the "we" used when speaking to young children—as in "now we're ready to eat" when only the child will be eating, and the caregiver has made the meal and will be feeding the child? In A4, Araya explained again that he had evaluated the first part (the pros) but not the second (the cons). In T5, Sarah again ignored, or did not understand, what Araya had said. She then signaled the end of the topic under discussion by stating repeatedly, "OK. All right" and repeating that Araya needs to do what she had just indicated to him. (Sarah used this same signal— "OK. All right."—when lecturing to indicate that she had completed one topic and is about to introduce a new topic for discussion or that she has reached the end of the lecture altogether.) Sarah ended the discussion of this topic despite the fact that Araya had indicated that he had already evaluated only one portion of the paper. Instead of turning then to Araya's paper to look at his evaluation of the arguments against welfare and discussing how he could expand upon or revise his evaluation and, further, instead of looking at his arguments in favor of welfare and then discussing how to evaluate them, Sarah dismissed the topic outright. By doing so, she denied Araya the one opportunity in the conference that had emerged in which he could have begun to enter into, on some level, a discussion of the ideas and arguments he had presented in his paper. By dismissing the topic, Sarah also denied Araya access to engaging in the discourse of the academy—in this instance, the discourse of the writing conference—and, in particular, the speaking and writing through texts that the academy requires and values. Throughout the first, as well as the second, conference, Araya engaged in only two forms of academic discourse: he listened to lectures and he gave short answers to his teacher's questions.

Access Denied

In suggesting that Sarah denied Araya access to more literate forms of academic discourse, I by no means suggest that she made a conscious decision to do so. On the contrary, at various points throughout the study, Sarah expressed a genuine and deep concern about the problems Araya was having in the course. Further, when she offered Araya suggestions about how to find more information for his paper, she genuinely felt this was what he needed from her.

Unfortunately, as is often the case, the student who most needed opportunities to engage in dialogue about his writing so that he could develop and expand upon the ideas he presented in his paper ended up working with his instructor at a very basic skill level. In this instance, Araya was presented with lists of general sources for his paper. It would have been far more helpful, perhaps, for Sarah to ask Sam, the tutor, to go to the library with Araya so that they could search for sources together. This would have helped Araya far more than did the grammar exercises he went over in tutoring sessions with Sam, the very exercises Tan skillfully avoided so that he could use Sam as a resource for finding sources. Had Sarah suggested this approach at the first conference, then the second conference might have been a time when she and Araya could talk about the ideas he presented in his paper. Instead, during the second conference Sarah once again outlined possible sources for his paper. She reiterated the perceived need for him to find editorials favoring and opposing welfare and, using much the same phrasing as she did in the first conference, she described to Araya what an editorial was. She also attempted, in the second conference, to focus Araya on a specific time frame in the *Reader's Guide*. She suggested that he look for articles published in the 1960s and 1970s rather than articles published more recently (and therefore listed in more recent issues of the *Reader's Guide*), as he had done thus far. Sarah had already used the timetable strategy in class as a means by which to point students in the right direction to find sources for their papers. Further, had Sarah made explicit the ways in which students were to behave and interact in conference with her, Araya would have had a much better chance of receiving the sort of feedback necessary for him to develop his paper. In addition, if Araya had received explicit directions about how to interact in conference and the conferences therefore been more productive, Araya might have received a grade better than the C– he received on his final draft of the paper, and he might have learned a little about writing and speaking in the academy. Finally, and most important, if Araya had had the opportunity to begin to engage in forms of discourse acquired in the academy, he might have been just a bit more prepared to interact in the next situation that made such demands on him.

Araya and Sarah engaged in discourse structures or patterns that "simply reproduce the interpersonal relationships of conventional schooling," thus intensifying "teacher-centeredness, magnifying the teacher's authority and more powerfully denying the student any access to control" (King, 1993, p. 17). Again, the writing conferences between Sarah and Araya were destined for the outcomes described by King. The process writing discourse that Sarah had been exposed to did not suggest that teachers explicitly delineate the behaviors expected in conference; the assumption was that providing the opportunity for face-to-face interaction between student and teacher, in and of itself, would be sufficient to lead to improved writing. What is not considered in process writing theory and practice is the fact that students bring with them to the conference differing assumptions regarding the ways in which student and teacher interact. As a student in Ethiopia, Araya would not have had the opportunity to engage face-to-face with an instructor, so the very positioning of student and teacher in an office, seemingly on equal footing, must have been quite unsettling.

Further, the opportunity I had to observe two conferences between Sarah and each of the four students participating in the study allowed me to bring to a conscious level thoughts of power differentials between student and teacher, disparity in time given to students with whom one feels comfortable, versus the habit of hastening the ending of meetings that create a feeling of unease—behaviors that I, too, have engaged in. I realized that I, too, had failed to explicitly characterize many of the expected behaviors in conference, and I had made many false assumptions regarding my assumed-to-be progressive approach to teaching when teaching writing. Sarah never acted with ill intent, yet there was considerable variation in outcome based on her interactions with students. I, too, never proceeded with a conference or ended one with ill intentions. In the former case, I proceeded because of a feeling of connection, a sense that what was occurring would end in a productive manner for the student. In the latter, I ended conferences with a sense of unease, a discomfort that I could not characterize with any specificity but that left me feeling that I had not assisted the student with whom I felt uncomfortable in a manner that would enhance writing competency. And then, of course, there were those conferences that did go ahead but did not seem to lead to much improvement in student writing.

I remember clearly that when I first started teaching writing I was enamored with the thought of providing for students the opportunity to write and rewrite their papers and to have the opportunity to meet with me to discuss their work. I had never had this experience as an undergraduate, and I felt it was extremely important for students to learn to interact with, and not fear, instructors. Magnanimous was I in the scheduling of time for students outside of regular class hours. This was the case until the time one of my students arrived at her scheduled conference with her young daughter—I had handed out a sheet of paper for students to choose a conference time from among the time slots I had provided, and she was one of the last to receive the list. The fact that she had arrived with her daughter was not a problem. But when I learned that she had traveled for an hour and a half, and had had to make numerous public transportation exchanges, in order to meet with me on a day when she normally would not have traveled to UMB, I realized that I, too, had failed to see outside of my own world; and by doing so, I had asserted my authority in such a way that I was embarrassed by my failure to interrogate my own power in requiring what I had of this woman. I had not even considered the difficulties scheduling a conference outside of the regular class hour would possibly impose on students. I do not fault Sarah for her failure to explicitly map out conference behaviors, behaviors that might not have even existed at a metalevel in her consciousness, as they were so taken for granted as to be unknown.

13

THE WRITING COURSE OVERALL AND AFTER ALL

The fundamental message of a pedagogic practice is the rule for legitimate communication.—Basil Bernstein, *The Structuring of Pedagogic Discourse*

When you assess something, you are forced to assume that a linear scale of values can be applied to it. Otherwise no assessment is possible. Every person who says of something that it is good or bad or a bit better than yesterday is declaring that a points system exists; that you can, in a reasonably clear and obvious fashion, set some sort of a number against an achievement.—Peter Hoeg, *Borderliners*

This chapter discusses student choice of topic, the overall structure of the writing conferences Sarah arranged for students as they wrote the first and second drafts of their research paper, and the grades Sarah gave each of the four students for the work they produced in the course. The chapter includes a discussion of Sarah's postcourse impressions and reflections and, finally, ends with a summary analysis of her ideological perspective toward writing and teaching writing.

Alan, Zola, Tan, and Araya met twice with Sarah in her office, as did all the students in the course: once to discuss the first draft of their final research paper and a second time to discuss the second draft of the final research paper. Sarah set aside a fifteen-minute block of time for each student. Students were directed to arrive at her office at least ten minutes before the scheduled appointment time so that they could pick up the draft of their paper and review Sarah's comments prior to meeting with her. Sarah left the papers outside her office so the conference in progress would not be interrupted by a student requesting his or her paper. During the days on which conferences took place regular class sessions were not held; thus students had more time to work on their papers. Further this gave Sarah the time to meet with students, though the time she spent in conferences far exceeded what she would have spent in class.

The extra time allotted for students to write their papers was very important because students in the summer session had to research and write their final papers for 102 in far less time than students taking the course during the regular fall or spring semesters. In addition, if Sarah had not canceled classes on conference days she would have been even more exhausted than she already was. This was a grueling period of time for students, but it was also especially exhausting for Sarah, who had to read and comment on approximately six student papers a night, three nights in a row, in order to be prepared to meet the next day with the students whose papers she had read the evening before. Many of the student drafts were handwritten, making the task of reading them quite difficult. To compound the situation the Boston area was in the midst of a record-breaking heat wave that continued without mercy during the period in which Sarah and the students were most pressured.

Students' Topic Choices

In this section I discuss briefly Alan, Zola, Tan, and Araya's choice of topic for the essay and the research paper and then I argue that choice of topic had a direct impact on the relative success each of the four students experienced in the course. Students were free to choose any topic they wished to pursue both for the essay and for the research paper. As noted earlier, the only restrictions Sarah placed on choice of research paper topic were that it be something about which people argued and that it not be about something that had just recently occurred because there would be a limited number of and limited types of sources available discussing such a contemporary issue.

Sarah directed students to a list of possible topics given in the research writing text assigned for the course (Memering, 1983, pp. 7–9). The only other advice Sarah gave students regarding choice of topic was that they should avoid abortion as a topic because some of her past students had had difficulty researching the topic because articles were torn out of magazines and other sources were missing from the library. Sarah attributed this to the popularity of abortion as a topic for research. This is interesting because abortion is the first topic presented in the list of possible research topics in the textbook assigned for Sarah's course. This book, *Research Writing: A Complete Guide to Writing Research Papers* by Dean Memering, is used in many of the 102 courses at UMB. One wonders whether students were driven by interest to pursue the topic or whether the topic was chosen because it was first on the list.

Alan's Choices

For the argumentative essay Alan chose as his topic "Should College Students Participate in Student Government?" Sarah had required students to write their essays without doing any research. She stipulated that the content of the paper be based solely on student personal knowledge and opinion. Alan not only had strong opinions regarding student participation in student government but also was privy to considerable information regarding student government because he had participated in, as an employee in the student activities office, organizing student government elections the previous March. As a result of this involvement he had considerable background knowledge upon which to base his argument in favor of student participation in student government. Alan felt strongly about the issue, and during the student government campaign and election he had voiced to me dismay at the lack of student participation in the process.

For his final paper Alan choose the title "Should Students Have Part-time Jobs?" Once again this was a topic Alan could relate to very strongly and about which he had considerable background knowledge. Alan had worked in a professional position for seven years prior to entering the university (see the first section of chapter 7), and as a full-time student at UMB he held a part-time position on campus. He was self-supporting, had been for years, and he was used to balancing schoolwork with the demands of a job. Alan recognized the extent to which his job in Hong Kong had contributed to preparing him for university work, and he was also well aware of the benefits of working part-time, particularly on campus as he did, while going to school full-time. Thus he once again chose a topic about which he had both considerable knowledge and strong opinions, and so he was prepared prior to doing his research to present a strong argument in favor of students working.

Zola's Choices

Like Alan, Zola chose topics for both her essay and research paper about which she had considerable background information and strong opinions. For her essay Zola chose the topic "English, an official language!" Zola related to this issue personally because she had grown up bilingual in Arabic and French and had learned English as an adult. She was not in favor of monolingualism and considered the English Only movement to be prejudiced against foreigners. In addition, Zola's 101 English class had spent considerable time discussing the English Only movement. The instructor for the course, Vivian Zamel, had provided for students readings on the movement, led by former U.S. senator Samuel Ichiye Hayakawa, to pass legislation to make English the official language of the United States. If such legislation were passed, bilingual programs would be outlawed, as would bilingual ballots, street signs, and any other official use of a language other than English in the United States. The instructor in Zola's 101 course used the English Only movement to generate debate among students, and the readings became the basis upon which students wrote papers for or against the English Only movement. Zola had thus spent considerable time arguing about, reading about, and writing about the issue of the adoption of English as the U.S. official language before she entered Sarah's research writing course. Zola chose to do her final research paper on the same topic, using the readings provided by her 101 teacher as references for her 102 paper.

Tan's Choices

Tan, in contrast to Alan and Zola, wrote an essay and final research paper on topics with which he was only somewhat familiar. For his essay Tan chose to write about age restrictions for drinking alcohol. In his essay he argued that there should not be a drinking age restriction in the United States. Tan came from Vietnam, a country in which there were no age restrictions on drinking. In his essay he mentions Vietnam, Greece, Italy, and Japan as countries where there are no "serious laws regulating the legal drinking age yet they do not really have many drinking problems." In addition, he commented more extensively on the philosophical perspective toward drinking in other countries, giving Italy as an example. The information Tan used in the Italy example came from Joe, Tan's friend/mentor who was a high school teacher. Tan had definite opinions about the drinking age, but he had difficulty with the topic because he was unfamiliar with the historical and cultural foundations of anti-alcohol legislation in the United States. However, because Tan had developed a strong network of support he was able to rely on Joe, who was familiar with the American views toward alcohol consumption and the historical and cultural contexts in which these views came to be translated into law, to help him with the information and arguments necessary to write the required argumentative essay.

For his research paper, Tan initially chose as his topic the Vietnamese refugee situation. As a Vietnamese refugee, Tan certainly had considerable background knowledge of the issue. However, the direction he chose to take in his paper led more to an attempt to sort out official policy on the part of Vietnam and the United States, a subject about which Tan was not knowledgeable. He soon found himself in a muddled state, unsure of where to go with his topic. At that point, with Joe's assistance, Tan chose a new topic, condom advertisements on television. For this topic Tan was able to find information in support of both sides of the argument. Tan was in favor of television advertisements for condoms, and considerable information on the topic was readily available in the library because the topic was directly related to the issue of AIDS. Thus, even though Tan did not have background knowledge in the area of condom advertising on TV, the topic was sufficiently narrow and clearly defined to make it an appropriate topic for a ten-page argumentative research paper.

Araya's Choices

Unlike Alan, Zola, and Tan, Araya relied solely on the list of possible research topics in the assigned research writing text in order to choose the topics for his essay and his research paper. Sarah had suggested that students choose from the list of topics in the text, although she by no means insisted that they do so. For his essay Araya chose to argue against the legalization of drugs, which was the second topic on the book's list.

In the introductory paragraph of his paper Araya wrote,

> Drug is a main problem in United States. THAT'S why people, who are in big government positeon always explain on tv. and radio about drug problem in our society. They always trie to find away how to get over this problem. Same of them say that the main solution for this problem is to legalized drug but the others dont whent to legalize it. So, there is same differens betwen them but it is very clear that drug shouldn't be legalized.

Clearly Araya presents here a topic with which he has become somewhat familiar through viewing television news. In this introduction Araya provides the reader with no information about the issue other than the fact that it is something about which people argue. In other words he establishes in his introduction that there are two sides to the issue of drug legalization, fulfilling Sarah's requirement that the essay topic be an issue about which people argue. However, although Sarah had spent considerable time in class focusing on the need to choose a topic that interested them, about which people argue, and for which information would be available in the library, she did not emphasize the need to choose a topic with narrow boundaries, one for which students could clearly identify with and under-stand the overriding issues. In fact, directing students to the list in their textbook ensured that some students would choose a topic that was unmanageable, because that list contained overarching issues that would have to be narrowed down in order for students to write a succinct and coherent ten-page paper.

Araya chose his topic for his final research paper, welfare, in much the same way, picking it from the list of suggested topics in the research writing text. In fact, Araya used the exact wording listed in the textbook, "Welfare: Social Benefit or Ripoff," for the title of his research paper. This topic was third from the end of the list of topics; thus, Araya chose one of the first topic suggestions for his essay and one of the last for his research paper. Of the four students, only Araya chose both his essay and research topics from the list in the textbook. Araya listened and followed through with all that Sarah said in class. He took her advice and her rules as absolutes, and he carried them out without question. Yet Araya had no back-ground experience with the welfare system, knew no one on welfare, and he did not know how complex the issue really was, so he had great difficulty sorting through information. Although Araya was clearly in favor of providing welfare to individuals in need, he did not have strong supporting arguments and data at hand initially to substantiate his position, nor had he ever had the opportunity to discuss and argue about the issue of welfare with others whose feedback might have served to further develop his thinking on the issue. Essentially Araya's isolation from people other than his family members led him to rely on the textbook assigned for the course for his paper topics, placing him at an extreme disadvantage in writing his papers. The difficulties Araya faced, however, were not due predominantly to linguistic issues, though certainly the fact that he struggled with English had an impact on his work (this was the case for all students in the class, though). Instead, his difficulties stemmed more directly from the cultural dissonance so apparent in his topic choices, his lack of a network of support, and his apparent desire to listen to and do exactly what Sarah directed him to do (she was his one and only connection to the English-speaking/writing world of the academy). In the end, his hard, hard work failed to lead to the success a writing teacher would hope for for her students.

Student Grades on Papers and in the Course

And how did each of the students fare in terms of the bottom line? Table 13.1 shows the students' grades on their essays, research paper drafts, and final research papers as well as their overall course grades.

Table 13.1. Student Grades

	Essay	Draft 1	Draft 2	Final Paper	Course
Alan	B+/88	B–/80	A–/92	A+/100	A–
Zola	C+/78	C/73	B/83	A–/92	B+
Tan	B/85	C+/79	B+/89	A–/92	B+
Araya	C–/72	D/64	C/75	C–/72	C–

The final grades Alan and Zola received conform to expectations: deemed proficient writers at the outset of the course, they remained classified as such at the end of the semester. Zola, however, failed somewhat to meet expectations in that she had been an A student in her first (101) writing course and she expected to receive an A in research writing also. Her persistent resistant behaviors discussed previously (see chapter 10), her failure to ingratiate herself with Sarah during conferences, and the unfortunate experience of having witnessed an armed robbery certainly negatively impacted on the final grade she received in the course. A B+ is not a bad grade, however, and it situates Zola nicely in the proficient category. Tan, on the other hand, had exceeded all expectations in terms of final grade. Most certainly his social skills displayed when in conference with Sarah, and used to his advantage in networking for help, enhanced his grade. Again, Araya, deemed less proficient at the outset, remained as unskilled in all areas of discourse anticipated in the writing class, and in the academy, as he was at the beginning of the course.

Writing Conference Analysis

Conferences were established by Sarah so that all students in the class would receive equal time to discuss their research papers and to receive feedback from her about revisions they needed to do before submitting their second drafts and the final versions of their research paper.

Time Spent in Conference

Although conferences were scheduled for fifteen-minute blocks of time, Sarah spent variable amounts of time with each student. Table 13.2 shows how much time Sarah spent with Alan, Zola, Tan, and Araya.

Table 13.2. Time Spent with Students in Conferences

	Conference 1	Conference 2
Alan	29 min. 30 sec.	26 min. 44 sec.
Zola	15 min. 59 sec.	17 min. 37 sec.
Tan	19 min. 01 sec.	18 min. 26 sec.
Araya	6 min. 13 sec.	7 min. 54 sec.

Alan, the most proficient at oral and, to a degree, written discourse, was able to capture and hold Sarah's attention for the longest period of time during both conference sessions. It was not until I timed the taped conference sessions that I became aware of the extreme discrepancy, particularly between the time Sarah spent with Alan and the time she spent with Araya. As an observer, I was not aware of the huge time discrepancy, for the exchanges between Sarah and Alan in conference were, for the most part, so smooth that while listening to and observing them I felt no discomfort. I noticed Alan to seem a bit frayed for only a second or so, so the time did not appear to drag on. Alan was quick to recover, so his time with Sarah placed no strain on her; time moved on without notice and, in fact, the first conference might have gone on for far longer had Zola not made her presence known. Zola got the allotted time for the first conference and just a couple of minutes more for the second. A bit domineering, and in control at times, she was driven by a desire to discuss issues then hampered by Sarah's concern that Zola structure her paper according to guidelines. Although Tan was unable to capture Sarah's attention and time to the degree that Alan was, Tan was, nonetheless, able to push the limits of the allotted time to his advantage. Araya, in striking contrast, did not even get half the officially allotted time. His discomfort and unfamiliarity with the notion of conferencing created the need on Sarah's part to fill the silence. Members of mainstream culture do not tolerate silence well and seek to fill the void silence seemingly creates (Scollon & Scollon, 1981). Sarah did just that when confronted with Araya's silence. After each conference with Araya she appeared to be exhausted by the effort it took to meet with him. Araya appeared relieved to have the experience end when Sarah asked him if he had any more questions, and he freely responded "No," thus allowing the possibility of exiting the office. The question remains: how are we to meet the needs of the underprepared so that they too may gain access to the forms of discourse that will provide further access to the academy and, perhaps, to future success in life?

Purpose of Conferences

The explicit purpose of the first conference was to discuss issues related to research and writing, not grammar, spelling, punctuation, or endnotes. On a comment sheet Sarah prepared for each student she segmented research into the following subcategories, each of which she graded based on the corresponding percentages: quality of research (25 percent), quantity of research (25 percent), integration of research into paper (25 percent), and effectiveness of quotes (25 percent). She subcategorized and graded on writing as: basic organization (20 percent), clarity of ideas (20 percent), development of ideas (30 percent), transitions (10 percent), unity within paragraphs (10 percent), and sentence structure (10 percent). The comment sheet also contained a category dealing with grammar, punctuation, and spelling. However, Sarah did not grade or comment on this area until the second draft.

Sarah firmly believed that revising and conferencing positively affected the development of student writing. She felt it was important to structure the process of revising and meeting to receive feedback into the course so that all students in the class would go through the revision process and would also have an equal amount of time with her to receive feedback on their work in progress. Nonetheless, despite Sarah's attempt to structure equality into the process by allotting equal time to each student, there was extreme variation among the four students in terms of the type of feedback they received from Sarah, the amount of feedback they received, and even the amount of time they spent in conference with her.

The differences relate in many ways to quality of feedback. In this instance, the more-proficient writers, Alan and Zola, received the most feedback from Sarah. And Tan, a less-proficient writer, was able to elicit considerable help from Sarah because of his extensive verbal ability—essentially his communicative competence gained through close association with Joe and others. Still, the type and quality of feedback received by Alan, Zola, and Tan did differ. However, it was Araya, the least-proficient writer of the four, who was given the least feedback. In fact, striking differences in quality and type of feedback occur in Araya's case. Thus, overall, there was considerable variation in what occurred during Sarah's writing conferences with Alan, Zola, Tan, and Araya. And, despite the fact that Sarah was committed to the egalitarian perspective of the cognitive approach, she unwittingly engaged in a process that accorded differential access to literate forms of language to students based on their proficiency, or lack thereof, in oral and written language and based on their previous cultural knowledge regarding the manner in which the academy expected a paper to be developed and discussed.

Along with Sarah's explicit beliefs about how students should behave in the context of the writing conference and throughout the revision process, however, came the tacit assumption that students understood her expectations and these expectations did not need to be explained explicitly. I discussed the ramifications of Sarah's assumptions in chapters 9 through 12, in which I analyzed the writing conferences. For example, Araya, who appeared to be totally unaware of what was expected of him in conference both in terms of physical actions as well as verbal behaviors, was able to elicit from Sarah very little assistance with his research paper. In fact, he was provided with a repetition of information Sarah had already lectured on in class. Araya's situation contrasted sharply with Alan's; already socialized into the expected discourse of the writing conference, Alan was able to elicit from Sarah the greatest amount of assistance. In addition, as a result of his facility with the discourse of the conference, Alan made an extraordinarily favorable impression on Sarah, while Araya, on the other hand, made a most unfavorable impression.

Although Sarah had been entirely explicit during class about the expected form and format for the students essays and research papers, she never made explicit her expectations about how to work together effectively in conference or about what she expected them to do in making revisions to their papers. And while Sarah had been totally directive in class, she expected students to take control during the conference. This required that the students behave in a manner quite in contrast to the way she expected them to behave in her class. For Sarah to assume that a student like Araya, who was so new to the university context, would take control during the writing conference was entirely misguided. By suggesting that Sarah was complicit in creating a context in which Araya was unable to participate—or, rather, begin to participate—in the discourse of the academy, I am by no means suggesting that she acted out of malice. I do suggest, however, that it is important to uncover these implicit, yet complicit, occurrences and to link them to specific ideologies. In this case, Sarah believed that Araya was at fault because he did not act appropriately in the conference. He was acting, however, in the very way he had experienced others behaving in the context of Sarah's classroom. In this instance a specific rendering of the ways of behaving in the conference would have been extremely helpful for all students. Opportunities to practice the expected behaviors would have been most beneficial as well. Sarah could have met with Alan to discuss his paper in front of the whole class. Or she could have called upon a proficient writer in the class to role-play the conference with her. Rather than put a student on the spot, Sarah could have had the tutor assigned to the class role-play a conference situation. Students would then have been provided a model of the expected behaviors required in the conference. And before this acting-out of the writing conference, Sarah could have made explicit the rules of the conference.

Explicit Rendering of Expected Writing Conference Behaviors

Had Sarah rendered explicit the behaviors she expected students to display in the writing conference they would have included the following. The first two she did explicitly state to students, but I have added many more items to this list of behaviors that Sarah seemed to assume her students would engage in.

1. Make sure you arrive at my office at least ten minutes—even earlier is better—before our conference is scheduled to begin.

2. This early arrival will allow you the opportunity to review all the comments I have made on your paper. Start reading from the beginning of the paper all the way to the end. Your paper will be placed outside my office door.

3. Bring with you to the conference a notebook that has a solid surface that you can use as a writing board upon which you can place your paper when you are in the conference.

4. Bring a pen (bring more than one in case you run out of ink) so you can write down on your paper the suggestions I give you for revision. Have the pen, paper, and notebook in hand when you enter my office for your conference.

5. When it is time for you to begin the conference I will invite you into my office. You may then sit in the empty chair next to my desk. It is important that you not interrupt me if I am with another student or on the phone.

6. When I invite you into my office we will exchange greetings—"How are you?" "Fine thanks, and you?" "Good, thank you"—then get right to your paper. I may or may not get up to greet you.

7. During the conference I will sit at the corner of my desk facing you. You will place the notebook on your lap, put your paper on the notebook. Your pen will be in your hand.

8. I will ask you whether you have any questions. This is a signal for you to go through my comments one by one, not a signal for you to ask questions that don't focus directly on the text of your paper.

9. You will start with the first comment I have made on your paper.

10. One strategy is to read my comment and then ask what you need to do to revise. For example: I might write, "What do you mean by this?" You will read my comment out loud, and then I will look at your paper.

11. I will read the sentence or section of your paper that I did not understand. This means that your paper is central to our discussion. It will be passed back and forth between us as we discuss the comments I have made on your paper and the questions you have in reaction to these comments.

12. You will then have the opportunity to explain what you mean by what you have written. One way to do this is to try to restate the sentence or section we are discussing. Try to look at me as you explain what you are trying to say in your paper.

13. Once you restate what you have written I may better understand you. Remember that my misunderstanding could be based on something as small as the fact that you have written a run-on sentence, for example. We might get stuck between grammar and meaning and you may be confused. Persevere. And always smile, acknowledging that you welcome the help I am giving you.

14. If I still do not understand you I may ask more specific questions as I try to understand better what you are attempting to communicate.

15. The focus of our discussion will always be on your paper, specifically the comments I have made on it. We will speak through and about the text—the paper you have written.

16. Please do not ask any other questions until all the comments I made on your paper have been discussed.

17. We only have fifteen minutes so I want to make sure that you have the opportunity to understand the steps you need to take to revise based on my concerns with your paper.

18. Once we have covered all of my comments on your paper, you may then ask other questions.

19. Please do not ask me to repeat what I have already said in class or to provide information that you can find in the textbook.

20. The conference is your time to get direct help from me so that you can revise and develop your paper. But, if I have noted an error in grammar, for example, you may suggest a correction, even if you do not know the correct grammatical form. By doing so you indicate to me that you are trying, and this effort on your part might just get me to provide you with the correction needed.

21. Do not ask simple questions about spelling or grammar. A dictionary or grammar book can help you with these concerns. I will not answer you if you ask me how to spell a word or what the correct grammatical form is. Once again, however, if you try to offer a correction, I just might provide you with the correction you need (but I may not).

22. When the conference is over, I will let you know by saying: "Well, I guess the time is up. Good luck with your revisions." This is the signal for you to put your paper in your notebook and stand with notebook in hand.

23. At this point you should say: "Thank you very much for your helpful comments. I'll start working on the revisions you suggested right away. Thanks again. See you." Then you should leave the office because I will probably have another student waiting to see me.

I have created this rendering of the implicit rules of Sarah's writing conferences through analysis of my observations of Sarah in conference with Alan, Zola, Tan, and Araya. These rules do not capture totally the subtleties, the nuances that came into play during Sarah's conferences, either enhancing or lowering Sarah's impression of each student. Such subtleties include a student's ability to insinuate humor into the encounter at the appropriate moment—so difficult to characterize prior to the fact—or, in turn, to appreciate the instructor's efforts to be humorous; a student's dressing in such a way that communicates order, control, and respect for the instructor; or, even, a student's ability to make a connection on a human level, through a shared interest, for example, quite apart from the topic of the paper being discussed.

How does one communicate to students the need for them to move in rhythm with the instructor so as to convey the message the two are in sync with one another not only verbally but also physically? Even if a student understands that particular behaviors, gestures, manners of dress, discursive choices, and so forth are necessary, it still might be nearly impossible to engage in the required behaviors. The further the required behaviors are from those expected in a student's previous home and academic contexts, the more difficult it will be for the student to engage in the newly expected behaviors. Assuming a new set of communicative behaviors—in this case, the language of academia expected of the beginning university student—may, in fact, require that the student take on a whole new personality, a whole new sense of self in relation to others (Scollon & Scollon, 1981). But we cannot expect that students will be able to immediately assume a whole new persona just because it has been articulated and modeled. What is necessary are repeated opportunities for the student to practice the expected behaviors—to serve an apprenticeship, if you will. The more opportunities the instructor presents, the more likely it is that the student will eventually become socialized into the new cultural models.

Self-Reflection: My Behavior with Students

Now that I have made explicit Sarah's implicit rules of the writing conference, I realize that they are very similar to the rules that I, too, have employed when discussing the development of a paper with a student. In my conferences I am in control and the student is there to perform, but I have never expressed this explicitly to a student. I have appreciated those who seem to intuit what I expect and, in turn, behave accordingly, because this makes encounters with students so much more pleasurable.

Since observing Sarah I have spent much time reflecting upon my own behaviors and the behavior of those I experienced and observed when I was but a student myself. It is extremely uncomfortable to admit this, but I know that I have tried to avoid encounters with students who make me feel ill at ease, and when I meet with such students I often make every effort to cut short our conference. With students with whom I am comfortable—often this means that we share an ideological perspective—I spend more time. Of course spending more time with the students who make me comfortable increases the likelihood that they will advance farther in academia while reducing the chances that the students who cause me discomfort will ever acquire the behaviors deemed appropriate in the academy. I know also that the behaviors I display in meetings with my students reflect the experiences I had as a student myself—I am a socially constructed academic, as are all who are in academia.

I remember clearly meeting with my advisor to discuss a paper as a beginning graduate student. I had not yet written the paper, so I arrived at the meeting with all my notes in hand—I wanted to communicate at least that I had been working on the project. The professor was appalled and asked me directly how I expected him to respond to notes. I had expected a discussion of the topic, and he had expected a paper to read and respond to. Never again did I arrive at such a meeting without a completed text in hand. I also remember clearly the initial conferences with my dissertation advisor. I knew these meetings were designed to initiate discussion of my topic and to frame the structure of the dissertation more fully. During the first meeting, my advisor started providing me with sources and a possible structure. I listened intently, with an unopened notebook on my lap. He stopped, incredulous, and asked, "Aren't you going to take notes?" Well, I had never taken notes when meeting with faculty members in their offices before—that was what I did in class; but I frantically opened my notebook and started writing. I never made that mistake again either.

And I remember another lesson I learned in graduate school, when I left a class with my professor to discuss further a linguistic issue that had intrigued me during class. We made our way to his office and continued our intellectual conversation. The professor suggested I read a dissertation written by one of Noam Chomsky's first students (this professor had been one of Chomsky's first students as well), a copy of which he provided to me. At our next meeting, another graduate student asked through the open doorway, "Do you have a minute?" My professor stood up, walked to the door, and swung it shut. This was the moment that I knew, truly knew, that I had made it through the gates that would eventually lead to the Ph.D. Although this fellow student would finally get a degree, she never received the recommendations and support that I did. Academia, like life, is very unfair, and many times the advantages go to those who manage to learn the discourse and behave in the expected manner.

When I think back to that early time in graduate school I remember answering many questions about my family background. I often felt that I was being read for pedigree, not degree. But I knew how to perform. That is not to say that I did not work hard, so hard, as I continue to do today and will in the years to follow, but the pedigree was important. It got me through doors that were often closed to other students. The more access I had to professors, the more I learned about the expected practices in the academy. Each professor seemed to want to know how I was able to insinuate myself into contexts so easily. I knew what to say, whom to reference, what to do, what to wear, how to be subservient yet seemingly in control. One professor even mentioned to me on a number of occasions that talking to me about intellectual issues was like talking to a man, which he considered to be a high compliment indeed. I began graduate school with the foundation upon which to build, with behaviors that allowed me further access to the academy. And I did not make the members of the academy uncomfortable. They did not fear they would have to fail me, they did not fear that their valuable time would be wasted in my presence—they felt that I had something to offer: intellectual curiosity, cultural capital, and, finally, access to the academic press when I became student editor of a journal.

The more practice—greater access—a student has had with academic behaviors and contexts before an encounter with a gatekeeper (instructor, admissions officer, dean), the better able the student will be to perform, to display the behaviors the situation demands. Thus, no matter how explicit an instructor is, there is always an advantage for some. This is a harsh reality. Nonetheless, I believe it is incumbent upon those teaching writing to make every effort to enunciate their expectations for each communicative encounter students must engage

in. Otherwise, only those students who already possess the principal components of the discourses of power—obtained through association with those
in power—will continue to succeed. Those who have no access to power yet
try so hard, like Araya and so many others I have known throughout the years,
will not make it. This sad story is one I have sought to fracture, to tell, to over-
turn, and to prevent from happening again and again, though I, too, have
wittingly and unwittingly been complicit in keeping the gates open to the spe-
cially chosen few.

What, then, is the relationship between the explicit expression of an ideological perspective and the realities of the classroom or other academic context in
which more tacitly held beliefs—the unconscious playing-out of our social histories—might dominate and thus determine practice? Are many instructors truly
aware of the relationship between the explicit expression of ideological perspectives and our own worlds of teaching and research? This relationship becomes
most exposed in the teaching of writing, I would argue, because of the lowly
position of writing as a nondiscipline and the mainly denigrated contexts in which
it is taught. The places and spaces that writing instructors and students inhabit—
the very bottom rungs of the academic ladder—serve to create contexts rife with
contradictions. Instructors, for the most part, want out; the students just want to
get through the requirement and on to something of substance.

The Nature of Beginnings and Endings

My work with Sarah, Alan, Zola, Tan, and Araya was an intense, exhilarating, and
intellectually stimulating experience. My observations of Sarah's class and writing
conferences and my interviews with her and her students opened my eyes, allowing me not only to reflect critically on the theoretical, practical, and research-
based concerns I have addressed in this book but also to assess critically my own
ideological perspectives and practices. My on-site ethnographic work came to an
end with a final interview I conducted with Sarah after she had completed the
grades for the course. In what follows, I discuss this final interview, thus marking
the end of my work with Sarah. Prior to this discussion, I looked to Harold Rosen's
work to help characterize the story I have recounted of one extraordinary writing
teacher and her four fine students. Rosen notes, in a discussion of narrative, that

> The unremitting flow of events must first be selectively attended to, interpreted as
> holding relationships, causes, motives, feelings, consequences—in a word, mean-
> ings. To give order to this otherwise unmanageable flux we must take another step
> and invent, yes, invent, beginnings and ends, for out there are no such things. . . .
> This is the axiomatic element of narrative: it is the outcome of a mental process
> which enables us to excise from our experience a meaningful sequence, to place it
> within boundaries, to set around it the frontiers of the story, to make it resonate in
> the contrived silences with which we may precede and end it. . . . The narrative
> edits ruthlessly the raw tape. (1984, pp. 12–14, cited in Cazden, 1988, p. 24)

This Is the End, My Friend

I met with Sarah after she finished the course—grades in and all—and asked her to tell me what her perceptions were of each of the four students. I did not prompt Sarah's memory or establish the order in which she was to discuss the students, yet Sarah discussed Alan, Zola, Tan, and Araya with me, in that order, mirroring the hierarchical organizing structure I had bestowed upon the group. The organizational pattern to emerge repeatedly throughout this study placed, perhaps not so innocently, Alan at the top, followed by Zola and then Tan, with Araya always discussed last, thus implicitly at the bottom of the heap. Here we have best student first, worst student last; best known first, least known last; most in control first; least in control last. Stepping out of my own text I can see that I have for the most part devoted the most attention, and foremost attention, always to Alan and the least to Araya.

At this point I continue the discussion of Sarah's perceptions of the four students so that they may be juxtaposed to my own. "My student" was Sarah's "excellent student"; my "resisting student" was Sarah's "good writer, with problems"; my "networker" was Sarah's "unorganized student"; and finally, my "silent(ced) one" was Sarah's "struggler." Why did Sarah characterize Alan as an excellent student, Zola as a good writer with problems, Tan as unorganized, and Araya as really struggling? I present Sarah's perceptions of the four in a bit more detail in order to answer that question.

Alan First

Sarah needed no prompting to help summon her thoughts on Alan.

> When I think of [Alan] the first thing I think of is an excellent student, and then you have to think what makes an excellent student. Well, he seems to know or to be able to pick out in a course what's important and what's not important. What things the professor is talking about that he needs to really work on in his writing and the things that really need to stand out, and he can differentiate that from, you know, details, things that aren't that important. He also is very well organized; he meets deadlines; he seems to be able to handle time very well. He works incredibly hard. He did a lot of background reading before he even started writing his paper. That's my impression, anyway, that he had a body of knowledge before he sat down to write, and he knew a lot more about his topic than what he put into his paper.

Sarah also remembered that when she had asked him a question during conferences, Alan "not only could answer my question, but he usually could talk about it in more depth or talk about other sources he had read, why he included this, why he didn't include other things." My analysis of the transcripts of the writing conference tapes reveals that Alan and Sarah did not talk about his topic, but they did, in fact, talk about his variety of sources for the paper. And Alan's background knowledge may have been more a reflection of the fact that he understood his topic from a personal perspective rather than that he had learned about it by reading sources. Sarah remembered also that Alan "had an awful lot of notes, note cards and things like that."

Zola Next

Sarah remembered Zola also as "an excellent student, but for very different reasons than Alan's." Sarah felt Zola had "a real love of learning and wanted to learn, but [Zola] also in that summer semester had a really hard time. I mean she had, was it her friend that was working at the hotel who was robbed at the club? So at the beginning she had a lot of personal trauma, and so I think that affected her performance at the beginning of the course." Actually the robbery had not occurred until midway through the course, and though no doubt it did affect Zola's overall performance in the course it did not have an effect on her first essay.

Sarah also considered Zola to be "a real live wire." She remembered her as also asking "very perceptive questions" and felt she "was always thinking." However, Sarah also had the impression that Zola "was kind of cluttered," though "she knew where everything was, and she could pull out whatever she needed to work on." This Sarah contrasted to her memory of Alan, who she felt had "everything in its proper little place" and knew "where to find what in what folder and all that." Sarah felt also that Zola "seemed to be always pressed for time," whereas Alan "seemed to have plenty of time to get things done." Sarah felt that perhaps Zola had not been able to get things in to her on time because she was working. This was not the case, however. Zola did not work during the summer semester.

Then Tan

And how did Sarah remember Tan? Sarah recalled Tan as "a really good student, but he wasn't quite as good a student as [Zola] or [Alan] mostly because I think he still has problems with English." Sarah recalled further,

> I think it takes him a lot, it took him a lot longer to read his material for his paper. I think that it took him a lot longer to pull things together. If I remember correctly, he had a real hard time at the beginning settling on a topic and in a six-week course that's something that really hurts a student if they can't decide right away what they want to do. There really isn't time to flounder around because they have to begin researching right away, and I think that he floundered a little because he couldn't decide on his topic, and it might have been because he wanted to so do something argumentative. I think that's maybe what it was; he had a hard time coming up with something.

Sarah felt also that Tan did not always understand what he read, though she felt he always worked hard, and that perhaps he had too many constraints against him as he was working and had to leave the course early because his brother was getting married. Sarah was left with a perception of Tan as having problems, which he in fact did have, but she did not recall, or at least does not recount explicitly, that Tan received an A– on his final paper and a B+ in the course.

Strangely, or perhaps not so strangely because he had a lot of help from his network of support, Tan received higher grades than Zola on all assignments, and he earned the same grade she did in the course. Despite the fact that Tan and Zola earned the same overall grade in the course, Sarah remembered Zola—who also got a B+—as a "good writer." Sarah recalled more specifically, "My memory of her writing was that she was a fairly sophisticated writer, and she really had a good vocabulary and good, sophisticated sentence structure. She was handling the language a level well above some of the other students in the course." But Sarah recalled Tan in the following way: "I think he was probably one that could have benefited from more time, but even though I say that, still in my mind I don't know how much he really understands about revision, or he really understood what revising was, you know." Once again Sarah relied on Alan as a basis of comparison:

> I think that a student like [Alan]—when he got his paper back with my comments on it he would read over and come into my office with his list of questions and we'd go boom, boom, boom right down the list. You know, he's incredibly organized about the whole procedure, and I think [Tan] kind of looked at and he read it and he kind of understood the comments, but if he didn't understand them, he didn't really act, and I think that he also may have just been concerned with getting through the course and that was it. I mean, students have different motivations, but I think Alan was one who really, really wanted to do well, and I don't know about Tan. I mean, on the one hand I think he did really want to do well, but I think on the other hand he just, I don't know, maybe halfway through kinda looked at it and said, "I have all these different things I'm trying to do and I'm just going to get through this the best I can."

Tan, in fact, wanted desperately to do well in the course in order to be accepted into the engineering program. And, in fact, he did do well in the course. Tan's final grade of B+ was one of only three given in the course. Alan's A– was one of only three in the course, and no one received an A.

And at Last, the Last: Araya

Initially Sarah had difficulty recalling Araya's work, although she did recall what he looked like. Once she was able to bring him to mind she remembered that she felt he had "really struggled" in the course. She felt this was the case because he still did not have a complete grasp of the English language, so I think writing was really, really a struggle for him I don't know . . . maybe if he had more time he would have done better, or maybe it's a case that he needed another course like between 101 and 102, but I do remember that Araya really struggled, and I think that, now he's coming back to me, one of his problems is that he didn't talk, and the conferences that I had with him he rarely said a word, and I would say, "Do you understand what I want you to do?" and he always said "yes," but then when the revised draft came in it was kind of obvious that he hadn't understood, or if he did understand he didn't know how to do it. I think that was one of my frustrations with him, that I never knew when he was understanding and when he wasn't. He never asked any questions in class.

Once again, as she had with both Zola and Tan, Sarah called upon her memory of Alan as a basis of comparison.

Although it seems like maybe whereas [Alan] kind of took control of the whole situation, [Araya] just kind of went along, and he wasn't able because of language or culture or whatever, to take control of his paper or writing conference. . . . It's a hard kind of difference to describe, but I think [Alan] was much more in control of things, you know, and I think maybe the whole process of a research paper was so overwhelming for [Araya] that he really didn't know what to do with it, and he was just gonna kinda get through the best that he could.

Once I reminded Sarah of the topic of Araya's final research paper—the welfare system—she was able to remember more about him and his performance in her course.

All right now, and I think that was probably another one of his problems with the course, is, the welfare system is just—I don't think he probably had the background knowledge to even begin to understand what he was reading about. Maybe I should have steered him away from that, but one of the problems in a six-week course is you don't really get to know your students well enough . . . that when you start to begin to get to know them it's too late to have them change their topics or whatever.

Sarah at this point in the discussion paused to look over the first and second drafts and final version of Araya's research paper.

Well, looking at it now, he did improve from the first draft; the last draft is a lot better. I mean, he did go out and find more sources and explored the topic a little more in depth, but he picked an incredibly difficult topic. . . . I mean, it's something very difficult for even an American to understand, let alone someone who is coming to this country without, you know, the background on the government to begin with. . . . Yeah, so it really is a difficult topic, and especially for someone whose grasp of English isn't as sophisticated as some of the other students in the course.

Thus Araya, who struggled with the most difficult topic, managed only to raise his grade from a D on his first draft to a C– on the final paper. In contrast, Alan was able to formulate the arguments he presented in his paper from his own personal experience and thus needed only to find supporting evidence for his assertions. In fact, Alan described the process of writing his paper as merely an exercise in data collection, one he said involved little thought. One might think that Alan had read Henry Giroux (1988), who argues forcefully that critical educators should create contexts in which students can draw on lived experience as a foundation for gaining access to academic discourse.

Sarah's Final Overall Perceptions of the Four Students

In conclusion, I present a brief summary, in list form, of Sarah's perceptions of each of the four students.

Alan

Positive
excellent student
able to assess what teacher wanted
   in course
on time
meets deadlines
organized
hardworking
understood revision process
understood teacher comments
in control
asked questions in conferences

Zola

Positive
excellent student
love of learning
asked perceptive questions in class
always thinking
good writer
sophisticated sentence structure
good vocabulary

Negative
pressed for time
did not meet deadlines
cluttered
appeared disorganized

Tan

Positive	*Negative*
good student	problems with English
	did not understand revision
	indecisive
	floundered
	wanted just to get through the course
	took too long to read material

Araya

Positive	*Negative*
tried really hard	problems with English
	did not understand revision
	did not talk
	not in control of writing
	not in control of conferences
	chose difficult topic
	really struggled

Sarah resigned from her two adjunct writing positions to travel to a third-world country to work in a development program for three years. And while she continues to work with nonnative speakers of English, she will not teach writing. As the interview drew to a close, I asked Sarah whether she thought she would miss teaching writing. She responded, "Right now, I don't think so, because I'm still coming off the overload. I just taught too much writing for too long and it got to be that I just was so sick of always grading papers."

Tertiary Knowledge

Clearly, Sarah repeatedly displayed in her interactions with students both as she lectured and as she met with them individually her tertiary knowledge of writing. Sarah consistently related to students bits and pieces of "rules for writing," rules that often had no true or absolute basis in the real-world contexts of academic writing, or within any other genre, for that matter. Sarah's insistence, for example, that "one-sentence paragraphs don't exist" is a mere construct of writing-textbook writers and has no basis in reality, because one-sentence paragraphs do exist in academic writing. Her insistence that "a good paragraph has anywhere from seven to fifteen sentences" is also a construct of textbook writers, one that Sarah accepted without question and conveyed to students as a hard and fast rule for writing. The notion itself that "good" writing is equated with numbers of sentences totally discounts the nature of writing as a communicative act or a performance art that may at once be graceful, dense, obtuse, critically acclaimed, or just plain boring and, as such, considered either good or bad depending on one's notions about what is graceful, dense, obtuse, worthy of acclaim, or just plain boring. To say that writing can be both a communicative act and at the same time a performance recognizes that student writers may in fact be writing more to display competence in the "mechanics" of writing, such as punctuation, spelling, paragraph formation, and structure, and an ability to use the library to find reference materials, than to really communicate their ideas. In fact, all of Sarah's rules for writing can be classified as forms of tertiary knowledge.

Writing in Sarah's course was taught from a text or from bits and pieces of texts reconstituted as class handouts. Writing was not considered as a process or form, that is, as something variable across genres and disciplines and thus available for analysis and critique. Nor was writing considered as a social construct embodying ways of acting and communicating that are linked to particular social practices and social groups. Rather, Sarah presented writing as a set of rules constituting a self-contained body of knowledge. Sarah expressly conveyed the message, through words and actions, that this body of knowledge was to be uncritically conveyed to and, in turn, uncritically absorbed by pliant, compliant students. Sarah conveyed this tertiary knowledge of academic writing acquired from textbooks and her own experience teaching with the best of intentions; she wanted her students to improve as writers. She wanted them to take from the course an understanding of academic writing that would serve to their advantage in other courses that they would take in the future.

Ideological Perspective

Sarah's ideological perspective links directly to the perspective of the traditional approach to teaching writing. This perspective assumes a hierarchy in which the teacher, as authority, possesses a body of knowledge that, once conveyed to and stored by students, will ensure each student's ability to write. If a student fails to write in a manner deemed appropriate by those who, in turn, are assumed to possess this body of knowledge, then it is the student's fault for not having studied enough or—as was the case when Sarah assumed that Tan's failure to understand her comments concerning his run-on sentence was due to his failure to complete the assigned run-on sentence exercises with the tutor—not having yet done one's homework. Sarah's perspective is also aligned to the traditional approach in that Sarah viewed the teaching of form, in this case the teaching of the argumentative essay and the argumentative research paper, as divorced from any social context. The form was taught because it was the form displayed and discussed in the rhetoric chosen for the class, not because it had any linkage whatsoever to an academic discipline or, for that matter, to the form required in the writing proficiency exam.

Writing was thus totally removed from any meaningful context related to the world of academic or personal writing.

In addition to holding an ideological perspective toward teaching writing that conformed to the traditional approach, Sarah also held beliefs supporting the cognitive approach. Her belief in the revision process and the need to institute writing conferences into the structure of the writing course were overt examples of her adherence to the cognitive approach to teaching writing. Along with these beliefs, however, came the tacit assumption that students understood her unstated expectations regarding the manner in which one should behave in the context of the conference and throughout the process of revision.

Finally, how closely did Sarah's teaching conform to her espoused beliefs regarding the manner in which writing should be taught? There was not a close conformity between expressed ideology and the reality of Sarah's classroom practice. While Sarah explicitly expressed an adherence, for the most part, to a process approach to teaching writing, her classroom practice revealed a greater adherence to a traditional approach. This fact—a dominant reliance on a traditional orientation—became clearer to Sarah as she reflected through discussions with me the ongoing nature of her research writing class. What also became clearer to Sarah was the degree to which her practices were in effect an outgrowth of her prior experiences teaching both ESL and writing.

When Sarah and I taught at UMB, the writing program was directed by Vivian Zamel, a prominent researcher in the field of process writing. The director's ideological perspectives created a powerful lens through which the whole program was viewed and supposedly understood both by members of the community and by those in other contexts engaged in teaching, researching, or theorizing about writing. I had assumed process writing was the dominant approach in the department, and Sarah had assumed the same; yet both she and I learned that perhaps this was not the case and that certainly Sarah's practice did not demonstrate such a perspective. Even Zamel's article "Responding to Student Writing" leaves open to question the degree to which the faculty in the program actively carried out the tenets of the professed ideological perspective of this writing program.

In conclusion, what the close attention and analysis of the writing class and conferences confirms is that the role of writing instructors and the world of students attempting to access academic prose are infinitely complex, often contradictory sites that differentially affect students from outside mainstream contexts and place extraordinary demands on instructors who are overburdened and underpaid.

SPEAKING BITTERNESS, OFFERING HOPE: CONCLUDING COMMENTS

> The first symptom of oppression is the repression of words; the state of suffering is so total and so assumed that it is not known to be there. "Speaking Bitterness" is the bringing to consciousness of the virtually unconscious oppression; one person's realization of an injustice brings to mind other injustices for the whole group.—Juliet Mitchell, *Woman's Estate*

Historical and Present-Day Racism

As a country, the United States has a sad, well-documented history of imposing on minority students restrictions and requirements that seek to erase students' histories, languages, and ways of thinking and behaving so that they will conform to the expected ways of behaving, thinking, speaking, and writing of the dominant community: middle- and upper-class, mostly White America. In his song "Wounded Knee," Floyd Red Crow Westerman movingly addresses this reality for Native Americans, and in so doing opens the door for "speaking bitterness" not only for his community but for all oppressed peoples.

> You put me in your boarding schools,
> Made me learn the white man's rules,
> Made me leave my home, my friends,
> Think I'll go back there again. (1982)

221

Wrenched from their communities, young Native Americans were sent to live in U.S. government boarding schools, punished for speaking their native language, and forced to assume the cultural and linguistic ways of dominant society. This dominant society was so powerful that, with legal justification, it stole children from their families to educate them far from home.

Linguistic minority students have experienced these same pressures from the dominant U.S. society time and time again, to the degree that as these students acquire English they often lose connection with their home language and culture. These students are frequently punished severely in schools for speaking their own languages. Massachusetts, for example, passed in November 2002 a statewide referendum to impose English-only classes for nonnative speakers of English, trying to do away completely with the bilingual programs that have been in place for more than twenty-five years. California has done the same.

To this day, in order to "make it" in the White man's world, Blacks need to adopt the behaviors of successful White students, thus becoming what William Labov designates as "Lames": essentially, lost souls in their own communities, destined to live in a shadow world between the Black and White communities, without full membership in either. Clarence Thomas, the only Black member of the Supreme Court, most recently typified his Lame status by being the only member of the court to vote against Thomas Miller-El, a Black "death row inmate who claimed prosecutors stacked the jury with whites and said he was not allowed to present evidence of the alleged bias" (Associated Press, 2003, p. 1). Evidence presented before the Supreme Court included the "claim the Dallas district attorney's office once specifically trained prosecutors to get rid of minority juror candidates because 'they almost always empathize with the accused'" (p. 1). Writing for the majority, Justice Anthony M. Kennedy states, "Irrespective of whether the evidence could prove sufficient to support a charge of systematic exclusion of African-Americans, it reveals that the culture of the district attorney's office in the past was suffused with bias against African-Americans in jury selection" (p. 1). Siding with Kennedy were Chief Justice William H. Rehnquist and Justices John Paul Stevens, Sandra Day O'Connor, Antonin Scalia, David Souter, Ruth Bader Ginsburg, and Stephen Breyer. The only dissenting opinion was that of Clarence Thomas, the only Black member of the court, who has, perhaps, been so co-opted by the system that he is not only a Lame but a racist one at that.

Establishing Writing as a Discipline

I note these injustices to make clear that my arguments for access to the discourses of academia are made without the assumption that students must denude themselves of their home and primary community's ways with words. I am not naive enough to suggest that once students have accessed higher education they will not be changed as individuals, but that does not mean that they should also be asked or expected to forget their origins. I do not argue for an approach to teaching writing that would serve these ends; I do not want to clone Richard Rodriguez. I argue instead for an approach that will provide students with the knowledge base to critique and maybe change the institutions they have entered and, with hope, from which they graduate. In order to do this, we must provide students with opportunities to understand the complex and multiple discourses that inhabit the spaces and places they wish also to inhabit. This will not happen without an abandonment of a laissez-faire, paternalistic approach to teaching writing in the academy. This will not happen with a return to an authoritarian, traditional approach to teaching. This will happen only if institutions undertake the structural changes necessary to ensure that novice writers receive the same attention and quality teaching that comes with a commitment to incorporating writing fully— as a discipline—into the academy. Process should stay, but form—grammatical, syntactical, and textual—needs to be as much a part of the curriculum as are rewriting and revising. We all speak, teach, and write from ideological perspectives. And those who teach from ideological, and openly critical, perspectives incorporating both form—discursive practices—and process must be allowed to do so from and with the status accorded professors in discipline area courses. So, too, must other faculty who teach writing be open to the opportunity to do so from a position of power as represented in holding full-time, tenure-track positions providing them with opportunities to engage fully with colleagues. Students will never find true access to academia unless those who teach them are afforded the same.

To this day, writing programs are replete with adjunct faculty isolated from peers. This is the case because institutions do not support to any great extent opportunities for adjuncts to meet with colleagues to discuss issues related to teaching, such as those raised throughout this book. Further, adjuncts are often overworked and overextended, as Sarah was, and they often have to work at more than one institution to earn enough money to survive. Further, those who teach writing often do so without a Ph.D. in hand, many with a master's but some with only a B.A., often meeting their first students without any preparation in writing theory and practice whatsoever. I have seen entering M.A. students with teaching assistantships assigned to teach composition with absolutely no preparation whatsoever in the teaching of writing and no support system to guide them as they seek to find their way through the semester. With this in mind, I ask again a question I posed earlier: What can be done to deal with the sorts of inequities and the complicit, though unintended, behaviors teachers engage in that serve to undermine students' possibilities for obtaining the discourses of the academy? The answers are not easy, and thus I make no attempt here to design a new writing curriculum. What I do here is pose questions that call into consideration the very manner in which colleges and universities most generally organize writing courses and treat faculty who teach these courses. I then direct my attention to suggestions for teachers, instructors—again, not professors—of writing.

Institutions Need to Change

Clearly, institutions must change to accommodate writing faculty. These changes would in turn allow institutions to more adequately accommodate the needs of students. Institutions must grant writing instructors the same status and opportunities that faculty in the more traditional disciplines are granted. Universities need to create full-time, tenure-track positions for writing teachers who have received a Ph.D. in rhetoric or a related field. Teaching writing needs to be considered central to the work of the academy. Here I speak as if I had returned to the turn of the century when the teaching of writing was first established among the rubble of classical rhetoric. The teaching of writing has not ventured far from this starting point, except for 1960s progressive efforts to reconstitute methodological approaches without an authoritarian stance.

Accomplishing the changes that I suggest will require a radical restructuring of an institutional context that seeks, and will continue to seek, privileged positions for those who speak, write, and act in the ways of the status quo. To consider a radical restructuring implies further the possibility that more and more students from underserved populations might have at least a chance of slipping into the dominant discourse communities that have heretofore served the powerful elite so well. Remember, at the turn of the twentieth century, very few students were entering the academy—though their number far exceeded the 1 percent who had previously had access to higher education before the twentieth century—and at that time even Harvard noted severe writing problems among its entering students. The door is open that much further today; the possibility exists that more and more students may find their way through the academy. But that is a frightening thought to many: thus the attack on affirmative action and bilingual education and thus the imposition of a writing proficiency exam at UMB and elsewhere.

The Assault against Access

President George W. Bush's attack on affirmative action speaks to this very issue: Not only do institutions fail to provide status to students and instructors of writing but also the dominant class now seeks to do away with a program intended to help level the playing field for minority and nonnative students, one that helps them overcome their lack of experience with the expectations of those in academia in order to gain entrance to institutions of higher learning. As noted throughout this book, members of minority communities, speakers of nonstandard English, nonnative speakers of English all seek entry to institutions of higher learning without having had the experiences that prepare one for success in academia, those experiences that are taken for granted by members of dominant groups. The playing field, indeed, is not level. At the same time Bush and others forcefully attack minority opportunity, they fail to make explicit the inherent contradictions in their attack. Bush, though but an average student, attended Andover and went on to Yale, due to the weight—both in money and status—afforded his family name. Why is it that the elite are provided opportunities that continue to enhance their already obtained access to others in positions of power, thus allowing them yet more status, power, and access—in the long run—to greater power and financial gain? Bush's educational record made him a more likely candidate for a state college, or a fifth year at Andover, not Yale. Bush's inattention to academic matters and his serious problems—now surmounted to his credit—with alcohol left him partying heartily, while most Blacks, minorities, and members of the working class and underclass spent their youth fighting a war in Vietnam, many dying without ever having the chance to seek admission to a university such as UMB (Yale would have been out of the question). UMB does now count among its student body many dazed, maimed, and traumatized veterans of Vietnam and the wars and military encounters that have followed, seeking an opportunity to access a better life that has been far from their grasp. Bush did serve in a reserve unit during the Vietnam War, though records are sketchy regarding his attendance and commitment to service. Why is it that contradictions so blatant seem not to faze a population quite willing to anoint its aristocracy and allow its underclass to drown? The catchy phrase "sink or swim" still maintains its mantra status among members of the far right and even for some closer to the middle of the political continuum. Do merit and hard work alone ensure success in academia, or in other contexts for that matter? Clearly merit and hard work are not the only factors underlying success.

Legacy, Athletes, and Affirmative Action

In "Critical Faculties" in the *Boston Sunday Globe,* Christopher Shea reported that an anonymous source from an elite Ivy League school gives "alumni kids a 25 percent boost over non-legacy applicants with comparable SAT scores. Athletes got a 48 percent boost. Minority students, in contrast, received only an 18 percent advantage" (2003, p. D5). This is the huge minority advantage Bush seeks to eliminate. Athletes are given an advantage so that alumni dollars will continue to roll in, but will these athletes graduate after leading their benevolent colleges and universities to victory? Derrick Jackson reported in "Losing the Graduation Game" (2003, p. A15) disturbing figures documenting the failure of schools to educate athletes fully so that they will not only win but also graduate with a degree. Jackson focuses on the National Collegiate Athletic Association basketball tournament and presents first graduation rates of his alma mater, the University of Wisconsin–Milwaukee. "Based on the 2002 NCAA graduation report," which "covers freshman scholarship athletes who entered school beginning in the 1992–93 school year and ending in the 1995–96 school year," the graduation rate for Blacks was zero. Overall, once again based on the 2002 report, Jackson reports that a "staggering 13 tournament teams have a black graduation rate of zero." For the sixty-four teams in the league, the overall graduation rate for Blacks is 35 percent as recorded in the 2002 report. When examined more closely, figures reveal that the top twenty schools in the league have a graduation rate of 71 percent, while the "bottom 42 teams have an average black graduation rate of . . . 18 percent." The University of Kentucky basketball team, the top-ranked team in the 2003 NCAA tournament, has a graduation rate for Blacks of only 13 percent, while the "black graduation rate of the top five teams in the final regular-season Associated Press poll, which also includes Arizona, Oklahoma, Pittsburgh, and Texas, is 15 percent." As Jackson comments: "remember this every time you see a college promo during the tournament." I would add, try to keep these figures in mind when considering the importance of writing classes as the foundation for entering into academic discourse and for obtaining the discourse strategies, behaviors, and practices necessary for further access to and through academia. If colleges and universities had a true commitment to access and education, writing courses and those who teach them would be central to the academy, and they would have the status accorded rhetoric during the 2,500 years prior to the onset of the twentieth century.

Before 1964 Yale recruited almost exclusively from elite private schools, accepting all students—and they were all male—who received As and Bs. The few slots left went to overachieving students from public schools (Shea, 2003, p. D5). In 1964 Yale did away with the private school selection process and sought to solicit students from the public schools. The average SAT scores for the first entering class not to rely solely on legacy rose by over one hundred points. William F. Buckley, the arch-eyebrowed, nose-in-the-air, vocabulary whiz kid of the Yale class of 1950, was appalled. In a 24 January 1964 op-ed piece he argued, "There are tribal instincts in life and colleges and universities are part of life" (quoted in Shea, 2003, p. D5). Buckley was arguing that Yale and other elite institutions had every right to select from among their own kind. Now I do accept, and have made it abundantly clear throughout this book, that humans are far more comfortable with those who share with them particular ways of thinking, acting, speaking, dressing, and so forth. We like to be with members of our own "tribe" or discourse community. Diversity causes tension; it fractures tribal boundaries established in an effort to keep outsiders out and traditions intact. What Buckley failed to make clear in his op-ed piece, however, was that he was not really speaking of "tribes" but was playing oh-so-cleverly with word association, that "tribal peoples"—Native Americans, Blacks, Arabs, and so forth—should stick with their own kind so that he and his tribal compatriots would not have to deal with these outsiders. Buckley was chagrined that Yale's new admissions policy meant that "the son of an alumnus who goes to a private preparatory school now has less chance of getting in than some boy from PS109 somewhere" (Shea, 2003, p. D5). Imagine being a silver-spoon elitist beaten out for a place at Yale by a ratty public school brat!

Chris Kahn of the *Boston Globe* (2003, p. A3) reported in "College Legacies Face Scrutiny" that today "sons and daughters of alumni make up more than 10 percent of students at Harvard, Yale, and Princeton. They are 23 percent of the student population at Notre Dame. At the University of Virginia, 11 percent of this year's [2002] freshman class were children of alumni, and more than 91 percent of them are white." The University of Virginia's "current student population, which is about 70 percent white, 11 percent Asian American, 9 percent black, and 3 percent Hispanic" certainly is not representative of the percentages of individuals from the "tribes" mentioned who want, and deserve, a place and space in the academy.

Rethinking the Teaching of Writing

In conjunction with faculty and students in graduate programs in rhetoric, applied linguistics, literacy, or other related fields, institutions need to reconceptualize, retheorize, and rethink the teaching of writing. Should writing courses, for example, be structured within the walls of classrooms? Or should more programs adopt writing centers? Should students like Araya be promoted after earning a grade of C–, thus ensuring limited progress at the next course level? Or should students be provided opportunities for working closely with faculty until they reach a greater level of proficiency? Does the possibility exist for the establishment of an apprenticing system in which students would work closely with professors in their major and would begin to see and hear what these professors produce both orally and in writing? And could the possibility exist for these students of not only seeing but also interacting, and eventually participating in, a new community? Work-study programs and teaching assistantships begin to create models for students of the varieties of discourses displayed and employed in various fields of study. But to extend this opportunity for apprenticeship to large numbers of students would indeed be difficult, if not impossible.

And what of peer tutoring? Are students who are deemed proficient writers adequate tutors for those who seek access to academic writing? Is commitment to service, which motivates many well-intended peer tutors, enough to ensure that they can adequately provide for the uninitiated the strategies necessary for obtaining academic discourse(s)? Or are institutions of higher learning providing the least qualified teachers for those who are most in need of explicit and qualified teaching? How much less expensive is it to place peer tutors and part-timers—many of whom are seriously unqualified to teach writing—in positions in which they meet and teach the students least likely to access academic prose? Not only do institutions fail to provide full or even adequate access to Blacks, women, members of the working and lower classes, nonnative speakers of English, and those who constitute the underclass, but they also call upon academia's underclass—students and adjuncts—to teach the members of these communities. The situation speaks explicitly to the issue of cost effectiveness and implicitly to the maintenance of boundaries.

Could disciplines themselves instead have their faculty members teach explicitly the discourses required, yet so taken for granted, by those who are already privileged by membership? This model is what the UMB English Curriculum

Committee on which I served attempted, and royally failed, to institute. Should students be asked to write in forms dictated by instructors and writing texts, forms that often have little connection to forms of writing used in the academic environment, or should they have the opportunity to explore genres within their chosen areas of interest with the guidance of their professors? This suggestion is problematic because many faculty willingly rely on prepackaged materials, particularly for testing, that can be analyzed and graded by computer. These materials further distance students from access to the discourses of disciplines and from the opportunity to speak, write, and act within these communities. But these materials also save professors a tremendous amount of time and the energy required to read student essays. So much time is spent on evaluating faculty production—research, publication, contributions to one's field—that little time is left for faculty members to fully address the needs of students.

And what of the paternalistic role of journal writing? Does it serve to empower students, or does it merely create contexts in which writing instructors can glance quickly through texts they need not correct and on which they comment only superficially? Is a happy face an appropriate response to a student's journal entry? I think not. Or should students have the opportunity to explore genres from a variety of disciplines and, in so doing, engage in a metalevel analysis and discussion of how genres vary across disciplines? Is talk about how texts are structured an important avenue to access to a metalinguistic awareness of the roles different texts play in different contexts? Further, need institutions require writing teachers to grade students, since good grades more often reflect the extent to which students have engaged in forms of writing and interaction congruent with what is expected in the classroom and poor grades generally reflect lack of experience with certain forms of academic discourse? Mike Rose speaks in *Lives on the Boundary* of the need for students to have

> More opportunities to write about what they're learning and guidance in the techniques and conventions of that writing. They need more opportunities to develop the writing strategies that are an intimate part of academic inquiry and what has come to be called critical literacy—comparing, synthesizing, and analyzing. They need opportunities to talk about what they're learning: to test their ideas, reveal their assumptions, talk through the places where new knowledge clashes with ingrained beliefs. They need a chance, too, to talk about the ways they may have felt excluded from all this in the past and may feel threatened by it in the present. They need the occasion to rise above the fragmented learning the lower-division curriculum encourages, a place within a course or outside it to hear about and reflect on the way a particular discipline conducts its inquiry. (1989, pp. 193–94)

And What of Writing Teachers?

These questions imply the need for change, of course, but they do not provide a specific writing curriculum (that is not my intent here). With this in mind, I turn now to suggestions for teachers. Once again, I point out explicitly that those who teach writing most generally do not have the status that implies the honorific "professor," except to students uninitiated into the academy who are inclined to use it because they are unaware of the lowly part-time or adjunct status of most writing instructors. Further, I make these suggestions from the position of teacher, not just from the position of researcher, theorist, or writer. I am no dictating authority making pronouncements with no connection to practice. Instead, I have taught for more than twenty years, and I have found teaching to be both exhilarating and exhausting.

Stepping outside Oneself

Pierre Bourdieu argues that

> In choosing to study the social world in which we are *involved,* we are obliged to confront, in *dramatized* form as it were, a certain number of fundamental epistemological problems, all related to the question of the difference between practical knowledge and scholarly knowledge, and particularly to the special difficulties involved first in *breaking* with inside experience and then in reconstituting the knowledge which has been obtained by means of this break. (1988, p. 1)

I have sought to do this throughout my study and this book. I have asked of others; I have acknowledged the need to break with that which is taken for granted in order to reconstitute "the knowledge which has been obtained by means of this break." In order to begin this process teachers need, first, to be aware of the ideologies—overt and tacit, explicit and implicit—that inform their practice. I only came to begin to understand this in terms of teaching writing when I had the opportunity to enter another instructor's writing classroom to have students complete a questionnaire related to research I was at that time undertaking. These questionnaires were filled out before my study of Sarah's class, and perhaps the information gathered in them precipitated my desire to seek answers to the questions I posed when observing Sarah and her students. This first encounter with a space and place outside of that which I inhabited occurred when I entered a writing class for native English speakers taught by a tenured member of the English Department at UMB. Upon first entering the class, I was almost struck dumb by the fact that there were but ten students in the class. I had never seen a writing class so small, because I had only seen my own large classes and listened to my colleagues in ESL complain of the large numbers of students they too had in class. My mind reeled with the immediate mathematical computation that resulted in the realization that I read more than twice the number of papers each time an assignment was completed than did this full-time, tenured member of the English Department faculty. Then I started to calculate the time I spent dealing with students and student papers, rather than with my other lives. I thought: "This professor has twice the time I have to spend with her children, plant flowers, write what needs to be written to gain stature in her field." I had not known of this disparity between the time and attention that native speakers received compared to the time and attention I was able to give the more than twenty students per class—every class—I served.

Further, upon seeing the syllabus for the course, I was struck by the fact that the writing that these native English speakers were asked to do focused on analyzing literary works and on weaving into their analyses themes dominant to various schools of literature. In contrast, I focused student writing on issues related to their own lived experiences, which allowed me to learn much about their histories and cultures and allowed them to speak from a position of authority. I wanted to learn from my students, and I did learn so much about political repression in Argentina under Pinochet that I could see the ear of my student's friend being sliced from his head, and the blood, pain, and loss pouring forth. I could understand the unsettling repercussions of the Vietnam War on people's lives or learn firsthand what it meant to flee from bombs in Lebanon or to be displaced from one's homeland due to a corrupt, fanatical regime as was the case in Cambodia under Pol Pot. I mourned my students' losses, and I wanted them to be documented, not for me but for them. My approach was to learn, to critique, and to seek along with these students some understanding of the power of political forces to control the fate of one's life and, further, the power of the printed word—writing—to capture for eternity these injustices. If they were rendered only orally, there was the distinct possibility that these stories would vanish with the wind. This lesson, in and of itself, was a lesson portending the power one held when in control of the printed word. I wanted this power for my students.

My Writing Courses

I was a political scientist and applied linguist critically interrogating a mean and violent history that was at the foundation of many of my students' lives. Their words made me cry; their drive made me rejoice. Our class discussions about the need to capture in writing the experiences that they and others had encountered, writing that would serve as an enduring testament to the wrenching experiences that had for the most part led them to UMB, became the goal of the courses I taught and the foundation upon which I communicated to students that texts serve particular purposes and that the forms and intentions of texts vary by context.

In this case, student texts would lead to the documentation and communication of a history that emerged from the voices of those that were not yet heard. This interrogation sought to allow students to communicate and critically assess their present status and presence in the United States. These examples, and many others, emerged through incorporating first-person narrative of each student's own experiences prior to entry in the United States and upon resettlement. We discussed the purposes of personal narrative, its structure, and its place in writing both within and outside of the academy. Students then moved to developing a case study of an individual who had also experienced relocation to the United States. One student, from Nigeria, chose to study migration and interviewed an elderly Black woman who had migrated from the South to Boston in the 1920s with what was left of her family. She and her relatives sought release from the fear of cross burning and lynching. George Miller, the Nigerian student who did this primary research, then incorporated this woman's story into the secondary research he did documenting, through texts, the research that became the foundation for his final research paper. I had lofty goals; the students did incredible work.

One young woman I remember in particular had arrived in the United States as a typical foreign student from Japan. She asked me how she could enter this dialogue, because she had simply flown here and was supported by her parents. I suggested that she try to find a Japanese individual who had lived in the United States during World War II and interview this individual about his or her experiences during the war. Through her community contacts my student found an older Japanese American man who told her what it was like to live in enclosed camps, far from the home he and his family had previously known as U.S. citizens, because their Japanese heritage made them suspect after Pearl Harbor. My student supported and provided a larger context for the interpretation of this elderly man's recollections by doing secondary research—hard work in the library, as had George and all the other students in the class. But by the time my student entered the library she had acquired from the man she interviewed the necessary background knowledge to allow her to better access the books and articles dealing with Japanese internment during World War II.

My student was shocked, as were the others in the class, that people in the United States, the land of freedom, had been wrenched from their homes and imprisoned solely because of their ethnic identity. These were the stories that could only be told by those who had lived outside this land. All my students did primary as well as secondary research. George Miller went on to medical school. And the Japanese woman I have just discussed went on to earn a Ph.D. in sociology from Boston College. I had not seen her in a few years when one day, as I was going to a seminar at Boston University (I was still a graduate student) she stopped me as I exited my car. This former student thanked me for the course and for the opportunity she had had to engage critically in a subject, a part of U.S. history that she had not known existed. She told me that her doctoral advisor was astonished that she had done such extraordinary primary and secondary research as a first-year university student. I was late and in a rush, but I knew then that the curriculum that I had developed for the research writing course was perhaps unique. I knew this was the case, as well, when I entered the classroom of ten native English speakers taught by an English professor. These students were laconic; my students were not. I was overworked, but passionate; the English professor was not.

The Different Worlds of Teaching Writing

There is nothing wrong with writing literature and analyzing literature. But connecting the Romantic theme "man must not intervene in nature" as expressed in

Samuel Coleridge's epic poem "The Ancient Mariner," in Shakespeare's play *Macbeth,* and in Mary Shelley's novel *Frankenstein* is a far different task, one not uncommon in the writing class taught by an instructor with a degree in literature. The short period of time I spent in the writing classroom inhabited by native speakers of English and taught by an English professor allowed me to step outside of myself, so to speak, in a way that made what I had assumed to be natural most notably socially produced. My assumption, strange as it must now seem, was that other writing classes were more like mine than like the one taught by the professor of literature. I was living in a closed world, naive to the multiplicity of approaches to teaching writing that exists within and across institutions. I was ideologically motivated by my background in political science, the literature professor by her involvement in English literature studies. And one must remember that not all the students in my class, or in the English professor's class, planned to major in English. Two semesters of writing is required of all entering students at colleges and universities throughout the United States, no matter what their major is.

There was no way that the English professor would teach the same writing course that I taught. We inhabited different worlds, spoke and wrote from differing discourse communities, and harbored divergent ideological perspectives, yet we both taught research writing. The disparities, the differences, the goals were from opposite ends of the spectrum of life. Once I recognized this, I also recognized the power of ideology and previous experiences to shape our understanding of what the present moment should contain. I learned, too, about how different we are from one another, those of us who inhabit this space called "teaching writing." And no one in the institution seemed to really care, or even understand, that these inequities and differences played important roles in determining who made it through the gates and who had them slammed in their face—be they student or instructor.

Perhaps we all need to critically assess our ideological perspectives. By this I mean we need to honestly examine who succeeds in our classes and who does not. We need to consider, in turn, how our own behaviors, demands, and assumptions may affect particular students' successes or failures. We need to look closely at whom we spend our time with during office hours, whom we encourage to continue on to seek higher degrees, and whom we discourage. When teaching writing we need to consider which students garner our attention and why. We must step back from our own practice to critically assess it. By this I mean that we need to critically observe, scrutinize, analyze, and assess our own modes of interacting and behaving with students. Moreover, we need, for example, to interview students, find out who they are, what their background experiences have been, and what their needs are. Henry Giroux speaks to this issue: "If teachers are to take an active role in raising serious questions about what they teach, how they are to teach, and the larger goals for which they are striving, it means they must take a more critical and political role in defining the nature of their work as well as in shaping the conditions under which they work" (1989, p. 19). Giroux asserts that in doing so, teachers become "public intellectuals who combine conception and implementation, thinking and practice" (p. 19).

In conclusion, and here I draw heavily from James Paul Gee (1984, p. 25), we must remember that the decision about what a writing curriculum will contain is not a neutral decision. The pedagogical practices of institutions are never neutral. How an institution, or the representatives of an institution, works to create avenues to literacy acquisition is a political as well as an educational decision. I hope that educators will reexamine their practices in an attempt to ascertain whether these practices serve, ultimately, to ease students into the acquisition of academic literacy or, in fact, work to exclude those who come to school proficient in ways with words that differ from those valued in the academic setting. Individuals who have not been socialized into language practices that constitute mainstream school-based literacy must be socialized into them if they are ever to succeed. Of course, there is no guarantee that this socialization will lead to success outside of school, because such socialization does not erase a student's minority status; but control of the discourses of power does portend the possibility of circumventing one's previous powerless position within society. Teachers are gatekeepers and as such must provide opportunities for the acquisition of academic prose. Educational institutions must become places where access to academic literacy—in its many forms—becomes a possibility not only for those who already possess it but also for those who may not yet have had the opportunities, experiences, or contexts for engaging in academic discourses.

Writing Is a Social Act

Throughout this book I have argued that writing is a social act and that it involves far more than putting pen to paper. Ways of acting, behaving, dressing—one's membership in or nonmembership in a particular discourse community marks the foundation upon which "learning to write" begins or fails to begin. Words, both spoken and written, are involved in the process of writing. The interactions during Sarah's writing conferences with Alan, Zola, Tan, and Araya make this abundantly clear. Writers are members of communities. Some students, like Tan, have a large network of support; other students work in isolation, like Araya, who, despite being a student at the university and in a class on research writing, received from his community quite limited support in producing the written work required of him. Araya also received little, if any, support from the institution. Gaining greater access to a community of writers—writers who speak the language you are required to speak—is fundamental to an individual's growth and success as a writer.

Nowhere have I found the recognition of this social reality more clearly stated than in the writing of Lee Child, a successful writer of pulp fiction. His writing is as crisp and straightforward as freshly harvested stalks of asparagus. His ability to see beyond himself, and to recognize that his work is firmly supported and situated within a community, is clearly captured in the acknowledgments to his novel *Echo Burning*: "People think that writing is a lonely, solitary trade. They're wrong. It's a team game, and I'm lucky enough to have charming and talented people on my side everywhere I'm published. Accordingly, if you ever worked on or sold one of my books, this one is dedicated to you. You're too numerous to mention individually, but too important not to mention at all" (2001, p. ix). Writers do not write alone. Writers speak with others, seeking support and feedback—confirmation for their efforts. They learn to act in ways that allow others to perceive them as writers. Much of what writers learn comes from reading the work of other writers they admire and seek to emulate or even to supersede. Models are important. Meaning and textual structure are inextricably bound. When boundaries are broken and new forms created, these new forms are based upon the knowledge of accepted forms—now fractured, and thus avant-garde. Student writers need the same opportunities to access models as "real" writers do. Process writing abhors the use of models but in so doing obscures possibilities for access. Models must be not only presented but also analyzed—deconstructed—so that each component is understood in terms of both its form and function. For, as Jacques Derrida notes, "Everything begins with structure, configuration, or relationship" (1978, p. 286).

What role does a particular component of a text play? What is the function of the introduction or the conclusion? For many beginning writers of the essay, confusion exists over the fact that the introduction often mirrors the conclusion. Why just say the same thing again, my son asks me? Because the form requires that you do so and, more important, the two serve to provide a frame for the main body of your paper. Students need to be told explicitly that multiple linguistic forms exist within the academy and that to speak and write outside of the accepted genres of one's discipline may hold serious consequences. Student writers do not need to examine all genres; this would be impossible. But the more forms an instructor presents, and the more opportunities students have to critique, evaluate, and assess multiple forms, the greater are the chances that the students will come to understand from a metalevel the complexity of this nondiscipline called writing, composition, or rhetoric.

Placing forms in juxtaposition, one to the other, serves to create contexts for understanding the various purposes textual forms serve. This means also that forms not generally accepted within academia should also be included. As noted in chapter 4, rap serves for some students as an important linkage between community discourse and academic discourse. What appears in the community most generally in an oral form can in school provide the foundation for the beginning steps of putting pen to paper. Further, rap could serve as a point of departure for understanding the relationship between structure and function in and of itself and in juxtaposition to more canonical forms of poetry fully entrenched within the academy.

Identifying Oneself as an Outsider

In March 2003 a friend showed me a student response to an economics college exam essay question. The student began his response by writing "People on welfare are lazy." Now this student is entitled to his opinion, I will grant him that. But in response to an exam question based on lectures and readings in part dealing with economic models of welfare systems, this response is inappropriate and immediately marks the student as a nonmember of the academic community. Why? First, this opening sentence indicates that most likely the student has not read the section in the textbook required for the course (a full reading of the student response confirms this assumption). Second, the student's response indicates he or she has not applied the economic analysis discussed in class and in the textbook in responding to the question posed. Third, this student has not fully grasped the concept that academia requires that one speak and write of and through texts and not from personal experience—unless specifically required to do so. Perhaps this student has a future in talk radio. For in talk radio, too, a particular discourse is privileged above others, one that is decidedly ideologically based, as are all discourses; one that is decidedly nonacademic; one that privileges speaking from the gut, or is it the heart. I need to call in and ask.

Problematic Practices

Many problematic practices occur in education. John Dewey argued that the point of departure for better understanding and improving education should begin with an analysis of these problematic occurrences. For 2,500 years rhetoric was dominated by the dictates put forth by Aristotle. These dictates were played out in a closed world, a discourse community dominated by the elite, white men, those very few who had access to money and the opportunity for the discussion of ideas and, much later, access to print. Today we live in a far different world, yet the elite attempts still to placate its privileged few. But I really believe that this will not continue to occur. I really believe that if institutions would open their doors more fully to men and women of color, immigrants, refugees, Native Americans, the underclass, and those who are so disdained as to seemingly not exist, this would be a better world. It is a world that I would like my child and all children to experience. And I do truly believe that much that needs to be done can occur within the academy among those who have a modicum of power, though little money no matter the cultural capital the position implies. I do imagine a better tomorrow.

Appendix

INTERVIEWING SARAH AND THE STUDENTS

The interview process I used when meeting with Sarah and four of her students was modeled on an approach developed by Eliot Mishler (1986) as an outgrowth of his critique of traditional survey methods. Mishler maintains that meanings are contextually grounded. This assumption is the primary basis for his critique of current, dominant interview practices in the social sciences, which he argues are characterized by a "striking asymmetry of power" (p. 117). In the typical survey interview the interviewer works to elicit from the interviewee answers to a pre-scribed set of questions. The primary goal throughout the process is to get the interviewee to stick to the questions or, in other words, to the task at hand. Mishler suggests that this structure and process serve to constrain interviewees from making sense of their experiences.

The alternative method proposed by Mishler focuses on an investigative process that facilitates respondents' efforts to make sense of what is happening to them. This alternative method focuses on the use of open-ended questioning and interviewer–interviewee interaction. The restructuring of the interviewee–inter-viewer relationship is designed to encourage the individuals being interviewed to find and speak in their own voices (Mishler, 1986, p. 118). This occurs because in the open-ended structure interviewees are encouraged to produce narratives in response to questions posed by the interviewer. As Gee (1985) argues, one of the primary ways through which individuals make sense of and give meaning to their experiences is to organize these experiences in narrative form. Thus if interviewers allow for the expression of narratives, rather than emphasizing a rigid questionnaire format, they allow interviewees to give voice to their experiences, which is an empowering act. Each time Sarah and the students were interviewed I was careful not to interrupt before they had completed the telling of their stories, and I asked open-ended questions rather than those that would elicit one-word responses.

Narrative Analysis

The methodological approach to the analysis of the narratives elicited from Sarah and the four students is also based on an approach suggested by Mishler (1986). I undertook a thematic analysis of the narratives working as well with a model employed by Gee (1985) in his analysis of a sharing time narrative produced by a Black second-grader. Through his analysis Gee was able to uncover the underlying conflicts and themes addressed by the young girl. The analytical approach to narrative analysis outlined here provided me with the necessary data to reveal the overt and covert beliefs held by Sarah and the students.

I was most interested in determining the professed ideological perspective of Sarah; the manner in which her perspective was revealed in practice was the primary focus of the first component of the study. The goal of the initial interview was to situate Sarah historically, socially, intellectually, and ideologically so that the subsequent analysis of her practice would be as contextualized as possible. I was interested in learning, first, where Sarah was educated; second, what, if any, specific courses she had taken in preparation for teaching writing; third, what perspectives her instructors held regarding approaches to teaching writing; and finally, whether Sarah had in fact planned on becoming a writing instructor or whether she had other career goals in mind as she went through school. I was interested in characterizing Sarah's relationship to the University of Massachusetts Boston (UMB) because the university's commitment to her, that is, whether she was hired for a full-time position or as an adjunct, could have had an impact on her commitment to students. Further, I elicited Sarah's views regarding the university's imposition of the writing-proficiency exam. I interviewed Sarah at least once weekly during the course, and I spoke with her at length prior to the onset of the study and again at the completion of the course.

As part of this component, I also had students from the class respond in writing to a questionnaire at the outset of the course. The written questionnaire was administered during the fourth class meeting. Students were asked questions relating to their background experience with writing instruction. I was interested, for example, in determining whether they had been exposed to a process writing approach to teaching in the past, or to a more traditional approach, and whether they had had much previous experience writing at all. I also asked what grades students had received in previous writing classes and about their attitudes toward writing.

The classroom observations became the basis on which to determine how Sarah's ideological perspective was revealed in practice. In other words, the observations were the basis for determining whether or not there was a congruence between teacher-expressed ideology and the reality of her classroom practice. More specifically, the observations provided the basis upon which the following questions could be answered: Would a teacher who philosophically advocated a process writing approach in fact follow through with the approach on a daily basis, or would aspects of a more traditional approach emerge in practice? Would the teacher focus on the writing process itself, that is, would her focus be on writing and rewriting? Would the teacher focus on the search for the student's meaning as revealed in the texts each produced, or would she be concerned with the form of student texts? If Sarah were concerned with one or more of these features, or others, how would she communicate these concerns to students?

Case Studies

The second component of the primary research I undertook involves the development of detailed case studies of four students in the class. Sarah and I identified two of the better writers and two less-proficient writers based on an in-class writing sample from the first class session. Once the student writers—Alan, Zola, Tan, and Araya— were chosen, they were interviewed so that a case history incorporating social, cultural, class, and educational background could be compiled. Again, I conducted the interviews with students based on Mishler's suggestions (1986). Emphasis was placed on attempting to determine each student's attitudes toward writing and how each had used writing both formally and informally in the past. Although the four students would already have completed a written questionnaire dealing with these issues, the interviews provided an opportunity to pursue background and attitudinal information much more fully. I began the student interviews reviewing the previously completed questionnaire in order to provide students the opportunity to clarify and expand upon their earlier written responses. I asked students what their goals were for the course, what they anticipated learning in the course, what their attitudes were toward being required to take the course, and how they felt they would perform in the course and why. I interviewed each student twice. During these interviews I referred back to comments and information gathered from the initial interview with the student in order to determine what, if any, attitudinal changes might have taken place as the course progressed.

During the classroom observations I focused on Sarah's expectations regarding student writing and, in turn, how these expectations were understood or, as the case may be, misunderstood and subsequently carried out on the part of the students. Specifically, what I focused on was the identifiable points of disjuncture, if any, between Sarah's expectations and the students' processes of carrying out these expectations. This focus led to the possibility of ascertaining whether or not disjuncture might possibly lead to student resistance (Chase, 1988; Giroux, 1983) or whether, perhaps, shared expectations would lead to conformity with Sarah's expectations. In fact, it is often through analysis of the points of disjuncture in the educational process that a better understanding of what students are being asked either explicitly or implicitly to do will emerge (Giroux, 1983). Upon completion of the course, I attempted to ascertain why students received the grades they did. Sarah was asked to specify how she arrived at her final evaluation. Did she evaluate based on how hard a student worked or, in a sense, on how actively the student engaged in the process of writing? Or did she focus on the student's search for meaning? Or did she grade on the basis of the overall structure of the student's text, thus focusing on form?

Overall, the research process outlined above was designed to shed light on the following questions: First, how do teachers' assumptions about what constitutes good writing inhibit or facilitate students' learning of academic prose? And second, how do the beliefs of the teacher and the beliefs of the student interact and affect the development of student writing?

Student–Teacher Interactions

The third component of the primary research focuses specifically on Sarah's ideological perspective and practice as well as on her relationships with the four students identified for the case studies. The methodology I employed here was used by Sarah Michaels (1981) in her research on sharing time as a literacy event in a second-grade classroom. Michaels incorporated the notion of key situation as discussed by Fredrick Erickson (1975), John Gumperz (1976), and John Gumperz and Jenny Cook-Gumperz (1982). This notion holds that life in complex, stratified societies offers certain gatekeeping encounters that determine access to occupation, official redress, and educational opportunities (Michaels & Collins, 1984). The key situation for Michaels was sharing time, or what is often referred to as show-and-tell. In my study I focused on the writing conference as key situation in much the same way Michaels did in her work on writing at the elementary school level (Michaels, 1985). I define "writing conference" as any encounter between instructor and student during which the two discuss issues relating to the development of a student's paper. As the study unfolded the definition of the key situation narrowed to specific, predetermined encounters between Sarah and her students. I attended as a nonparticipant observer all the writing conferences Sarah had with the four students. The conferences were audiotaped and I took field notes as well. In addition, throughout the course I read all student work, both before Sarah commented on it and after.

Tertiary Knowledge

It was through a focused analysis of interactions, both during class and in student conferences, between the teacher and the four students that the distinction between implicit and explicit expression of ideological perspective was explored. The distinction between overt and covert, or explicit versus implicit, ideological perspective can be illustrated in the following hypothetical example. If a teacher explicitly stated to students that she wanted their papers to have an introduction, and in so stating she also outlined for the students what her expectations for an introduction were, this would be counted as an explicit expression of expectation. If, on the other hand, the teacher commented to a student, orally or in a written response to a student draft, that the student needed to write an introduction to his or her paper but the teacher had not prior to this comment stated that this was a requirement or what this required component was to consist of, this exchange would be classified as implicit. In other words, I was interested in whether or not the teacher would react to students with a little bit of theory for which she did not have the context and, in so doing, display her tertiary knowledge.

Here, the term "tertiary knowledge" is used as it is by Paul Atkinson (1985) in his discussion of Basil Bernstein (1977), a well-known British sociolinguist who considers both the relationship between class and language use and the relationship of the two to academic success. Tertiary knowledge, as explicated by Atkinson, refers to the form knowledge takes after it has undergone the simplification process that permeates pedagogical practice. This process evolves in the following manner: A theoretical perspective developed a decade or two before in a university setting may later be adopted by textbook writers so that the theory, in now more simplified form, may be taught to students at, for example, an undergraduate level. These same students will then take some even more simplified version of the original theory and incorporate these notions in their own practice, such as the writing of academic papers. At each movement away from the original source further simplification occurs. This very process, I believe, will be reflected in the relationship to be drawn between teacher ideology and practice and the discussion of the historical roots of this ideology and practice. What comes to be expressed whether implicitly or explicitly by teachers and writing theorists, for that matter, may in fact be but bits and pieces of far more comprehensive theoretical notions the sources of which teachers and theorists are unaware.

REFERENCES

Applebee, Arthur N. (1974). *Tradition and reform in the teaching of English: A history.* Urbana, IL: National Council of Teachers of English.

Arthur, Chris J. (Ed.) (1970). *Karl Marx and Fredrick Engels: The German ideology.* London: Lawrence & Wishart.

Associated Press (2003, February 25). Justices side with death row inmate on jury bias. *New York Times,* nytimes.com, 1.

Atkinson, Paul (1985). *Language, structure and reproduction: An introduction to Basil Bernstein.* London: Methuen.

Baron, Dennis E. (1982). *Grammar and good taste: Reforming the American language.* New Haven, CT: Yale University Press.

Bartholomae, David (1985). Inventing the university. In Mike Rose (Ed.), *When a writer can't write* (pp. 134–165). New York: Guilford.

Belsey, Carol (1980). *Critical practice.* London: Methuen.

Berlin, James A. (1984). *Writing instruction in nineteenth-century American colleges.* Carbondale and Edwardsville: Southern Illinois University Press.

Berlin, James A. (1987). *Rhetoric and reality: Writing instruction in American colleges, 1900–1985.* Carbondale and Edwardsville: Southern Illinois University Press.

Berlin, James A. (1988, September). Rhetoric and ideology in the writing class. *College English, (50)5,* 477–494.

Berlin, James, & Inkster, Hillard L. (1980, Winter). Current-traditional rhetoric: Paradigm and practice. *Freshman English News,* 1–4, 13–14.

Bernstein, Basil (1977). *Class, codes and control: Towards a theory of education transmissions* (2d ed.). London: Routledge, Chapman and Hall.

Bernstein, Basil (1990). *The structuring of pedagogic discourse: Class, codes and control.* New York: Routledge.

Bernstein, Richard J. (1983). *Beyond objectivism and relativism: Science, hermeneutics and praxis*. Philadelphia: University of Pennsylvania Press.

Berthoff, Ann (1982). *Forming, thinking, writing*. Portsmouth, NH: Boynton/Cook.

Bizzell, Patricia (1986). Composing process: An overview. In Anthony R. Petrosky & Donald Bartholomae (Eds.), *The teaching of writing eighty-fifth yearbook of the National Society for the Study of Education*. Chicago: University of Chicago Press.

Bizzell, Patricia (1992). *Academic discourse and critical consciousness*. Pittsburgh: University of Pittsburgh Press.

Bjork, Daniel W. (1993). *B. F. Skinner*. New York: Basic Books.

Bourdieu, Pierre (1977). The economics of linguistic exchanges. *Social Science Information, (16)6*, 45–68.

Bourdieu, Pierre (1988). *Homo academicus*. Stanford, CA: Stanford University Press.

Bowles, Samuel, & Gintis, Herbert (1976). *Schooling in capitalist America*. New York: Basic Books.

Brodkey, Linda (1987). *Academic writing as social practice*. Philadelphia: Temple University Press.

Bruffee, Kenneth (1986, December). Social construction and the authority of knowledge. *College English, (48)8*, 773–790.

Bruner, Jerome S. (1960). *The process of education*. Cambridge, MA: Harvard University Press.

Cazden, Courtney B. (1988). *Classroom discourse: The language of teaching and learning*. Portsmouth, NH: Heinemann.

Chase, Gerald (1988, February). Accommodation, resistance and the politics of student writing. *College Composition and Communication, (39)1*, 13–22.

Child, Lee (2002). *Echo burning*. New York: Jove.

Chomsky, Noam (1967). A review of B. F. Skinner's *Verbal Behavior*. In L. A. Jakobovitz & M. S. Miron (Eds.), *Readings in the psychology of language* (pp. 142–171). New York: Prentice-Hall.

Chomsky, Noam, & Macedo, Donaldo (1999). Democracy and miseducation: A dialogue. Unpublished manuscript, University of Massachusetts Boston.

Clifford, John (1988). Burke and the tradition of democratic schooling. In Louise Z. Smith (Ed.), *Audits of meaning: A festschrift in honor of Ann E. Berthoff* (pp. 29–34). Portsmouth, NH: Boynton/Cook, Heinemann.

Cody, Sherwin (1903a, revised 1922). *The art of writing and speaking the English language: Composition and rhetoric*. Sherwin Cody Publisher.

Cody, Sherwin (1903b, revised 1922). *The art of writing and speaking the English language: Word study*. Sherwin Cody Publisher.

Coe, Richard M. (1987, January). An apology for form: Or, who took the form out of the process? *College English, (49)1*, 13–28.

Cohen, Lawrence (2002, August 1). Getting along. *The Boston Globe*, p. H3.

Coleman, Arthur, & Tyler, Gary R. (1987). Writing about literature: A guide to research. *The Little, Brown guide to writing research papers* (Suppl. 1 of 8 vols.). New York: Prentice-Hall.

Collins, James (1991). Hegemonic practice: Literacy and the standard language in public education. In Candace Mitchell & Kathleen Weiler (Eds.), *Rewriting literacy: Culture and the discourse of the other* (pp. 229–254). New York: Bergin & Garvey Publishers.

Connors, Robert (1991). Rhetoric in the modern university: The creation of an underclass. In Richard Bullock, John Trimbur & Charles Schuster (Eds.), *The politics of writing instruction: Postsecondary* (pp. 55–84). Portsmouth, NH: Boynton/Cook.

Connors, Robert, Ede, Lisa S., & Lundsford, Andrea A. (1984). The revival of rhetoric in America. In Robert Connors, Lisa S. Ede, & Andrea A. Lundsford (Eds.), *Essays on classical rhetoric and modern discourse* (pp. 1–15). Carbondale and Edwardsville: Southern Illinois University Press.

Delpit, Lisa (1995). *Other people's children: Cultural conflict in the classroom.* New York: New Press.

Derrida, Jacques (1978). *Writing and difference.* Chicago: University of Chicago Press.

Doctorow, E. L. (1985, August 25). The passion of our calling. *The New York Times Book Review,* 1.

Eagleton, Terry (1984). *The function of criticism.* Thetford, Norfolk: Thetford Press.

Emig, Jane (1971). *The composing processes of twelfth graders.* Urbana, IL: National Council of Teachers of English.

Erickson, Fredrick (1975). What makes school ethnography "ethnographic"? Unpublished manuscript, Harvard University.

Faigley, Lester (1986). Competing theories of process: A critique and a proposal. *College English, (48),* 527–542.

Faigley, Lester, & Hansen, Kristine (1985). Learning to write in the social sciences. *College Composition and Communication, 36,* 140–149.

Finegan, Edward (1980). *Attitudes toward English usage: The history of a war of words.* New York: Teachers College Press.

Flower, Linda, & Hayes, John R. (1981). A cognitive process theory of writing. *College Composition and Communication, (32)4,* 365–387.

Fowler, H. Ramsey, & Aaron, Jane E. (1984). *The Little, Brown Handbook.* New York: Longman.

Freire, Paulo (1970). *Pedagogy of the oppressed* (Myra Ramos, Trans.). New York: Seabury Press.

Freire, Paulo (1998). *Pedagogy of freedom: Ethics, democracy, and civic courage.* Lanham, MD: Rowman & Littlefield.

Freire, Paulo, & Faundez, Antonio (1992). *Learning to question: A pedagogy of liberation.* New York: Continuum.

Freire, Paulo, & Macedo, Donaldo (1987). *Literacy: Reading the word and the world.* South Hadley, MA: Bergin & Garvey Press.

Freire, Paulo, & Macedo, Donaldo (1994). *Letters to Cristina.* New York: Continuum.

Freire, Paulo, & Macedo, Donaldo (1995, Fall). A dialogue: Culture, language, and race. *Harvard Educational Review, 64(3),* 377–402.

Gee, James Paul (1984). The narrativization of experience in the oral mode. Unpublished manuscript, Boston University.

Gee, James Paul (1985). The narrativization of experience in the oral style. *Journal of Education, (167)1,* 9–35.

Gee, James Paul (1987, March). *What is literacy?* Paper presented at the Mailman Foundation Conference on Families and Literacy, Harvard Graduate School of Education.

Gee, James Paul (1988). Personal communication.

Gee, James Paul (1989). Ideology and theory: Intellectual and moral foundations of discourse analysis. Draft of chapter to appear in James Paul Gee, *Ideology, Literacy, and Linguistics.* Bristol, PA: Falmer Press.

Gee, James Paul (1996). *Social linguistics and literacies: Ideology in discourses* (2d ed.). Bristol, PA: Falmer Press.

Giroux, Henry (1983). *Theory and resistance in education: A pedagogy for the opposition.* South Hadley, MA: Bergin & Garvey Press.

Giroux, Henry (1988). *Teachers as intellectuals: Toward a critical pedagogy of learning.* South Hadley, MA: Bergin & Garvey Press.

Giroux, Henry (1989). Textual authority, voice, and the role of English teachers as public intellectuals. Unpublished manuscript, Miami University, Miami, Ohio.

Giroux, Henry (1992). *Border crossings: Cultural workers and the politics of education.* London: Routledge.

Gould, Stephen Jay (1981). *The mismeasure of man.* New York: W. W. Norton.

Graff, Gerald (1987). *Professing literature: An institutional history.* Chicago: University of Chicago Press.

Gramsci, Antonio (1971). *Prison notebooks* (Quentin Hoare & Geoffrey Smith, Trans.). New York: International Publishers.

Graves, Donald H. (1983). *Writing: Teachers and children at work.* Portsmouth, NH: Heinemann.

Graves, Donald H. (1990) *Discover your own literacy.* Portsmouth, NH: Heinemann.

Greene, Maxine (1986, November). In search of a critical pedagogy. *Harvard Educational Review, (56)4,* 427–441.

Greene, Maxine (1995). Educational visions: What are schools for and what should we be doing in the name of education? In Joe L. Kincheloe & Shirley R. Steinberg (Eds.), *Thirteen questions: Reframing education's conversation* (2d ed.) (pp. 305–313). New York: Peter Lang.

Gumperz, John (1976). Language, communication, and public negotiation. In P. Sanday (Ed.), *Anthropology and the public interest.* New York: Academic Press.

Gumperz, John (1982). *Discourse strategies.* New York: Cambridge University Press.

Gumperz, John, & Cook-Gumperz, Jenny (1982). Introduction: Language and the communication of social identity. In John Gumperz & Jenny Cook-Gumperz (Eds.), *Language and social identity* (pp. 1–21). New York: Cambridge University Press.

Hairston, Maxine (1982). The winds of change: Thomas Kuhn and the revolution in the teaching of writing. *College Composition and Communication, 30,* 76–88.

Hatlen, Brian (1988, November). Michel Foucault and the discourses(s) of English. *College English, (50)7,* 786–801.

Havelock, E. A. (1963). *Preface to Plato.* Cambridge, MA: Belknap Press.

Heath, Shirley Brice (1982). What no bedtime story means: Narrative skills at home and school. *Language in Society, 2,* 49–76.

Heath, Shirley Brice (1983). *Ways with words: Language, life and work in communities and classrooms.* Cambridge: Cambridge University Press.

Herzberg, Bruce (1991). Composition and the politics of the curriculum. In Richard Bullock, John Trimbur, & Charles Schuster (Eds.), *The politics of writing instruction: Postsecondary* (pp. 97–117). Portsmouth, NH: Boynton/Cook.

Hirsch, E. D., Jr. (1987). *Cultural literacy: What every American needs to know.* Boston: Houghton Mifflin.

Hoeg, Peter (1995). *Borderliners* (Barbara Haveland, Trans.). New York: Dell.

Inghilleri, Moira (1989). Learning to mean as a symbolic and social process: The story of two ESL writers. Unpublished manuscript, Boston University School of Education.

Jackson, Derrick (2003, March 28). Losing the graduation game. *The Boston Globe.* Opinion section, A15.

Kahn, Chris (2003, March 9). College legacies face scrutiny: Critics contend such admissions benefit whites. *The Boston Globe,* A3.

Kincheloe, Joe L., & Steinberg, Shirley R. (1995). Introduction: The more questions we ask, the more questions we ask. In Joe L. Kincheloe & Shirley R. Steinberg (Eds.), *Thirteen questions: Reframing education's conversation.* New York: Peter Lang.

King, Mary (1993). Introduction to section II. *Dynamics of the writing conference: Social and cognitive interaction.* Urbana, IL: National Council of Teachers of English.

Kintsch, Walter (1977). *On comprehending stories: Cognitive processes in comprehension.* Hillsdale, NJ: Lawrence Erlbaum.

Knoblauch, Cyril H., & Brannon, Lil (1984). *Rhetorical traditions and the teaching of writing.* Montclair, NJ: Boynton/Cook.

Kozol, Jonathan (1967). *Death at an early age.* New York: Plume.

Kuhn, Thomas (1970). *The structure of scientific revolutions* (2d ed.). Chicago: University of Chicago Press.

Labov, William (1972). *Language of the inner-city.* Philadelphia: University of Pennsylvania Press.

Lang, Berl (1991). *Writing and the moral self.* New York: Routledge.

Macedo, Donaldo (1994). *Literacies of power: What Americans are not allowed to know.* Boulder, CO: Westview Press.

McLaren, Peter (1991). Working paper, Miami University Graduate School of Education.

Memering, Dean (1983). *Research writing: A complete guide to research papers.* Englewood Cliffs, NJ: Prentice-Hall.

Michaels, Sarah (1981). Sharing time: Children's narrative styles and differential access to literacy. *Language in Society, 10,* 423–442.

Michaels, Sarah (1985). Hearing the connections in children's oral and written discourse. *Journal of Education, (167)1,* 36–56.

Michaels, Sarah, & Collins, James (1984). Oral discourse styles: Classroom interaction the acquisition of literacy. In Deborah Tannen (Ed.), *Coherence in spoken and written discourse.* Norwood, NJ: Ablex.

Mishler, Eliot (1984). *The discourse of medicine: Dialectics of medical interviews.* Norwood, NJ: Ablex.

Mishler, Eliot (1986). *Research interviewing: Context and narrative.* Cambridge, MA: Harvard University Press.

Mitchell, Juliet (1971). *Woman's estate.* New York: Vintage Books.

Murray, Donald (1976). Teaching writing as process, not product. In Richard Graves (Ed.), *Rhetoric and composition.* Rochelle Park, NJ: Hayden.

Murray, Donald (1985). *A writer teaches writing.* Boston: Houghton Mifflin.

Nespor, Jan (1991). The construction of school knowledge: A case study. In Candace Mitchell & Kathleen Weiler (Eds.), *Rewriting literacy: Culture and the discourse of the other* (pp. 169–188). New York: Bergin & Garvey.

Ong, Walter J. (1982). *Orality and literacy: The technologizing of the word.* London: Methuen.

Paul, Robert A. (1988, August 21). The living dead and the puffer fish. *The New York Times Book Review.*

Perl, Sondra (1979, December). Understanding composing. *College Composition and Communication, (31)4,* 363–369.

Phelps, Louise Wetherbee (1991). The institutional logic of writing programs: Catalyst, laboratory, and pattern for change. In Richard Bullock, John Trimbur, & Charles

Schuster (Eds.), *The politics of writing instruction: Postsecondary* (pp. 155–170). Portsmouth, NH: Boynton/Cook.

Raimes, Ann (1984). Anguish as a second language: Remedies for composition teachers. In Sandra McKay (Ed.), *Composing in a second language* (pp. 81–96). Rowley, MA: Newbury House.

Rodriguez, Richard (1983). *Hunger of memory: The education of Richard Rodriguez.* New York: Bantam.

Rosaldo, Renato (1989). *Culture and truth: The remaking of social analysis.* Boston: Beacon Press.

Rose, Mike (1989). *Lives on the boundary.* New York: Free Press.

Roskelly, H. (1988). The dialogue of chaos: The unthinkable order. In Louise Z. Smith (Ed.), *Audits of meaning: a festschrift in honor of Ann E. Berthoff* (pp. 96–106). Portsmouth, NH: Boynton/Cook, Heinemann.

Schank, Roger C., & Abelson, Roger (1977). *Scripts, plans, goals, and understanding.* Hillsdale, NJ: Lawrence Erlbaum.

Schwegler, Robert A. (1991). The politics of reading student papers. In Richard Bullock, John Trimbur, & Charles Schuster (Eds.), *The politics of writing instruction: Postsecondary* (pp. 203–225). Portsmouth, NH: Boynton/Cook.

Scollon, Ron, & Scollon, Suzanne (1981). *Narrative, literacy and face in interethnic communication.* Norwood, NJ: Ablex.

Shaugnessy, Mina (1977). *Errors and expectations: A guide for the teacher of basic writing.* New York: Oxford University Press.

Shea, Christopher (2003, February 9). Critical faculties: Advantage card; William F. Buckley's affirmative action legacy. *The Boston Sunday Globe,* D5.

Shore, Ira, & Freire, Paulo (1987). *A pedagogy for liberation: Dialogues on transforming education.* South Hadley, MA: Bergin & Garvey Press.

Skinner, Burrhus F. (1957). *Verbal behavior.* New York: Appleton-Century-Crofts.

Slevin, James F. (1991). Depoliticizing and politicizing composition studies. In Richard Bullock, John Trimbur, & Charles Schuster (Eds.), *The politics of writing instruction: Postsecondary* (pp. 1–21). Portsmouth, NH: Boynton/Cook.

Sommers, Nancy (1996). Responding to student writing. In Bruce Leeds (Ed.), *Writing in a second language* (pp. 148–154). Boston: Addison-Wesley.

Street, Brian (1984). *Literacy in theory and practice.* Cambridge: Cambridge University Press.

Tannen, Deborah (1984). *Conversational style: Analyzing talk among friends.* Norwood, NJ: Ablex.

Thayer, V. T. (1926). The university as a training school for college and university teachers. *School and Society, 24,* 773–779.

Tuman, Myron C. (1988, February). Class, codes, and composition: Basil Bernstein and the critique of pedagogy. *College Composition and Communication, (39)1,* 42–51.

University of Massachusetts Boston (2003, 4 August). President's office student profile report: Fall 1996–Spring 2002. Boston: Office of Institutional Research.

Volosinov, Valentin N. (1973). *Marxism and the philosophy of language.* New York: Seminar Press.

Westerman, Floyd Red Crow (1982). "Wounded knee" from the album *This land is your mother.* Woodland Hills, CA: Full Circle Productions.

Williams, Raymond (1984). *Writing in society.* London: Verso.

Young, Richard (1978). Paradigms and problems: Needed research in rhetorical invention. In Charles Cooper & Lee Odell (Eds.), *Research in composing: Points of departure* (pp. 29–47). Urbana, IL: National Council of Teachers of English.

Zamel, Vivian (1976). Teaching composition in the ESL classroom: What we can learn from research in the teaching of English. *TESOL Quarterly, (10)1*, 67–76.

Zamel, Vivian (1983). The composing processes of advanced ESL students: Six case studies. *TESOL Quarterly, (17)2*, 165–187.

Zamel, Vivian (1985). Responding to student writing. *TESOL Quarterly, (19)1*, 79–97.

Zamel, Vivian (1996). Responding to student writing. In Bruce Leeds (Ed.), *Writing in a second language* (pp. 155–172). Boston: Addison-Wesley.

INDEX